2nd Edition

New Directions in Social Work Practice

Kieron Hatton

 |

Los Angeles | London | New Delhi
Singapore | Washington DC

Series Editors:
Jonathan Parker and Greta Bradley

Learning Matters
An imprint of SAGE Publications Ltd
1 Oliver's Yard
55 City Road
London EC1Y 1SP

SAGE Publications Inc.
2455 Teller Road
Thousand Oaks, California 91320

SAGE Publications India Pvt Ltd
B 1/I 1 Mohan Cooperative Industrial Area
Mathura Road
New Delhi 110 044

SAGE Publications Asia-Pacific Pte Ltd
3 Church Street
#10-04 Samsung Hub
Singapore 049483

Editor: Kate Wharton
Development editor: Kate Lodge
Production editor: Chris Marke
Copy-editor: Solveig Gardner Servian
Marketing manager: Camille Richmond
Cover design: Wendy Scott
Typeset by: C&M Digitals (P) Ltd, Chennai, India
Printed by CPI Group (UK) Ltd, Croydon, CR0 4YY

First published 2008
Second edition 2015

Library of Congress Control Number: 2015933160

British Library Cataloguing in Publication Data

A catalogue record for this book is available from the
British Library.

MIX
Paper from
responsible sources
FSC
www.fsc.org   FSC® C013604

ISBN 978-0-85725-876-2
ISBN 978-0-85725-813-7 (pbk)

New Directions
in Social Work
Practice

WITHDRAWN

Contents

Series editors' Preface

Since the first edition of Kieron Hatton's important book outlining many of the *New Directions* facing social work practice in the UK there have been continued changes demanded. Some of these are politically driven, of course, and represent areas ripe for critique, whilst some of the new directions being promoted are concerned with improving practice and enhancing the lives of those who use social work services. Portentously, the attacks made in changes to social work education and practice have damaged internationalisation and our capacity to learn from and contribute to global perspectives on social work.

Hatton's book is a welcome antidote to stagnation and moribund thinking in contemporary professional practice and readers will gain much from engaging with the concepts he sets out and the challenges he raises.

In a world of increasing standardisation, we can sometimes fail to critique our positions within social work, the impact of changing structures, practices and thinking. Hatton makes this explicit and challenges social work students to deepen their appreciation of the world around them and the social and political contexts inhabited by their service users.

This book re-establishes an important contribution to learning from which students, their service users and ultimately society should benefit.

Jonathan Parker

Acknowledgements

Thanks to all members of the social work team at the University of Portsmouth for their support, inspiration and openness to new ideas.

Thanks also to all those colleagues, whether they be academics, social workers/ social pedagogues or people who use services, who contributed, directly and indirectly, to the theories and practices underpinning the book. A particular thanks to staff at the Department of Social Education, Frobel University, College in Copenhagen and Evangelische Hochschule, Freiburg whose support and contribution to international debates is so important. Thanks also to colleagues in France who have helped me sharpen and widen my knowledge. Particular thanks to members of the Social Work Inclusion Group at the University who continue to demonstrate why the link between inclusion and creativity is so central to good practice. It is to the University of Portsmouth's credit that it remains so committed to international, inter-professional and inclusive strategies.

The book is dedicated to Helen, Cal and Ruari without whose support my work would be much more challenging.

Introduction

If you don't risk anything, you risk more.

Erica Jong

I risk crossing the road because otherwise I risk standing still,

I risk being honest because otherwise I risk never knowing,

I risk being in a relationship because otherwise I risk never learning to care,

I risk eating chocolate because otherwise I risk missing out,

I risk a sense of humour because otherwise I risk going mad,

I risk being misunderstood because otherwise

I risk never being understood at all.

Creative Writing Working Party, Social Work Inclusion Group,
University of Portsmouth, 2006

The first edition of this book noted that 'Social work is confronting significant challenges at the beginning of the twenty-first century'. It commented on the fact that despite the development of a newer, more mature professional identity (since the introduction of the Care Standards Act 2000, the introduction of a three-year prequalifying degree programme, and the processes of regulation and accreditation through the General Social Care Council – now the Health and Care Professions Council, HCPC), social work faced challenges on a number of fronts.

Among those highlighted were:

- The increased emphasis on partnership working which could often seem to leave social work as the junior partner in relationships with big spending professions such as health and education.

- The workforce below social work qualification level was still poorly qualified and new types of worker were being put forward as potential rivals or alternatives to social work.

- Service users and carers were articulating their own agendas in ways which questioned the right of professionals, including social workers, to make decisions about people's lives without full consideration of the voice of these previously ignored or marginalised groups.

- The book sought to examine these challenges and posed a set of alternative scenarios for social work which aimed to cement its place in welfare provision in ways which were accountable, democratic and innovative. (Hatton, 2008)

The book was organised around three key themes:

- **Inclusion** – If social work is to make a real impact on the lives of those people who are marginalised and excluded it needs to develop a frame of reference which values, hears and works in partnerships with the people who are experts in social work, those who use social work services.

- **Inter-professionalism** – Too often inter-professionalism is seen as an unequal relationship in which the most powerful partner – statutory as against voluntary organisations, health or education as against social work – sets the agenda and structures the way services are developed and delivered. This book suggests a different way in which these partnerships can be framed which enhances the role of social work.

- **Internationalism** – It sometimes appears as if social work sees itself as solely a national activity which is impermeable to international or global influence. This view is being increasingly challenged and if social work is to continue to demonstrate its relevance it needs to listen to and learn from practitioners and theorists in other countries.

Central to these themes was the idea of innovation. It noted:

> If social work is going to grasp the opportunities available to it, it needs to be innovative, creative and critical. New forms of practice are emerging which encompass these emerging themes. However, they are often imperfectly developed, unevenly practised and poorly theorised. This book seeks to explore the dilemmas around these issues, and to suggest, drawing on UK and European examples, ways in which they can be incorporated into new forms of welfare practice.
>
> (Hatton, 2008)

The notion of creativity was, and remains, central to this reconfigured social work agenda. The poem which opens this chapter resulted from the collaboration of service users/carers from the Social Work Inclusion Group (SWIG) at the University of Portsmouth with UK and international students in the development of a creative workshop to explore issues of identity, difference and diversity. The decision to use creativity to enhance this process was the result of SWIG members' frustrations with traditional methods of collaboration and a desire to show that they had the capacity and ability to explore complex issues around their experience without having their views mediated by professionals. The poem powerfully reflected a major concern of service users and carers that current social work practice had become risk averse. This was despite the views expressed in policy developments such as Valuing people; Independence, wellbeing and choice; and Our health, our care, our say (see Chapters 1 and 5). The safety-first practice of much current social work, reinforced by a managerialist focus on outcomes rather than the social work task (Dominelli and Hoogvelt, 1996) made the achievement of such risk enhancing practice even less likely to occur.

The possibilities for a new creative agenda to frame social work practice was a key theme within the book. At the heart of this was, and still remains, a belief that social work and other forms of welfare practice, need to be critical, reflective and utilise an intellectual understanding of the contribution the social sciences can make to an improvement in the theory and practice of social work.

The task therefore becomes one of utilising the possibilities that exist to recognise uncertainty and embrace it as a means of understanding the complexity of the social work task. As Lymbery notes, 'the application of ... creativity will be linked to a number of factors: the level of complexity of the work, the degree of familiarity of the practitioner with the type of work, and so on' (2003, p109). He suggests that in particular creativity is likely to be embraced more by higher-level practitioners, especially at post-qualifying level. He suggested that it is in the areas of assessment and evaluation that the potential for creativity is most likely to be found.

Although we can welcome this attempt to reintroduce creativity into UK social work, the analysis of Lymbery and others suffers from an over-concern with the national context. As noted earlier, social work needs to embrace the lessons of practice in other countries. The work of Cameron, McQuail and Petrie (2007) points to the potential of integrating a European tradition – social pedagogy – into the UK. Other writers have sought to demonstrate how a more radical perspective can contribute to new forms of practice (Lavalette and Ferguson, 2007; Ferguson and Woodward, 2009; Hatton, 2013, 2015). A central element of these practices concerns the use of creativity to build relationships between professionals and the people they work with. Creativity in this context can therefore be seen as part of a process of collaboration and empowerment (see Chapters 5, 6 and 7).

The author has suggested elsewhere that social pedagogy may provide a link to these notions of creativity (Hatton, 2013). The use of creativity should be part of a strategy to improve services.

This book therefore seeks to develop a definition of creativity which encompasses both the desire to improve current practice and new forms of practice. Creativity in this definition can therefore be seen to have four central elements to it:

- To modify existing ways of doing things to make them more relevant to people providing and experiencing services.

- To challenge current ways of doing things and in particular to expose the limitations of forms of practice that focus on outcomes and which neglect relationships as an integral part of practice.

- To develop new ways of doing things that build on the best elements of current practice but which also draw on European traditions of social education and social pedagogy (Hatton, 2013).

- To promote the use of the 'creative imagination' (Vygotsky, 2004) to envision new forms of activity that replace and challenge the more conservative discourses which often seem to frame welfare priorities.

The contemporary context

Six years on from the first edition of this book, *where does this leave social work?* Undoubtedly contemporary social work faces a significant number of challenges from central government, the direct providers of social work services and those who use those services. The context within which social work is practised has changed significantly since the first edition of this book was published in 2008. The second Laming report (into the death of Peter Connelly) and the subsequent work of the Social Work Task Force, Social Work Reform Board and The College of Social Work have sought to (re)professionalise social work and provide it with a coherent professional identity. At the same time the Hackney model and the Reclaiming Social Work agendas have aimed to reconfigure the way social work is delivered and the Munro Report has emphasised the importance of looking at social work practice (particularly around child protection) and reaffirming the importance of direct work with people using social work services through an emphasis on relationship work rather than proceduralism and managerialism. A number of these developments were predicted in the first edition, which argued for social work to take a new direction which was 'innovative, creative and critical' (Hatton, 2008, p2). Central to such an approach, the author argued, was a framework for social work which 'examined the way debates around inclusion, interprofessionalism and internationalism are key to the future direction of social work' (p143).

The second edition of this book will examine how far such an explanatory framework can take us in understanding the theoretical and practical challenges we face as we approach a post election period where there may well be changes of emphasis in welfare provision. They are likely to occur within a similar neo-liberal paradigm that provided the context for the first edition and which continued to frame developments after 2010. The initial Task Force report came out in May 2009 and was closely followed by the Interim report in July 2009, which said:

> When people are made vulnerable – by poverty, bereavement, addiction, isolation, mental distress, disability, neglect, abuse or other circumstances – what happens next matters hugely...good social workers can and do make a huge difference in these difficult situations. They are needed now as much, if not more than before.

> (Social Work Task Force, 2009, p10)

Prior to the publication of the final report there were widespread concerns that the agenda was being driven by large statutory employers who were laying the blame for the difficulties that social workers were experiencing, not at the management practices and lack of resources being devoted to front-line practice but at the lack of preparation for practice evident in social work education programmes. At this time the author questioned this approach and suggested that there were a significant number of silences and omissions in the employer and government discourses around these issues (Hatton, 2009). These included:

- Questions around the way we *perform* social work. We need to be aware of the control and regulatory functions of what we do. But also need to be aware of the need to engage with creativity so that we enhance the wellbeing and potential of the people we work with (see discussion of social pedagogy, Hatton, 2013).

- An overall *silence on notions of power* as reflected in the minimal attention given to users/carers role in social work education or practice within these discourses.

- The question of whether the changes suggested, especially the focus on the enhanced professional status of social work as a profession, disempower people who use those services (Tew, 2006).

- Noticeably the proposals were silent about *hierarchical power relationships* in organisations. This raised the question of whether this new professional identity will enable social workers to exercise control over their work, or is managerialism so entrenched that this will not happen?

These questions remained current throughout the subsequent abolition of the General Social Care Council and its replacement by the Health and Care Professions Council and the establishment, and subsequent closure, of The College of Social Work. The latter was envisioned as an attempt not only to confirm the identity of social work as a profession, but also to provide a voice for social work and those who use social work services. However, a number of these issues remain central to current practice and will be revisited throughout the book and addressed specifically in the Conclusion.

Post Reform Board reviews of social work education and practice

The first published review of social work education after the establishment of The College of Social Work was commissioned by Michael Gove and undertaken by Martin Narey (2014). Perhaps not surprisingly, given this Minister's hostility to public services, Narey's report was highly critical of social work education's focus on *non-discriminatory practice* at the expense of the practicalities of the social work task. He alleged, without research evidence to back this up and mainly on the basis of unattributed sources, that:

> Anti oppressive practice in academic social work is closely linked to concepts of empowerment and working in partnership. While a number of social work academics reject them, these are not extreme notions at the fringes of academic social work. One newly qualified social worker from a well-regarded University told me that the concentration in her course on non-oppressive practice was at the expense of understanding practicalities about the job.

> (Narey, 2014, p11)

This book rejects Narey's analysis of contemporary social work and is written within a tradition which recognises that those people using social work services have faced significant discrimination and oppression and that our task is to challenge such marginalisation and promote positive outcomes for the people with whom we work

(Ferguson and Woodward, 2009; Dominelli, 2010; Jones and Novak, 2014). This is not the same as seeing people as victims, as Narey suggests, rather it is about seeing people with capacity and agency to bring about change. The analysis in the report was underdeveloped and contained a largely inaccurate account of social work's commitment to social justice. However, given that it was commissioned by a Coalition minister who has also spoken of privatising child protection services (see later in this chapter) it serves as a useful reminder as to why we as a profession need, in conjunction with those using social work services, to organise and develop theoretically consistent and rigorous analyses of where we are going. It is intended that this book will contribute to that debate.

The only caveat in Narey's analysis is when he suggests that:

> Nobody – certainly not me – believes that when someone graduates with a social work degree they should be the finished product, battle ready for a job of extraordinary challenge. But there are too many employers and too many new social workers and students who think that standards are not always what they should be.

> (2014, p 25)

Given the significant reforms that social work education has undergone recently, and the lack of evidence in Narey's report to support such a statement, this is an extraordinary conclusion.

A more nuanced and balanced account is provided by the work of Croisedale-Appleby. The Care and Support Minister within the Coalition government, Norman Lamb, asked the independent Chair of Skills for Care to undertake a review of social work education, including looking at issues regarding the question of genericism versus specialism within qualifying programmes. Lamb said:

> I want to be reassured that social work education produces high quality practitioners and that the government's £100m investment is producing the high quality social workers that our society deserves and needs.

> (Croisedale-Appleby, 2014, p15)

Croisedale-Appleby concluded that the generic option provided the best starting point for qualifying social workers and that specialisation became more significant after qualification when practitioners were developing their expertise. Significantly, given the focus of this book, he commented on the importance of inclusion and internationalism in our current and future approaches to social work. He commented positively on the involvement of service users and carers in social work education, which he suggested

> compares very favourably with that of the clinical professions, and should be given much greater recognition. It is worthy of note that the HCPC has accorded due recognition to this good practice and has enhanced its regulatory requirements to this effect.

> (p42)

He is similarly positive about the importance of learning from other countries and argues that:

> As social work is an international profession, any moves made to develop or change social work education educational practices should be required to identify and take account of the differences of such moves in relation to the direction of educational practice internationally, and in particular to that being followed in the devolved nations of the UK.

(p82)

One of the significant elements of his analysis is, however, the way he correctly identifies the intellectual component of good social work, referring to the need to have both *theory informing practice* and *practice informing theory*. He suggests that social work education needs to 'be expressed in a new way' in which we see social workers through a three-part prism:

- **The social worker as practitioner** – who can show resilience under pressure, good communication and risk assessment skills.

- **The social worker as a professional** – who can apply appropriate ethical principles, engage in reflective practice, work with a wide variety of disadvantaged groups, provide a safeguard and, in line with the third core principle articulated within this book, 'learn to work effectively with and contribute other professions and disciplines' (p15).

- **The social worker a social scientist** – this is a welcome corrective to other commentators such as Narey who have sought to play down the intellectual traditions of social workers with a form of ant-intellectualism (Cowden and Singh, 2009). Croisedale-Appleby places a particular importance on evidence collection and research (p15).

A further challenge to the academic provision of social work education is provided by the range of fast-track programmes for 'high achieving undergraduates' wishing to enter social work such as Frontline, Step up to Social Work (both to train graduates to work in children's services) and Think Ahead (mental health practitioners). There is some concern within the social work community that such programmes devalue experiential learning and the recruitment of mature students, and that they appear to be based on a misunderstanding of the importance of intellectual learning as part of social work education. In this sense they appear to be more in tune with Narey's rather than Croisedale-Appleby's analysis with the implications mentioned above.

The work of the new Chief Social Workers suggests a further set of challenges. The Department for Education (2014) issued a document outlining the *Knowledge and Skills for Child and Family Social Work*, which was launched by Chief Social Worker Isabelle Trowler in late July 2014. If they wish to be awarded approved child and family practitioner status the child and family social worker will, it is suggested, be able to:

Apply a wide range of knowledge and skills to help build family relationships, resource and resilience so that the welfare of the child remains paramount; identify the full range of risks to children and help manage those risks; ensure proportionate intervention, including securing and supporting alternative homes for children, including those in and beyond public care placed with family and friends and for adoption; and to provide care and support to young people as they move towards independence and adulthood.

Explain and critically evaluate the role of social work as part of a system of welfare support to children and their families, including parents as vulnerable adults, and how this relates to the social contract between citizenship and the state and the role of family, kinship and community; explain the impact of poverty, inequality and diversity on social and economic opportunities and how that relates to child welfare, family functioning and the highest context of child protection.

(Department of Health, 2014, p1)

A similar review of the knowledge and skills needed for the adult social care work-force is currently out for consultation. The consultation document suggests that social workers in adult social services will need to

apply a wide range of knowledge and relational skills to understand and build relationships, and work directly with individuals, their families and carers to enable and empower them to achieve best outcomes. This should include undertaking assessments, planning care and support and making the best use of available resources to enable people to have better lives. Social workers should enable people to experience personalised, integrated care and support them to maintain their independence and wellbeing, cope with change, attain the outcomes they want and need, understand and manage risk, and participate in the life of their communities.

(Department of Health, 2014, p7)

Central to these proposals are claims that social workers in both children and adult services should focus on relationships, manage risk, ensure that people have access to appropriate resources, be aware of the impact of poverty, inequality and diversity and enable participation in community life. The key to achieving such aims is the need for social workers to be able to challenge their organisations – including the way they distribute resources and relate to people using services – and a society which is predicated on the promotion of poverty and social inequality (Wilkinson and Pickett, 2009). At present these statements provide little guidance on how this can be achieved. Our task as educators and practitioners is to mobilise resources to achieve these broader goals. This book seeks to make a contribution to this debate and to changes in practice.

The privatisation of social work

While at least some of these developments can be seen as an attempt to (re)profes-sionalise social work they are occurring within the context of a focus on reducing the role of the state and in particular, reducing substantially the public investment in welfare (see Chapter 1 and Jordan and Drakeford, 2012). In May 2014 the Department for Education announced plans to privatise child protection services and to outsource them to for-profit companies such as G4S and Serco (Patrick Butler, Privatise child protection services, Department for Education proposes, *Guardian*, 16 May 2014). Not surprisingly there was a strong response to this proposal from a wide range of experts in the field of child protection. The *Guardian* quoted Professor Eileen Munro, author of a major report into child protection (Munro, 2011), who argued that 'establishing a market in child protection would create perverse incentives for private companies to either take more children into care or leave too many languishing with dangerous families'. Munro's views were widely echoed by other commentators within the profession and in June the *Guardian* reported that the plans had been abandoned (Ray Jones, U Turn on children's services privatisation hides underlying problem, *Guardian*, 24 June, 2014). However, whether this policy returns and continues to form the policy agenda is likely to be determined by the election in May 2015, which returned a majority Conservative government.

The social work pilots

A modified way in which a proto-privatised agenda could be developed is illustrated by the social work pilots (SWPs) introduced in 2013. The pilots were located in Birmingham, Lambeth, North East Lincolnshire, Shropshire, Suffolk, Surrey and Stoke. Birmingham withdrew from the pilots in 2013 following a reorganisation of their adult social care workforce. In total there were seven across the country. A team from the Work Force Development unit at King's College London reviewed the operation of the pilots and reported that:

> For most participants in this study – social workers, other practitioners, SWPwA managers and commissioners alike, SWPwAs offered the potential for job satisfaction, autonomy and in some cases greater opportunities for team working than they had experienced working for the local authority. In other areas, such as supervision practice and access to training, form filling and resource pressures, there were strong similarities with local authority colleagues.

> (Manthorpe et al., 2014, p5)

It has been suggested that three possible models of practice could emerge from such a model:

- A *professional practice* (social enterprise) run by a partnership of social workers independent of the Local Authority.
- A *third-sector model* (not for profit) run by voluntary organisation.
- A *private sector* (for profit) model.

The Social Work Action Network (n.d.) pointed out how these SWPs 'argue that the long term solution lies in privatising social work services because state run services are monopolistic and do not promote innovation'.

The election of the Conservative administration in May 2015 could lead to an acceleration of these trends. The College of Social Work, the professional voice for social work, which emerged after the work of the Social Work Task Force and the Social Work Reform Board, was closed suddenly in July 2015. The process of privatisation of children's services continues, but through an understated and under-reported backdoor route, which will allow private companies to bid for contracts if they do so through affiliated 'non-profit' companies.

As Ray Jones noted in Community Care, 'It is also intended that they will not be registered, regulated or inspected when providing these services' (Luke Stephenson, Community Care, 07/02/15).

The introduction of the Care Act 2014 has resulted in significant changes to the delivery of health and social care services that, while providing some improvements for carers and increased accountability for local authorities in their decision making with respect to adult social care, also promised to cap carer costs to £72,000. Already this has been dropped as a government commitment and a re-emphasis placed on cutting further public spending on welfare services. The Government announced in the July 2015 budget projected cuts of £12bn to the welfare budgets. These cuts fall disproportionately on people who use social work services. The Institute of Fiscal Studies estimated that the poorest would be worst hit, with some low-income families losing up to £3,000 per year. The *Guardian* reported the IFS analysis as suggesting the budget changes could lead to the following:

> Most working-age benefits, tax credits and housing benefit will be frozen for the next four years, and once inflation is taken into account that will mean 13 million families losing an average of £260 a year.

> The other big change – making the new universal credit less generous – results in much bigger losses, but to a smaller number of people. What the chancellor has announced is that people will not be able to earn as much before their tax credits start to be removed. Previously the limit was £6,420, but it will be reduced to £3,850, costing around 3 million people around £1,000 a year on average.

(Larry Elliott, Guardian, 09/07/15)

Within such a financial context the challenges to social work practice will be substantial over the coming years. However, we should see this as an opportunity, not just a challenge. It is clear from this context that social work needs to develop new strategies to engage with people who use social work services. We should not sit passively in our offices while the people we work with, and ourselves, become increasingly impoverished. We need to develop more collective approaches to oppose these policies, which begin to challenge them at community, regional and national levels. This will mean developing alliances with people using services, community organisations and trade unions representing public sector workers. This book is an attempt to suggest ways in which we can begin to do this. At its core is a belief that we need to work in an inclusive, accountable way with the range of people using services and being affected by austerity.

The structure of this book

Given this challenging agenda, this new edition is predicated on the belief that we need to understand policy developments in social work and how we can influence as well as be influenced by them. The book identifies a number of key characteristics of the wide-ranging legislative timetable which has been introduced since 1997 (encompassing successive Labour governments and the Coalition). Chapter 1 seeks to delineate the way these new policies have developed and to suggest continuities across policy development in social work, particularly around issues of independence, choice, wellbeing and partnership. It points out, however, how these objectives are also cross-cut with the contradictory policies of regulation and advocacy. It locates these developments within a discussion of a framework for understanding the development of the policy process that encompasses pluralistic, elite theory and structuralist explanations of how policy emerges, is implemented, and problems that may occur with the implementation process. This edition has, however, developed a further explanatory model around *street-level bureaucracy* (Lipsky, 1980), which it is argued can allow us to understand the way social workers are able to exert power (negatively or positively) when they exercise discretion.

Chapter 2 demonstrates how the issues we are currently confronting do not present new dilemmas, but that they can be traced back to earlier debates around radical social and community development. Chapter 3 looks at the way in which these shared traditions of radical, social and community work can be used to develop new forms of practice that utilise an agenda which promotes social change.

This in turn raises issues about the role of social work as a professional activity and the way in which social work is developing within the contemporary context. Chapter 4 looks at the importance of the voluntary or 'third sector' in promoting alternative ways of delivering services. It also points to the way in which debates around communitarianism have led to an attempt to dampen down the radicalism of the sector and the way in which the government has sought to promote those elements of the voluntary sector that concentrate on service delivery rather than oppositional work or an agenda promoting social change. It takes forward discussion of the future of social work by looking at the potential importance of debates around the 'underclass', social exclusion, the role of social enterprises, social entrepreneurs and the way these debates are currently framed within discourses around the 'Big Society'. It points to the way concepts such as the Big Society, localism and social action have been used to divert attention from the wider policy of retrenchment and the diminution of those resources previously available to the public sector.

One area where there does appear to have been a commitment to a more radical agenda, which promotes new forms of practice, is in the emphasis placed on the involvement and participation of people who use services. Chapter 5 demonstrates the wide-ranging nature of this commitment and points to the legislative and policy framework within which these developments have occurred. It draws attention also to the way in which these debates are not only taking place in the UK but are part of a wider European debate about the nature of welfare provision. It suggests that involvement has to mean a tangible rather than tokenistic change in services. Drawing initially on Arnstein's (1969) ladder of citizen participation, the chapter seeks to develop a model of involvement and inclusion which promotes the idea of service users and carers being the agents of change within social work by integrating a more sophisticated analysis of power within the discourses around participation and inclusion.

Chapter 6 addresses the implications of the analysis in previous chapters for social work and its emerging professional identity. Redefining social work within discourses of professionalism, the chapter traces the way social work interacts with other professionals, both within the UK and in relation to other professionals internationally. In particular it traces the development of interest with European models of social care such as social pedagogy. It demonstrates the implications of social pedagogy for new forms of practice.

Chapter 7 then provides a more detailed focus on social work in three European countries – Ireland, Denmark and the Czech Republic – and looks at the implications for practice in the UK. The chapter seeks to draw together the key themes in the book and suggest a model for understanding the way social work in the UK is going which acknowledges the challenges of meeting the demands of service users, other professionals and the international social work agenda.

Chapter 8 seeks to draw these lessons together and relate parallel debates around internationalism, inter-professionalism and inclusion to debates around professionalism, participation and partnership. It concludes with a focus on the potential for good practice to improve wellbeing and to offer a transformatory and optimistic perspective for the future.

Learning features

The book seeks to engage the reader with the key issues raised by providing a number of pivotal examples of the way particular approaches have been developed (for instance, see examples in Chapter 7). It provides a number of activities in each chapter to test the reader's understanding of the key issues, and each chapter ends with a summary of the key issues, suggestions for further reading and a range of useful web addresses. For more detailed discussion of particular areas of social work practice readers are referred to other titles in the series such as:

Introduction to social work: Horner, N. (2013) *What is Social Work? Context and Perspectives,* 4th edn. London: Sage/ Learning Matters.

The legal framework: Johns, R. (2014) *Using the Law in Social Work,* 6th edn. London: Sage/Learning Matters.

Service user involvement: Warren, J. (2007) *Service User and Carer Participation in Social Work.* Exeter: Learning Matters.

Children and families: Jowitt, M. and O'Loughlin, S. (2012) *Social Work with Children and Families,* 3rd edn. London: Sage/Learning Matters.

This book has been carefully mapped to the new Professional Capabilities Framework for Social Workers in England (The College of Social Work, 2012) and will help you to develop the appropriate standards at the right level. These standards are:

- **Professionalism** – Identify and behave as a professional social worker committed to professional development.

- **Values and ethics** – Apply social work ethical principles and values to guide professional practice.

- **Diversity** – Recognise diversity and apply anti-discriminatory and anti-oppressive principles in practice.

- **Rights, justice and economic wellbeing** – Advance human rights and promote social justice and economic wellbeing.

- **Knowledge** – Apply knowledge of social sciences, law and social work practice theory.

- **Judgement** – Use judgement and authority to intervene with individuals, families and communities to promote independence, provide support and prevent harm, neglect and abuse.

- **Critical reflection and analysis** – Apply critical reflection and analysis to inform and provide a rationale for professional decision making.

- **Contexts and organisations** – Engage with, inform and adapt to changing contexts that shape practice. Operate effectively within your own organisational frameworks and contribute to the development of services and organisations. Operate effectively within multi-agency and inter-professional settings.

- **Professional leadership** – Take responsibility for the professional learning and development of others through supervision, mentoring, assessing, research, teaching, leadership and management.

References to these standards will be made throughout the text and you will find a diagram of the Professional Capabilities Framework in Appendix 1 at the end of the book. Also appended are the relevant sections of the Subject Benchmark Statement for Social Work (QAA, 2008) and the National Occupational Standards for Community Development (Federation for Community Development Learning, 2009).

Chapter 1

A framework for understanding contemporary social work

Introduction: the changing context of social work

Contemporary social work is facing a number of significant challenges as it seeks to establish a distinctive identity in the face of competing and emerging professions. For social work professionals, academics, people using services, and those training to become social workers, these challenges seem to multiply and become more complex with every new government initiative or crisis facing social work. This chapter seeks to conceptualise those changes and challenges within broader debates about social policy and legislation.

The search for a new identity for social work can be mapped against the recognition that social work has failed to meet the expectations placed on it by a combination of significant actors including the government, the media, people using services, other professionals and those involved with social work as a professional activity. Prior to 1997 many of these discourses were framed by a hostility to social work which was at least partly the outcome of the previous Conservative administration's hostility to public-sector organisations (Savage and Atkinson, 2001), public concern about the outcome of a number of inquiries into child deaths (Department of Health, 1995), which social workers were held to be, at least partly, accountable for, and drives to create a professional identity which social work had previously been seen to be lacking (see Chapter 6).

One of the earliest initiatives under the Labour administration elected in 1997 to focus on renewing and making more accountable social work was *Modernising Social Services*, a White Paper presented to Parliament by the Secretary of State in the Department of Health in 1998. Subtitled *Promoting independence, improving protection, raising standards,* the White Paper can be seen to encapsulate the government's key priorities for social work as it began its period of governance from 1997 to 2010. The key problems identified by the White Paper included:

- protection – the improvement of safeguards to protect vulnerable children and adults;

- coordination – improving coordination between the different elements of the system;

- inflexibility – improving the ability of service to meet the needs of service users rather than service providers;

- clarity of role – a focus on expectations and standards;

- consistency – removing the imbalances between services provided across the country;

- inefficiency – a focus on minimising cost differentials between different providers.

While it is worth noting that many of these themes are at least the partial outcome of the move toward greater managerialism and control of public services, which can be traced back to the preoccupations of the previous administration (Dominelli and Hoogvelt, 1996), the themes did highlight a number of problems within existing provision which became the focus of policy initiatives over the next ten plus years. The White Paper drew particular attention to the need to promote independence, focus on individual need, achieve parity across the country in terms of provision, secure improvements to the looked-after care system –in particular a focus on improvements in safeguarding vulnerable children and adults, better training and greater public confidence in the work of social services. The latter would be achieved by improving the training of social workers and greater statutory regulation of social workers and social work agencies. At the heart of these proposals was the idea that these improvements should be attained through partnerships between the state, the market, the family and civil society or more specifically the third or voluntary sector (see Chapter 4) (Driver and Martell, 1998; Johnson, 1999).

Policy and legislative framework

Those people looking for a comprehensive account of the legislative changes implemented since 1997 are referred to one of the numerous texts that provide an account of social work law (e.g. Brayne and Carr, 2013; Brammer, 2010). They are also reminded that it was asserted that Labour had introduced over 3,000 new criminal offences between its election in 1997 and 2006 (Wilson, 2006). Clearly it would be impossible to do justice to such a wide-ranging legislative timetable within the confines of this book. They are in any event well dealt with in other titles in this series (O'Loughlin and O'Loughlin, 2008; Golightley, 2008; Horner, 2013). The discussion here is more concerned with the trends in social, political and legal policy that have impacted on social work. However, before these elements are drawn out it is important to highlight to a number of the more significant legislative and policy developments that have occurred within the period since the establishment of the modernisation agenda in 1998.

Arguably the Care Standards Act 2000 was the first and most significant of these developments. The Act was introduced because of concerns mentioned in the White Paper about the need to regulate social work and ensure a higher level of professional expertise among social work and social care staff. The Act established a new regulatory framework through the establishment of the General Social Care Council (GSCC) and the Commission for Social Care Inspection (CSCI). The GSCC replaced the Central Council for Education and Training in Social Work (CCETSW) and was charged with introducing a new qualification to replace the Diploma in Social Work (DipSW) and to regulate the social work and social care workforce.

The year 2003 saw the introduction of the new degree in social work based on the National Occupational Standards for Social Work developed by the Training Organisation for Personal Social Services (later replaced by Skills for Care) and the Benchmarking Statement for Social Work produced by the subject group for social work and social policy (Horner, 2013 – now replaced with the Benchmarking statement for social work, 2008). The new social work degree has replaced the DipSW as the qualification for trainee social workers. At the core of the degree is a commitment to provide a generic training programme which will equip students to work across a wide range of social work settings. It focused on six key roles that, it argued, would enable the student to work effectively as a social worker and meet the requirements laid down in the modernising agenda. This was subsequently replaced by the Professional Capability Framework (PCF) in 2012. Each chapter in this book begins with an account of the PCF relevant to that chapter and suggestions as to how the reading and exercises can help the student achieve the necessary level of competence. However, because a key underpinning theme of the book relates to the role of other traditions in social work intervention such as community development and community action (Kendall, KA 2000), the chapters also cross-reference to the National Occupational Standards (NOS) set out for community work by the training organisation for community work (FCDL, 2015). The relationship of the arguments in the book to the relevant NOS community work is mapped out in Appendix 1.

Understanding how policy development occurs

Hill (2005) has suggested that to understand the way policies are developed, enacted and implemented we need to be clear about the model of the policy process we adopt. He argues that we need to distinguish between policy content, policy output and the policy process itself. The first of these involves developing an understanding of the genesis and development of particular policies: *policy output* refers to the way particular services develop, and the *policy process* refers to the way decisions about particular policies are made and how they are shaped by those people and agencies responsible for implementing them. Such an approach enables us to understand how there may well be an imbalance between the perceived intentions of the policy-makers and the way policies are received and understood by the people for whom they are intended. In the current social work environment this means that it is not sufficient to simply assume that the intentions of the policy-makers are translated into practice, but also that we may need to read beyond the rhetoric of the policy-makers to see if the policy really is geared to meet the needs of the groups for whom it is intended.

This is at the heart of this book. If the identified key themes of inclusion, interprofessionalism and internationalism are to be achieved, we need to be able to evaluate the processes through which policy is formulated and implemented. For example, if policies are seeking to promote the involvement of people who use services, not just the professionals implementing policy, how is this realised? How can we make involvement real and not tokenistic? This dilemma is the focus of Chapter 5.

Hill (2005) also argues that to make sense of the way policy develops we need to understand the theories underpinning these approaches. He deals comprehensively with a wide range of theoretical approaches. For the purpose of this analysis it is sufficient to concentrate on four key theories: pluralism, elite theory, structuralism and an intermediate theory which examines the way workers in public organisations exercise a degree of discretion – street-level bureaucracy.

Hill describes pluralism (as defined by Dahl and his supporters) as a situation in which

> *sources of power are unequally though widely distributed among individuals and groups in society. Although all groups and interests do not have the same degree of influence, even the least powerful are able to make their voices heard at some stage in the decision making process.*

(Hill, 2005, p29)

Furthermore, any groups emerging through this process do so as representative of a wider societal view.

What does this mean for the analysis presented in this book? It suggests that although the groups of people with whom we as social workers interact are often the most marginalised and deprived within our society, it should be possible to redress this unfairness or inequality through developing organisations which are representative of the people with whom we work. In this context both social workers as an interest or professional group and the people who use social work services (users and carers) should also be able to express their aspirations, and to an extent have them met, within the existing social system. It therefore provides us with an optimistic view of the potential for social change and there should be clear evidence that the policy intentions and the policy outcomes should be beneficial for those involved with social work. A claim which this book seeks to challenge.

Elite theory is described by Hill as representing an alternative to pluralism in so far as it suggests that power is concentrated in the hands of

> *a variety of sources: the occupation of formal office, wealth, technical expertise, knowledge and so on. To a certain extent, these resources may be cumulative, but power is not solely dependent on any one resource.*

(Hill, 2005, p37)

Elements of such associations include bureaucratic and business elites.

In analysing policies impacting on social work agencies, professionals and service users/carers this conception of policy development would suggest that we would need to see whether policy initiatives reflected the power interests of significant powerful groupings within the social work sector, in particular the professional groupings within social work and the regulatory and controlling bodies within social work such as professional associations, registration organisations (The College of Social Work or any future equivalent, and The Health and Care Professions Council) and administrative agencies such as Skills for Care and key government departments such as the Department of Health and Department for Education.

Structuralist explanations, including Marxism, emphasise the way power is mediated through economic agencies and highlight the operation of systems of class stratification. In this conception actions, even of the most powerful groups, are determined by economic power so that structuralists '*see political action as determined by powerful forces ... which* act as *powerful constraints upon human action which have* to *be attacked* to *achieve fundamental change'* (Hill, 2005, p42). Such an approach mirrors the analysis of radical social work and community work outlined in Chapter 2, and those seeking to tackle structurally determined policy drivers face the challenges outlined in Chapters 2 and 3.

However, before leaving this discussion it is worth focusing briefly on a theory which has received an increasing amount of attention in discussions around rank-and-file social workers' capacity to influence the way services are delivered – street-level bureaucracy (Evans and Harris, 2004; Ellis, 2007, 2011). Lipsky (1980) argues that

> *the decisions of street-level bureaucrats, the routines they establish, and the devices they invent to cope with uncertainties and work pressures, effectively become the policies they carry out ... they believe themselves to be doing the best they can under adverse circumstances and they develop techniques to salvage service and decision making values within the limits imposed on them by the structure of work.*

> (pxii)

Hill notes that this suggests that street-level bureaucrats see themselves as oppressed by the system, yet they are often perceived by the user of the service to be the people with discretion and autonomy. He says that *'street-level bureaucrats make choices about the use of scarce resources under pressure; contemporary fiscal pressures upon human services make it much easier for officials to emphasise control than to try to put into practice service ideals'* (2005, p244).

Street-level bureaucrats therefore can be seen to have two key characteristics: a relatively high degree of discretion; and a relative autonomy from organisational authority (Hupe and Hill, 2007, p280.) Hupe and Hill (2007) argue that there are a number of key elements to street-level bureaucracy:

- They necessarily have discretion and are forced to use it. Rules may be ambiguous or contradictory, they work under an action imperative – they have to act, make choices.

- They seek to manage their own work.

- They are professionals – they may be policy-makers but they use their freedom to make policy to manage their work.

- In their interaction with users they are public officials – they have discretion because the nature of what they do calls for human judgement, managers have a difficult job managing them, as they define themselves expressly in the way they inter-relate to service users. In this sense they are more policy formers rather than implementers.

- There are a variety of types of agency, functionaries and tasks – these differences may be in even the same category of street-level bureaucrat.

- They work in a micro-network or 'web' of multiple networks, both vertical and horizontal relationships – they are not just working in organisations but are located at their boundaries. A simple model of hierarchical structure grossly oversimplifies this process. Horizontally they have workers in their own departments, peers may be members of their or ancillary professions; vertically they have structural relationships with users and public managers.

Hupe and Hill conclude that:

- Decisions determining action in public policy are nested in a multi-dimensional system, with a nested system of decisions about structure, financing and about the management of outputs – for which different actors may be accountable, in different ways.
- At the street level governance may be multiple, bottom up, top down and vertical.
- Different forms of accountability exist. The institutional context is important, as it raises questions as well about who should be in control (pp295–6).

However, Ellis suggests that

> *Lipsky's theory rests on the discretion which welfare professionals, including social workers, enjoy to interpret policy guidelines and organizational procedures in such a way as to determine who gains access to publicly funded provision. Policy and operational ambiguity allow for the possibility of choice, whilst the necessity to select clients is created by an excess of demand over resources available.*

> (2007, p408)

She argues that there is a powerful imperative for informal rationing because of the process in which front-line workers are encouraged to generate take-up yet manage scarce time and resources. This occurs partly because of the discretionary gap that allows social workers, in the circumstances she describes, to choose not to introduce direct payments, which they regard as *'illegitimate challenges to their decision-making power'* (p418). This is compounded by the way social workers (and other social professionals) face restrictions on resources, making it more difficult to keep up with expressed need.

In a later article Ellis argues that

> *[m]anaged environments create fresh conditions for street-level discretion but that managers collude in this exercise and, where accompanied by resource constraint, it is the negative manifestation of value discretion, paternalism, which is exercised in the spaces available for street-level bureaucracy … [moreover] … an emphasis on empowerment and rights appears only to invoke defensive practice.*

> (2011, p240)

Alden echoes this point when she maintains that among the people she interviewed who could be characterised as facing the dilemmas of street-level bureaucrats (in her case in relation to homelessness services),

> *[n]early all interviewees suggested a detachment from the central context of the policy they delivered, and many, including managers, appeared to view themselves within a linear top-down reality with little opportunity to influence outcomes. Many expressed what could perhaps be described as a fatalistic outlook; policy happened to them, and there was nothing they could do to prevent whichever trajectory the Government chose to pursue.*

> (2014, p6)

This book argues that this process occurs precisely because we, as social professionals, take on board the cynicism of neo-liberal ideologies, particularly their focus on individualism and the self, one dimensional views of power and lack of belief in the efficacy of collective and social action. Our task as educators, practitioners and as users of welfare services is to create and maintain positive alternatives so that we utilise all opportunities for discretion in favour of the people we work with. In other words, we can use the insights of theories such as those around street-level bureaucracy to fashion ways of working which are affirmative and progressive rather than aimed at maintaining an increasingly oppressive status quo.

Indeed there is evidence from other studies that street-level bureaucrats can have a more positive influence. Writing about the employment service in Denmark, Winter et al. suggest that

> [c]aseworkers who are more committed, pay more attention to rules, and work in organisations with more committed managers tend to place a greater emphasis on getting clients into jobs quickly than caseworkers where these considerations are less strong.

(2008, pp17–18)

This does not appear to be a function of the particular organisational or welfare type but is more to do with levels of commitment, and provides an interesting counterpoint to some of the more negative analysis of a worker's potential to promote change.

Key themes in recent policy developments

What then are the key themes in recent policy developments around social work and how do they relate to these above analyses? Clearly since the first edition of this book was published in 2008 there have been significant changes to the policy environment within which social work is practised – not least because there has been a change of government (see introduction and Chapter 4). However, it can be argued that the impact of the change of government has not been as profound as might be expected given that they operate within the same neo-liberal economic and social framework as the UK has experienced since 1979.

The next section looks at three important areas of development within contemporary social work that throw a light on these discussions: policies around children and young people; people with learning disabilities; and adults using social work and social care services. However, it is necessary to remind ourselves of those developments that are linked to the significant number of reviews to which social work and social work education have been subject. These include the second Laming report, the work of the Social Work Task Force and the Social Work Reform Board, The Munro Report (and Reclaiming Social Work) and more recently the changes to social work education proposed in the Narey and Croisedale-Appleby reports. These issues were highlighted in the previous chapter.

Children and young people

It is not the purpose of this book to look in detail at the policy context in which work with children has developed. Readers wanting more information are referred to the companion volume by Jowitt and O'Loughlin (2012) and key texts around social work law such as Brammer (2010) and Brayne and Carr (2013). The key policy framework for this area of work includes the Children Act 1989; the Children's Service Planning Order of 1996; Quality Protects (1998); the *Framework for the Assessment for Children in Need and their Families* (Department of Health, 2000); the Children (Leaving Care) Act 2000; the Victoria Climbié Inquiry 2003; *Every Child Matters: Change for Children* 2004; The Children Act 2004; the Children and Families Act 2014; and initiatives such as SureStart, Homestart and the recent Children's Centre initiative. For the purpose of this book, the focus will be on developments within services for looked-after children – particularly those around *Every Child Matters*. The key elements of *Every Child Matters* were:

- be safe;

- be healthy;

- enjoy and achieve;

- make a positive contribution;

- enjoy economic wellbeing.

Underpinning this approach was a commitment to partnership working (Chapter 6); the inclusion of young people using services (Chapter 5); and the development of a critical inter-professional practice (Chapters 4 and 6). In October 2005, the Commission for Social Care Inspection produced a report called *Making Every Child Matter*. They suggested from their inspections of children's services that services needed to be made more accessible; that social workers needed to respond effectively to children in need and their families; and that local authorities in particular needed to develop their role as corporate parents. In February 2007, the Commission for Social Care Inspection produced *Care Matters*, which analysed children and young people's views of *Every Child Matters* (HM Government, 2003). Among the key findings were that children wanted to be listened to more, have their different needs met, be kept safe and to have an effective social worker. Central to the last point was the idea of giving young people in care a say in decisions made about them.

At the same time as enhancing the rights of children and young people, the government has also been strengthening the statutory framework for young people through the new structure provided in *Working Together to Safeguard Children* (HM Government, 2015). Following on from *Every Child Matters*, it emphasised that

> [e]ffective safeguarding arrangements in every local area should be underpinned by two key principles:
>
> - safeguarding is everyone's responsibility: for services to be effective each professional and organisation should play their full part; and

- *a child-centred approach: for services to be effective they should be based on a clear understanding of the needs and views of children.*

(HM Government, 2015)

These themes of partnership, joint working and safeguarding vulnerable people find echoes in other legislation concerning learning disability and the needs of adults.

People with learning disabilities

The key policy agenda for people with learning disabilities was set out in *Valuing People: A New Strategy for Learning Disability for the 21st Century* (Department of Health, 2001).This White Paper outlined the problems and challenges faced by people with learning disabilities, which, they argued, included: poor coordination and planning of services; insufficient support for carers; the lack of choice and control experienced by people with learning disabilities; unmet health care needs; inconsistency in service delivery; and the frustrating lack of real partnership working across the health and social care sectors. It drew attention in particular to the problems faced by people from minority ethnic communities whose needs 'are often overlooked' (p3).

The White Paper argued that central to improving the life chances for people with learning disabilities were four key principles: rights, independence, choice and inclusion. The key to achieving these objectives were the principles of advocacy and person-centred planning. Money was made available for the development of advocacy services and the White Paper said:

People with learning disabilities have little control over their lives, few receive direct payments, advocacy services are underdeveloped and people with learning disabilities are often not central to the planning process. The Government's objective is to enable people with learning disabilities to have as much choice and control as possible over their lives and the services and support they receive.

(Department of Health, 2001, p4)

In 2009 the government produced *Valuing People Now*, which reviewed progress made since 2000. In a review of progress in 2010, it was concluded that

considerable progress has been made under the Valuing People Now programme across the key priorities in health, housing and employment up to September 2010. However, there is still more to do to make change happen for all people with learning disabilities and their family carers.

8.2 Learning Disability Partnership Boards have a critical role to play here in demonstrating transparency and continuing to drive change at a local level. This needs to be in real partnership with people with learning disabilities and their families – and people with learning disabilities and their family carers need to be supported to do this well.

(Department of Health, 2010, p63)

People using adult services

The government produced a Green Paper (consultation paper) in 2005 which looked at the future direction of social care services for adults. *Independence, Well-being and Choice* sought to produce a new vision and framework for social care in which the government expressed its desire to

> [m]ove toward a system where adults are able to take greater control of their lives. We want to encourage a debate about risk management and the right balance between protecting individuals and managing their own risks ... and to put people at the centre of assessing their own needs and how these can best be met.
>
> (Department of Health, 2005a, p10)

The Green Paper suggested a range of outcomes for adult social care which included:

- improved health – the promotion of good health and appropriate treatment and support;
- improved quality of life – access to leisure, social activities and lifelong learning and to universal, public and commercial services;
- making a positive contribution – active participation in the community;
- exercise of choice and control – maximising independence, choosing and controlling services, managing personal risk;
- freedom from discrimination and harassment – not being subject to abuse;
- economic wellbeing – access to sufficient income and resources;
- personal dignity – to be clean and comfortable, having available appropriate personal care.

> (Department of Health, 2005a, p26)

To achieve these goals the Green Paper suggested that it was important that people exercised control over the assessment of their own need through promoting direct payments and individual budgets over which the service user could exercise decision-making. In addition the Green Paper suggested the development of new models of service delivery and greater partnership between health and social care providers. A number of the respondents to the consultation on which the Green Paper was based indicated why these changes were necessary:

> People don't have high expectations, just to be treated with a bit of dignity and respect with some of the opportunities the rest of us take for granted.
>
> I've lost control of some things. I want control over my personal care.
>
> The professionals really need to listen to people who use services.
>
> (Department of Health, 2005a, p26)

In 2006 the government produced the *White Paper Our Health, Our Care, Our Say* which provided a guide to the way in which consumers of health and social care services wanted to see services develop in the future. In the introduction Patricia Hewitt, Secretary of State, said that she noted

> *how frustrating it is when the system seems to work against you rather than for you. Your answers give us great insight into the changes that need to be made, and in the government's white paper ... Our health, our care, our say: a new direction for community services, we show how we are going to make them happen.*

> (Department of Health, 2006, p3)

The White Paper was based on two major consultations in 2005 and from the responses of approximately 100,000 people. It promoted seven outcomes:

- improved health and wellbeing;

- improved quality of life;

- making a positive contribution;

- choice and control;

- freedom from discrimination;

- economic wellbeing;

- personal dignity.

More recently the government has introduced the ideas of personalisation (Department of Health, 2007) or person-centred planning, which has been defined as

> *a way of discovering what people want, the support they need and how they can get it ... Person-centred planning is both an empowering philosophy and a set of tools for change, at an individual, a team and an organizational level. It shifts power from professionals to people who use services.*

> (Department of Health, 2010, p3)

This emphasis has been further developed through the promotion of co-production, an approach which provides a new way of looking at organisational culture, the structure of services and everyday practices demonstrated between professionals and people using services. Co-production has been defined as including:

- co-design, including planning of services;

- co-decision-making in the allocation of resources;

- co-delivery of services, including the role of volunteers in providing the services;

- co-evaluation of the services.

> (SCIE, 2013, p8)

This approach is underpinned by core principles of equality, diversity, accessibility, and reciprocity and mutuality (SCIE, 2013, p9–13). Perhaps surprisingly these approaches were endorsed in *A Vision for Adult Social Care* produced by the Coalition early in its election term. The paper argued that *'Reform cannot and will not be top-down ... if power and control is devolved to communities, then people – including the most vulnerable – can lead more independent and fulfilled lives'* (Department of Health, 2010a, p7).

The document highlights the need for partnership and plurality in the delivery of services and appears to fit well within the best-practice philosophies discussed in this book. However, although there was an initial pledge to provide a stable financial base for the next four years to enable these aims to be translated into practice, we have seen significant cuts to frontline services and stringent economic policies which have significantly reduced the resources available to take forward this agenda. With this in mind it is useful to look at the challenges this has presented to state and third-sector agencies, a point explored in detail in Chapter 4.

Other relevant initiatives

From 1998 the Labour government pursued an agenda of tackling social exclusion and promoting social inclusion. This was based on partnerships between statutory organisations, voluntary and independent organisations and the promotion of market mechanisms to generate prosperity and opportunity for all. The Department for Work and Pensions produced its seventh *Opportunity for All* report in October 2005. The report set out objectives to break inter-generational disadvantage and underachievement, which included the eradication of child poverty in a generation, improving the quality of education to break cycles of deprivation, promoting work as the best form of welfare, supporting people to build personal assets and social capital (see discussion of social entrepreneurship in Chapter 4), providing security and independence in retirement and delivering high-quality public services.

The focus on the voluntary sector became increasingly important in policy development (see Chapter 4). Early in 2007 the Charity Commission published its survey of the work of charities which provide public services. Their findings threw a light on the way in which the voluntary sector came to play an important part in the delivery of public services. The report, *Stand and Deliver*, noted how

> *almost one third of all public services delivered by charities are in the field of health and social care ... Only 26 per cent of charities that deliver public services agreed that they are free to make decisions without pressure to conform to the wishes of funders.*

> (Charity Commission, 2007, pp3–4)

The report argued that charities needed to consider issues of independence and governance, funding and sustainability. These issues are discussed in detail in Chapter 4.

Sir Michael Lyons suggested in an article in the *Guardian* in October 2006 that 'in areas such as social care it is difficult to see how the public services will achieve their goals ... without a powerful alliance with the voluntary sector' (Lyons, *The best of both worlds* available at www.theguardian.com/society/2006/oct/04/publicservices.guardiansociety supplementsociety.guardian.co.uk/futureforpublicservices/story/ accessed 30/07/15). Craig et al. (2004) had previously noted that the government's emphasis on partnership was opening up opportunities for the voluntary sector. However, they suggested that government may be more interested in the service delivery role of voluntary organisations than more oppositional approaches. They point to the tensions in managing this relationship but expressed the view that the possibilities of a more mature rather than conflictual relationship existed. The Association of Chief Executives of Voluntary Organisations established the *Remaking the State* Commission (ACEVO, 2014) to look at ways in which the voluntary sector can become more involved in the delivery of public services (ACEVO, 2014). Will Hutton, who is chairing the commission, said:

> *The next few years are going to prove a crucial period for both the delivery of*
> *public services and the involvement of many more charitable and third sector*
> *providers in their delivery. Success will mean that we develop an ecosystem*
> *of partners that can provide services that are genuinely responsive to citizens'*
> *preferences. (available at www.acevo.org.uk/news/acevo-commission-chaired-will-*
> *hutton-and-rob-own-tackle-'care-deficit'-public-services, accessed 30/07/15)*

(ACEVO, 2014)

These issues are addressed in greater detail later in this book. Table 1.1 illustrates the continuities in the above initiatives.

Table 1.1 Key themes: Continuities and developments

Theme	Originating policy/ legislation	Continues in	Future/ contemporary developments
Regulation	Care Standards Act 2000	*Independence, Well-being and Choice*	Move to HCPC
	General Social Care Council	*Safeguarding Children*	
Training	Care Standards Act 2000	*New Social Work Qualification*	Professional Capability Framework, regulation through HCPC
Independence	*Values in Action*	*Independence, Well-being and Choice* *Our Health, Our Care, Our Say*	Personalisation and Co-production
		Valuing People Now	
Choice	*Values in Action*	*Every Child Matters*	Personalisation and Co-production
		Independence, Well-being and Choice *Valuing People Now*	
Wellbeing	*Independence, Well-being and Choice*	*Every Child Matters*	Personalisation and Co-production
		Our Health, Our Care, Our Say	
		Valuing People Now	
Community	*Values in action*	*Every Child Matters*	New enhanced role for voluntary/third sector in delivery of public services
Involvement	*Values in Action*	*Independence, Well-being and Choice*	Personalisation and Co-production
Partnership	*Values in Action*	*Every Child Matters*	Personalisation and Co-production
		Our Health, Our Care, Our Say	
		Valuing People Now	

ACTIVITY *1.1*

Table 1.1 shows how the plethora of policies which have emerged from successive governments since 1998 have important themes running through them. Using Hill's (2005) typology of pluralism, elite theory, structuralism and street-level bureaucracy, indicate how these policy developments fit within his framework. Then after reading Chapters 2, 3, 4 and 5, return to the Table and assess your conclusions against these earlier conclusions.

Risk, risk avoidance and advocacy

This discussion highlights two key issues which are currently impacting on contemporary social work in the UK: issues of risk and advocacy or what Baistow (1994) referred to as 'regulation and empowerment'.

Independence, Well-being and Choice (Department of Health, 2005a) was important because it recognised that much of modern social care had become risk averse and reintroduced the idea that part of the task of social care workers should be to enable people using services to take risks. As Lupton noted:

> *The language of risk is taking over from that of need or welfare in the literature on personal social services, such as probation, mental health and child care services, with risk assessment, risk management, the monitoring of risk and risk taking itself having become the raison d'être and organizing principle of agencies providing such services. Risk related discourses and strategies have taken on a key role in decision making about service delivery, including the rationing of services and decisions about need ... individuals and groups are increasingly expected to engage in practices identified as ways of avoiding or minimizing the impact of risks to themselves.*

> (1999, pp98–9)

Yet counter-tendencies exist and have become increasingly supported among policy-makers, although this is also taking place within a context of austerity and restrictions on social spending (Lymbery, 2010; Power, 2014). Service users are increasingly demanding that they be allowed to make their own decisions, not have their choices mediated by the intervention of a professional, as is illustrated in the debates around personalisation and co-production. Consultations across the service-user spectrum are redolent with service users calling for the opportunity to take risks and be responsible for their own actions. In *Care Matters*, young people talked eloquently about their right to have more say in decisions made about them. One young person said, 'Everyone wants to make decisions for me and it really hurts' (Commission for Social Care Inspection, 2007). Another said that children and young people need to be heard more. In *Real Voices, Real Choices* (Commission for Social Care Inspection, 2006a) the services users consulted articulated strong views around the question of risk. The report says that to reach their potential, an individual must be allowed and supported to take risks, have new experiences, and make mistakes (2006a, p12). They quote a participant in the *Shaping Our Lives* report who said that

> The right to manage risk should reflect the similar rights experienced by other people living in our community and society. Provided that access to help and advice is easily available I see no problem with this. Institutions with(in) the caring sector continually struggle with this in our blame culture and this is the main factor that has paralysed service providers to the point where they have become so ineffective radical change is required. Society punishes rather than learns from mistakes and this is very destructive. The balance for deciding on risk must swing drastically back to the individual service user.

(2006a, p13)

This commitment to choice and inclusion can be found in other areas. *Valuing People* talks of the need to provide even the most severely disabled person, with the right help and support, with the opportunity to make important choices and express preferences about their day-to-day lives (Department of Health, 2001, p24). *Independence, Well-being and Choice* recognised the dilemma posed by the need for protection, but also argued for the establishment of a debate about risk management and the right balance between protecting individuals and enabling them to take their own risks (Department of Health, 2005a, p28).

This discussion highlights how it is important that people are able to articulate their own needs and concerns, and points to debates in the following chapters as to whether social work needs to revisit a more radical agenda.

Advocacy is an important means of achieving such aspirations for many people and has been defined by the Independent Advocacy Campaign (seven key stakeholders representing people with physical, sensory, communication and profound multiple impairments) as '*taking action to help people say what they want, secure their rights, represent their interests and obtain services they need*' (Lewington and Clipson, 2004, p4).

Rapaport et al. (2005) suggested that there are five core types of advocacy:

- legal advocacy – the broad range of methods and activities used by lawyers and other skilled individuals;
- class (collective, corporate or group) advocacy – when groups come together to speak up for and represent a larger group (e.g. MIND);
- Self-advocacy – excluded people are empowered to speak for themselves, develop skills and gain knowledge and confidence to advocate on their own behalf;
- peer advocacy – people with similar experiences speak for each other;
- citizen (voluntary) advocacy – where a person with a need is linked to a volunteer to advocate on her/his behalf.

Underpinning this typology are a number of key components which promote the idea that:

- each person has value;

- every person has the capacity for growth and learning;

- people should be supported to achieve more valued social roles (normalisation);

- consumer participation and increasing accountability should be central to good practice;

- human and legal rights are observed (people who use services are citizens with the same rights as others).

Atkinson (1999) framed the key characteristics of advocacy as being empowerment, autonomy, citizenship and inclusion, echoing some of the key themes outlined in the above discussion of policy development and the framework within which policy operates. However, discussions of the potential of advocacy are often constructed by discourses on individual and social models of disability. Goodley has argued that self-advocacy sits uneasily with the individual model: *'if we are told that impairment is all important and unsurpassable, then ... self-determination can only go as far as these constructs of disability will allow: assumed inability hampering personal growth'* (1997, p370). He suggests that the social model of disability permits a different approach:

> [T]he social model encourages a context to be formed in which people can strive for self-expression, growth and determination ... when an advisor sees people ... not as passive individuals constrained by impairment, but as people actively striving for their own self-determination in the face of a society that denies such rights, then self advocacy can be supported in a far more empowering manner.

> (Goodley, 1997, p374)

This is a view supported by agencies working with users of services. People First workers who, 'provide training for Disabled Peoples Organisations and self advocacy groups' say self-advocacy includes:

- speaking up for yourself;

- standing up for your rights;

- making choices;

- being independent;

- taking responsibility for oneself.

(see www.peoplefirstltd.com/what-we-do)

Aspis (1997), quoting Dawson and Palmer, argues that to self-advocate you need to resist practices which oppress you by challenging people in power, and exercise the right to challenge others and be angry and challenge carers when the need arises (1997, p648). To Aspis, self-advocacy must include:

> *knowledge of how the institution and the system works; knowledge and use of the policy-making process in the institution and system; the understanding that service users and institutional or system staff and managers do not have equal power; knowledge and use of human and legal resources ... recognition of what level of change is needed, striving for changes that may include alternatives to the choices that are available ... one critical ingredient of understanding if self-advocacy has really worked is whether what has been asked for will be permanent or temporary.*

> (1997, p652)

ACTIVITY 1.2

1. *How does advocacy fit within the four policy frameworks discussed by Hill? Which is the most conducive to developing advocacy services?*

2. *Taking one of the policy areas discussed above – children and young people, learning disability or adults – explore three ways in which an advocacy strategy can be rationalised by the key legislation/policy discussed.*

Comment

You may want to draw on examples from your practice in answering these questions. Use the Professional Capability Framework to explore how you would use advocacy in the circumstances you are working within.

As we noted earlier, self-advocacy is only one of the approaches available within advocacy. Healy (2000) suggests that peer advocacy is

> *a structured programme to assist young people ... to develop the skills required to recognise, resist, report and replace bullying behaviours through representative advocacy.*

It represents:

> *the establishment of a partnership which supports self-protective responses to abusive behaviour, not a dependent relationship where passivity is reinforced. The process of accessing and collaboration with a peer advocate are in themselves proactive responses on the part of the victimised individual, which will assist in the development of further effective behaviours.*

Further, it challenges the dominance of social work in decision making about children and young people. As an example he points to ASC (Advice, Advocacy and Representation Services for Children and Young People), which was established in 1992. The starting point was that advocates had the same status as other professionals. This approach is now growing across a range of settings, including:

- specialist services responding to young people within certain social divisions;
- some wholly reliant on volunteers;
- others having paid workers.

Dalrymple argues that one of the advantages of advocacy is that it provides a potential focus on the notion of the 'committed practitioner' – 'an ally with a personal commitment to social change' (Dalrymple, 2004, p186). She also suggests that child and youth advocates can be either professional or radical:

> [T]he professional advocate uses particular skills to motivate children and young people to ensure effective delivery of services. The radical advocate will challenge oppressive structures ... the roots ... though, are far from the radical traditions and, arguably for both professional and radical advocates their role is more compatible with the model of committed practitioner than other professional models.
>
> (pp187–8)

This can be achieved by reducing the disempowering effect of the personal experiences of children and young people which has required them to need advocacy support. The advocate concentrates on the child or young person's feeling of self-worth and trying to enable them to strengthen the ability to control their lives. They in turn go further by seeking changes in the agency or wider systems which affect them. This is more like a systematic advocacy (Dalrymple, 2004, p192–3).

Boylan and Ing suggest that what young people want from their social worker is:

> Someone you can trust and won't let you down ... someone who will really stick up for you, who turns up when they say they are going to and is your friend (female 14, residential care).
>
> An enduring relationship.
>
> The appropriate exercise of power.
>
> She kicks arse, she's there for me (Care Leavers Group).
>
> Independence from social services.
>
> She's not from social services so they take notice (female aged 14, residential unit).
>
> (2005, p9)

Dalrymple and Boylan argue for the importance of linking social work values to a commitment to service user and carer perspectives. They believe that such an approach should be underpinned with a focus on the need to develop a critical practice which is based around the recasting or renewing of relationship practice as a central element of social work. Central to this, they argue, is the recognition that

> [t]he rights of service users can only be realised if there are changes in power relations in individual interactions and within structures and organisations ... this

involves changing who decides what information is shared, who decides whose voice is heard and what resources will be available in order that they gain self-esteem and the confidence that they advocate for themselves. Our approach to advocacy is a structural model which analyses empowerment from the standpoint of service user.

(2013, p166)

This focus on the empowerment of service users, the ability of people to self-realise, and the importance of a structural or macro-approach are central to the arguments in the rest of this book and are situated within a broad social work/community development and social pedagogic agenda in Chapters 2, 3 and 6.

C H A P T E R   S U M M A R Y

This chapter has sought to chart some of the key issues facing contemporary social work. Following Hill (2005), it suggests a framework for analysing policies impacting on social work and looks at the way a number of consistent themes are beginning to emerge in social policy discourse. These include issues of choice, control and independence. The chapter illustrates how these policy options are underpinned by contradictory discourses around risk, or rather risk avoidance and advocacy. The chapter provides a contemporary framework through which Chapters 2 and 3 will explore the way some of these dilemmas relate to the development of social work and the ways in which they can be resolved.

FURTHER READING

Dalrymple, J. and Boylan, J. (2013) *Effective Advocacy in Social Work.* London: SAGE.

A good account of the relationship of advocacy to contemporary social work, with a focus on inclusion and participation, the importance of relationship-based practice and the need for a structural model of advocacy.

Hatton, K. (2013) *Social Pedagogy in the UK: Theory and Practice.* Lyme Regis: Russell House.

Provides a framework for understanding the potential relationship of social pedagogy to UK social work and has a particular focus on how social pedagogy can link to discussions around personalisation and co-production.

Hill, M. (2005) *The Public Policy Process*, 4th edn. Harlow: Pearson/Longman.

Provides a good account of the policy process, theories of power, organisational processes and inter-organisational processes.

Horner, N. (2013) *What is Social Work? Context and Perspectives*, 4th edn. London: Sage/Learning Matters.

A good introduction to the history and current practice of social work. Includes discussion of social work with all major groups of service users.

Jordan, B. (2006) *Social Policy for the Twenty-first Century.* Cambridge: Polity Press.

A thoughtful, if complex, discussion of the present and future direction of social policy in the UK. Includes a particularly good discussion of human wellbeing and social justice.

33

WEBSITES

Association of Chief Executives of Voluntary Organisations: www.acevo.org/ (accessed 27/2/15)

The College of Social Work Professional Capability Framework: www.tcsw.org.uk/pcf.aspx (accessed 27/2/15)

Social Care Institute of Excellence (www.scie.org.uk) describes its visions as being:

- **Co-productive and collaborative** – We co-produce our work with people who use services and their carers to identify what works and how that knowledge can be put into practice. We promote equality and value diversity and human rights. We collaborate with partners to influence future policy and practice, and to increase our reach and impact.

- **Innovative and customer-focused** – We meet the changing needs of our diverse audiences and customers with new and better services and products that support the delivery of high quality services.

- **Enterprising and expert** – We seek new opportunities to promote our knowledge and skills throughout the care and support and other sectors. Our work is based on a rigorous approach to identifying good and developing practice

(Available from www.scie.org.uk/about/index.asp – accessed 27/2/15)

Chapter 2
Social work, community work and social change

This chapter will help you to develop the following capabilities, to the appropriate level, from the Professional Capabilities Framework:

Values and ethics. Apply social work ethical principles and values to guide professional practice.

Diversity. Recognise diversity and apply anti-discriminatory and anti-oppressive principles in practice.

Rights, justice and economic wellbeing. Advance human rights and promote social justice and economic wellbeing.

Critical reflection and analysis. Apply critical reflection and analysis to inform and provide a rationale for professional decision making.

Intervention and skills. Use judgement and authority to intervene with individuals, families and communities to promote independence, provide support and prevent harm, neglect and abuse.

Contexts and organisations. Engage with, inform, and adapt to changing contexts that shape practice. Operate effectively within own organisational frameworks and contribute to the development of services and organisations. Operate effectively within multi-agency and inter-professional settings.

See Appendix 1 for the Professional Capabilities Framework diagram.

The chapter will also introduce you to the following standards as set out in the social work benchmark statement (QAA, 2008).

4.1 Defining Principles

4.3 Defining Principles

4.6 Defining Principles

Community Development National Occupational Standards

Key Area 1: Understand and practice community.

Key Area 2: Understand and engage with communities.

Key Area 3: Take a community development approach to group work and collective action.

Key Area 6: Provide community development support to organisations.

(Federation for Community Development Learning, 2009)

Introduction: reintegrating the radical into contemporary social work

In the first edition of this book the author noted that social work is increasingly confronting pressures to refocus its gaze on the scope of individuals and to ignore or play down the way the problems individuals face are structured by broader social economic and political factors. In the UK the mixed economy of welfare (Johnson, 1999), increased marketisation of welfare services and the focus on assessment and regulation in social work practice (Humphries, 1996) had led some to argue that any potential or radical practice has become marginalised. Yet at the same time there was an increase in recognition of the role of the user of welfare services (or more recently 'experts by experience') as an 'active agent'. Williams and colleagues have suggested we could see the emergence of a new welfare paradigm which

> emphasises the capacity of people to be creative, reflexive human agents of their lives, experiencing, acting upon and reconstituting the outcomes of welfare policies. It also points to the complex, multiple, subjective and objective social positionings that welfare subjects inhabit.
>
> (Williams et al., 1998, p21; see also Chapter 5)

Below we will look at how social work activity continues to be constructed within the parameters of the increasing poverty and social exclusion of social work's service users. Increasingly it has become recognised that social work can make a contribution to the process of social inclusion (Barry, 1998; Dominelli, 2004, 2010; Jones and Novak, 2014). Social work has a role in empowering people to overcome their exclusion through promoting forms of social inclusion. However, as Barry noted,

> there seems to be a dichotomy between the philosophy behind the notion of social inclusion (which could be argued to be welfare-orientated and based on notions of a collective responsibility rather than individual blame), and the emerging trend within social work to move away from a more proactive welfare and collective approach to social problems and towards refocusing on reactive management of individual behaviour, irrespective of the wider social and economic context.
>
> (1998, p9)

If anything, this trend has accelerated, initially with New Labour's focus on the communitarian agenda of rights and responsibilities (Jordan and Jordan, 2000) and its increasingly punitive attitude to marginal groups and perceived anti-social behaviour and more recently the Coalition government's attacks on the poor ('the bedroom tax', cuts to disability benefits etc.). Jones and Novak (2014) have suggested that 500 years of history of dealing with poverty have meant that the UK state has become permeated with 'a particularly callous treatment [of the poor] which marks it off from many of its European neighbours' (p4).

There is, therefore, a tendency to emphasise the control and management functions of social work without examining or (re)examining the potential that social work may have for promoting processes of transformation. We need to address these problems by remembering again the issues raised by those theorists and activists who were promoting 'radical social work' or 'radical community work' in the early to mid–1970s and who have recently, at least, been seen to be swimming 'against the stream' of managerialism and the competency culture (Dominelli and Hoogvelt, 1996; Pinkney, 1998; Clarke et al., 2001; Dominelli, 2010; Lavalette and Ferguson, 2007; Ferguson and Woodward, 2009; Jones and Novak, 2014). These works provide the beginnings of a more systematic and structural framework against which we can evaluate social work's potential to engage with processes of change.

Remembering the radical alternatives: from casework to class struggle

An extensive selection of writings which could be said to fall within the umbrella of radical social work, including important literature on community work and community action, emerged around the mid- to late 1970s (examples include Leonard, 1975; Jones and Mayo, 1974; O'Malley, 1977; Mayo, 2002). To begin with we will examine those key collections which bore the sobriquet 'radical social work', specifically those by Bailey and Brake (1975, 1980) and Langan and Lee (1989), and to a lesser extent the work of the CaseCon collective which produced a magazine of the same name for a period in the mid- to late 1970s. We will then examine the literature which emerged from the Community Development Projects (CDPs) and radical community work around the same time.

Radical social work – what was (is) it?

Bailey and Brake, in the introduction to the first radical social work collection, argued that their aim was to move social work beyond its then preoccupation with casework and its 'over emphasis on pathological and clinical orientations to the detriment of structural and political implications' (1975, p1). This collection of readings promoted an advocacy/welfare rights approach, radical community action, and what Cohen called the 'politics of abolition', that is, maintaining a focus on abolishing the legitimacy of state organisations. In the same volume Leonard (1975) suggested that radical practice should be built around a process which involves working both within and against the structures in which the worker is employed. This, he suggested, involved a three-way process: the creation of dialogical relationships between worker and user; the development of group consciousness which entails 'the demystification of political structures and economic relations'; and the development of a complex range of organisation, administrative and planning skills (1975, p60 – the relevance of this analysis for contemporary practice will be discussed in later chapters).

This first collection drew extensively on the work of Paulo Freire (1972) and had a clearly oppositional stance to existing social work practice. However, although there is a focus on sexuality the paradigm addressed is essentially class based and there is no developed account of feminist or anti-racist struggles.

This absence was corrected in Brake and Bailey (1980). Wilson pointed to the tension between the personal and the political in any radical social work. As she argued, *it is not that help for the individual is inimical to social change (all political activists and movements have combined social aid for individuals for political campaigning); and social change cannot be brought about unless individuals feel that the politics will answer individual needs ... but the problems that face social workers who are concerned with social change is the rather brutalised and ativised nature of the groups with whom they have the most part to deal; groups whose rebellion against their conditions of life often comes out not as rebellion but as personal disaster in the sphere of private life ... Social workers never throw up an adequate strategy for dealing politically with these personal problems.*

(1980, p39; see also Jordan, 1996 and discussion below)

Husband (1980) focused on the issues facing 'black' professionals and clients within social work, arguing that the cultural understanding of white UK social workers, when combined with the routinisation of their professional practice, render white institutions particularly resistant to comprehending the new demands which they must meet in order to service multi-racial clientele (p85).

This analysis was taken further in Langan and Lee (1989), who argued that one of the most important elements of the early radical social work texts was that they provided a critique of existing social work provision, and they pointed out that one of the most useful things radicals can do is resist new attempts by the authorities to promote the idea that poverty is a problem of personal failure, rather than a social problem (1989, p15; see also section on poverty and social exclusion below).

Hudson (1989) took forward the feminist critique of social work and pointed out how it had developed a critique of psychological paradigms in social work and argued for social work to develop a more meaningful account of the ways in which social inequalities impact on the personal and emotional lives of service users. She pointed out how statutory and professional power are issues with which feminists have sought to critically engage. She also pointed to the need for feminists to engage with men and points out how the pursuit of great gender equality has sometimes been at the expense of recognising other oppressions, particularly those experienced by both black and working-class women and by lesbians (1989, p93). Shar (1989) made a similar point when she argued that it is not our responsibility to provide solutions for white women; they must find genuine ways of support by examining their own practice, ideas and motives (p190).

Running throughout these texts is also a commitment to other forms of practice, particularly radical community action. Writing in 1980, Mayo had warned against the dangers of allowing the state to dictate the agenda around community development (p135). In 2002 she argued for the continuing involvement of radicals in community work as a way of criticising local services when they need to be criticised, yet defending the very existence of those services (p275).

Similar arguments were also found in a number of other key texts during the 1980s. Jones (1983) sought to show how social work clients are separated off from those sections of the working class in employment. He pointed to the ways in which the focus of much social work is on the poor and disfranchised and argued that,

*for many clients, the sheer struggle to survive compels them to adopt the most
individualistic and introverted strategies which are completely at odds with the
traditions of collective action which have developed within the organised working
class both in their communities and in their work places.*

(1983, p57; see also comments of Jordan below
and discussion in Chapter 3)

Jones argued that socialists within social work should do their best to maintain a
broad front of oppositional work (p152). This would involve, he suggested, highlighting the inequalities that clients/service users face and arguing for the democratisation
of welfare services. He warned, however, against a simple process of democratisation,
pointing out that it can have negative consequences. Some of the most marginalised groups of service users often face marginalisation within their communities from
within a *'working class culture [with[long standing antagonistic strands towards
some clusters of the client population'* (p155).

There are similarities here with some of the earlier arguments put forward by Bolger
et al. (1981). They argued for an approach which operates within and outside the state
(see also Rowbotham et al., 1980) and pointed to the way in which, during the 1970s,
the welfare state had come to be perceived by the general population as external to
themselves, bureaucratic, paternalistic and dependency creating. This negative image,
particularly among working-class people, created a problem for socialists in that it *'is
absurd to expect that people who experience humiliation on a day-to-day basis at the
hands of the welfare state will then turn round and defend it when the right wing tries
to dismantle it'* (1981, p151). Bolger et al. called for a democratic restructuring of the
welfare state, suggesting a democratisation of the client–worker relationship as well as
the workers' relationship to the welfare state. This democracy, they suggested, is inextricably linked with the improvement of relationships, structure, politics, welfare policy
and revolutionary change (p154). Arguably it was precisely this disenchantment with
the welfare state that allowed the Conservative government elected in 1979 to introduce
neo-liberal policies aimed at rolling back the state (Johnson, 1999).

ACTIVITY 2.1

*Jane and Tom live in a three-bedroom flat in a high-rise block in Eastsea. They have two
children, Aaron who is 8 and Benji who is 5. The flat is damp and both children have
asthma. The family receive income support, but have no other source of income. Their
social worker has indicated that it is Jane and Tom's responsibility to ensure that their children are healthy and that she will intervene if the family do not carry out improvements to
their property. Examine the above scenario and evaluate the following:*

- *How should a local authority social worker intervene?*

- *Would a social worker with a more radical perspective adopt a different approach? If
so, how would it differ?*

Comment

Use the Professional Capability Framework and the National Occupational Standards for Community Work to look at the competencies both professions would expect a social worker to demonstrate within this work.

An example of how these debates were played out across a state-sponsored community work project is provided by the Community Development Projects (see below), which were funded by the Home Office in the early 1970s.

Community Development Projects 1970–74: from class struggle to difference and diversity

The Community Development Projects (CDPs) in Britain were announced following a statement from the Home Secretary in the Houses of Parliament in 1970 and were initially seen as a *'neighbourhood based experiment aimed at finding new ways of meeting the needs of people living in areas of high social deprivation'* (Community Development Projects, 1974, p1). They were designed to intervene in areas of between 10 and 20 thousand people, but were concentrated in 12 areas ranging from Liverpool in the Northwest, Coventry in the Midlands, to Glyncorrwg in Glamorgan.

The first project was started in January 1970 and the last started in October 1972. The inter-project report written in 1974 noted that,

> *despite their wide diversity, projects have all identified similar symptoms of disadvantage indicating the now familiar profile of poverty. All areas do not share identical elements but most include:*

> - *lower than average incomes,*
> - *disproportionately high rates of unemployment,*
> - *high dependence on state benefits,*
> - *poor health records ... and poor housing.*

> (Community Development Projects, 1974, p8)

The CDPs were a culmination of a decade of projects which had sought to deal with the rediscovery of poverty in the 1960s. The projects were originally based on a social pathology model of urban deprivation in which it was assumed that

> *problems of urban deprivation had their origins in the characteristics of local populations – in individual pathologies – and these could best be resolved by better field coordination of the social services, combined with the mobilisation of self help and mutual aid in the community even amongst those who experienced most difficulty in standing on their own two feet.*

> (Community Development Projects, 1974, p1)

By the time the inter-project report was published in 1974, many of the projects had changed emphasis and had moved towards a structural analysis of the urban deprivation that the communities they were dealing with suffered from. The report noted that

> the problems of the 12 CDP areas are not reducible to problems of employment,
> housing, income and education. They are not isolated pockets suffering from an
> unfortunate combination of circumstances, they are a central part of the dynamics
> of the urban system and as such represent those who have lost out in the
> competition for jobs, housing and educational opportunity.

> (Community Development Projects, 1974, p52)

Such comments were borne out by the final reports from a number of the projects. The North Shields project's final report notes how the inter-project report for them represented the decisive rejection of social pathology accounts of the problems of CDP areas and of the community therapy model, in the CDPs' work, at least by the majority of CDPs.

They note instead that on North Tyneside the CDP *'had adopted a class based account of these issues and origins'* (North Shields CDP, 1974, p10). The arguments against social pathology were taken up and extended in the joint report *Gilding the Ghetto* (Community Development Projects, 1977). The authors of *Gilding the Ghetto* noted that the emphasis on tackling social needs in isolation inevitably distracts attention from the root causes of the problem by focusing attention upon personal deficiencies.

To counter these factors, a number of projects developed an emphasis on community and group work solutions to the problems of their areas. The Benwell Project, in Newcastle, believed that it was valid to encourage people to engage in community action because their role was not to encourage people to, in their words, *'tolerate the intolerable'*. They argued that should people

> make unreasonable demands, or even to demand the impossible, we would only
> answer that in the circumstances in which residents of Noble Street in Newcastle
> were placed themselves, they had no responsibility whatever to be reasonable if by
> that is meant learning to adapt to such circumstances. Indeed we would argue that
> the only reasonable reaction to such an environment is to do everything possible
> to escape from it. They did not create the slums; they did not want to live in them,
> the argument that there isn't enough money to do anything about it cannot and
> must not be taken seriously. For it is precisely this type of argument that led to the
> creation of the slums in the first place.

> (Benwell CDP, 1974, p45)

Similar discussions led some CDPs to adopt a more intransigently action-based approach. For example, North Shields argued for more projects to engage in the process of 'radical reformism'. They defined this as

> a class model of society, it is a process which involves fairly substantial change in
> one aspect of society but that in the end has not challenged the fundamental base
> of society. It tends to be most applicable in areas of social welfare, for example,
> the National Health Service implementation 1946 was a radical reformist measure,
> where it can alter the distribution of income in society and is an expression of the
> existence of organized class power, but it does not alter the fundamental structure
> of the social market economy model.

> (North Tyneside CDP, 1974, p10)

This commitment to the radical reformist approach is described in detail in Volume 4 of the North Shields CDP's final report entitled *Organising for Change in a Working Class Area: The Action Groups*. The aims of this process are also through struggle to *'make people conscious both of the process they are facing and their ... power as a class to bring about unofficial changes'* (North Shields CDP, 1974, p6; see also Chapter 3).

Corkey and Craig (1978) note in their review of CDPs that the analysis developed by the CDPs frequently brought them into dispute with their local authorities, and potential funders; there is little support individual projects could call on outside the project areas in time of conflict. They point to the ways in which working on individual issues threw out broader issues; for example, the 1976 housing campaign resulted in alliances between tenants and local authority unions.

On the basis of their analysis of the work developed by the CDPs with trade unions, Corkey and Craig concluded that only the working class, through its collective action, is in a position to defend its class interests against the operations of capital. This leads them to generalise that

> *traditional forms of community work are dangerous and that they tend to socialize working class areas into the existing economic system and community workers who are developing such strategies must be challenged about their attempt to control and dispel working class action and protest on behalf of the state.*

> (1978, p64)

Waddington located the experience of the CDPs as a watershed in the experience of community work in the 1970s. As he noted,

> *CDP fulfilled a prophetic function in plugging community work's theoretical and ideological cavities with a structural perspective at least for a time. But after the ending of CDP many community workers found it difficult to operationalise or apply the theory to their own practice, partly because the material produced by the CDPs has tended to be longer on analysis than on applications.*

> (1979, p226)

The experience of the CDPs should be seen as important because of the way in which they moved from an individual social pathology model of social deprivation to an analysis based on an understanding of class structure and of the inter-relationship of industrial, economic and social policies. They were state sponsored and therefore, to the extent that they supported the development of community action initiatives and developed a comprehensive critique of the operation of the state nationally and locally, they can be seen as providing an important corrective to the individualising of social problems.

However, even within these criteria it seems clear that they were to some extent hindered by an overly deterministic class analysis of the role of the state. They sought to develop alliances between industrial and community groupings but seemed to have been guilty of putting forward an analysis which subsumed community interests below those of the industrial groupings with which they worked.

However, there is evidence from within the projects themselves that they made strenuous efforts to work with and empower the communities in which they were based. *Gilding the Ghetto* concentrates on how the state's commitment to tackling urban deprivation was merely empty rhetoric and argues that *'the basic dilemma for the state remains the same, how best to respond to the needs of capitalism on the one hand and maintain the consent of the working class on the other'* (Community Development Projects, 1977, p63).

And yet at the same time it is undeniable that the CDPs did extremely good and complex work with the communities in which they were based. The third and fourth reports of the North Shields CDP concentrated on the areas of group work within which they engaged. In Volume 4 of their report they demonstrate how the Percy Main Residents Group, a group made up of residents of a village near the River Tyne, maintained their militancy despite the fact that *'the kind of tactics they used generated a lot of antagonism in the area because it affronted the notions of respectable and legitimate behaviour of many of those who live there'* (p39).

For example, a local GP wrote to the press complaining of the activities of the CDP and their small band of 'puppet followers'. He asked, *'What is this country coming to when Local Authorities and Home Office combine to plant an extremist group like this in the community and allow to do as it pleases in the name of community development?'* (cf. pp24–6, Vol. 4). Similar attitudes to what are perceived as oppositional groups continued throughout the 1980s and 1990s as witnessed by the public statement of Cllr Derek Allinson, then Chair of Cardiff City Council's Environmental Services Committee, who when discussing an application for funding from Adamsdown Law Centre (an independent free legal service controlled by the local community) said that to give the law centre money *'would be like sending tanks to Saddam Hussein'* (*South Wales Echo,* 2 November 1990).

The rationale for such an oppositional approach is provided in the Tyneside report, which notes that *'collective work was regarded as desirable precisely because of a suspicion of case work approaches, suspicion not least of the long term effectiveness of any gains established in this way, even for individuals concerned'* (p42).

They go on to argue how *'individual case work legitimises the system and splitting is an essential mechanism for keeping things as they are',* a factor which *'was never squarely faced by North Tyneside CDP or anyone else for that matter'* (p43). By 'splitting', they meant the individualisation of problems, so that people were prevented from seeing the structural causes of the problems they faced. Finally, the projects do not seem to have dealt explicitly with questions of gender or ethnicity. In fact, there seems to have been a tendency throughout the projects to subsume such issues within the umbrella of class oppression. Some commentators at the time questioned whether there was any substance to the idea that a radical community was ever effective. Vass suggests that this was a myth sustained by radical community workers themselves because of a *'natural desire to believe in something regarded as new, different and alternative'* (1980, p3). However, despite the relatively short timescale within which the CDPs were operative, it is undoubtedly true that they enabled a wide group of community activists to see the potential of generating change at the very least at local and regional level (South Wales Association of Tenants; Wales Social Security Campaign, 1989).

Themes in radical social and community work

The above discussion of radical social and community work suggests a number of key themes, which can, and should, be incorporated into discussions of current welfare practice. Briefly, these are:

- The need to reinsert class into our analysis. Phillips (1999) has noted the way that attention has shifted from the focus on class inequalities to the way gender, racial or cultural hierarchies undermine equal citizenship. Radical social work and its attendant literature can remind us of this need to connect all forms of oppression. The discussions of race/ethnicity and gender relations are important for social work, not just because they describe the social relations between groups/collectivities but because they also provide a means of grounding their practice.

- The need to democratise the organisations in which we work.

- The need to build a critical consciousness which can empower the individuals and collectivities with which we work.

- The need for a transformative vision which looks beyond the situations we currently face.

Focusing on poverty and social exclusion

One way in which social work has 'remembered' these concerns with class and structural factors has been an increasing recognition in the last 20 years of the significance of poverty and social exclusion as determinants of the life chances of many of the service users with whom social workers engage (Beresford and Croft, 1995; Beresford et al., 1999; Davis and Wainwright, 2005; Shepperd, 2006; Jones and Novak, 2014).

However, even this focus on social exclusion is itself problematic. Before embracing the concept we need to ask what we mean by social exclusion and how it can help us build strategies to improve the life chances of people using welfare services (Levitas, 2005; Oppenheim, 1998; Byrne, 1999). Levitas (2005) has argued that the concept of social exclusion is problematic precisely because it dichotomises the experience of both the included majority and the excluded minority and draws attention away from the differences and inequalities among the included (p7). Driver and Martell (1998) pointed out how New Labour's debates on social exclusion were framed by their commitment to communitarian notions of rights and responsibilities so that the government will fulfil its side of the bargain by helping the socially excluded to find work; in turn, the socially excluded must fulfil their own responsibilities by doing something about their condition (p90; see also Byrne, 1998, and Chapter 4).

Levitas (2005) suggests that there are three distinct discourses around social exclusion, which she characterises as the redistributive discourse, the moral underclass discourse and the social integrationist discourse. Drawing on Levitas' analysis these discourses can be codified to suggest how they 'fit' with a conceptualisation of social work. The results are presented in Table 2.1.

Table 2.1   Discourses around social exclusion – typical features and relationship to social and community work (adapted from Levitas, 2005)

Redistributive discourse	Moral underclass discourse	Social integrationist discourse
Poverty prime cause	Underclass culturally distinct	Narrow definition exclusion – emphasises paid work
Increase in benefit levels	Focus on behaviour of poor	Does not imply increase in benefits
Can valorise unpaid work	Implies benefits are bad	Obscures inequalities between paid workers
Posits citizenship as obverse exclusion	Ignores societal inequalities	Obscures gender inequalities
Broad critique of inequality, not just limited to material inequality	Gendered discourse about idle, criminal young men and single mothers	Obscures class inequality
Focus on processes which cause inequality	Unpaid work unacknowledged	Unable to deal with question of unpaid work
Implies radical reduction of inequality and redistribution of societies' resources	Dependency on state problematised, personal economic dependency not problematised	Ignores unpaid work and its gendered distribution, implies increase in women's workload, undermines the legitimacy of non-participation in paid work
Social/community work response: Community action, self-organisation	Social/community work response: Casework, statutory, dependency creating	Social/community work response: Community development, interventionist, top-down

Each of these discourses has different implications for social and community work. The theory of social exclusion that underpins our interventions determines our ability to engage with service users in ways which lead to their empowerment rather than their oppression. For example, a moral underclass analysis would lead us to view service users in terms of their deficiencies and social pathology and would be likely to result in us problematising service users rather than looking at the broader social factors which impact on them (examples can be seen in the Coalition government's welfare reform proposals which are predicated on a moral underclass paradigm that blames people for their poverty). A social integrationist discourse is likely to lead us to see reintegration into the labour market and policies that aim to achieve this goal (under New Labour these included Working Families Tax Credit, Disability Tax Credit, personal advisers, job training) as being the most fruitful outcome. A redistributionist discourse is the one that is more likely to focus our attention on wider structural factors, minimise any tendency toward pathologising the service users/carers we work with and focus our attention on social change and societal redistribution.

Jordan (1996) argued that the choices open to people in poverty are in any event more constrained than those from more affluent communities and that these processes of social exclusion through community formation and *'voting with the feet'* (p169) indicate that the life chances of the affluent and the dispossessed are constrained by their occupation of *'communities of choice'* or *'communities of fate'*. He suggests that the latter should not be characterised as passive, anomic or resigned, but should be seen as generating strong resistance cultures which involve both solidaristic and supportive association and opportunistic, predatory action against the residents of *'communities of choice'* (p174). He points to the way in which these processes impact disproportionately on women and people from minority ethnic communities. He argues that

> [p]oor women, and especially women from ethnic minorities, constitute the basis for *'community'* and hence for social policies that try to define the relationship between public providers of welfare services and their clienteles in terms of *'partnership'*.

> (Jordan, 1996, p185)

This is an interesting attempt to introduce the notion of welfare recipients as active agents who consistently negotiate space for change. It connects with some of the concerns expressed within radical social and community work about the capacity of people to create collective solutions to the problems they face. Indeed, Jordan points to the way in which women in such communities often have to resist dual pressures in that public authorities exploit the community of women in the very manner that individual men exploit their partner (Jordan, 1996, pp182–3). This fits with the attempts to develop a new 'cultural perspective' on welfare, which shifts attention from the spheres of the market, and of the administrative state, to the networks and social relations of society itself (Freeman et al., 1999, p280). It is also consistent with Williams et al.'s (1999) suggestion that we need to develop a new paradigm of welfare.

Lister sees poverty as spelling exclusion from the full rights of citizenship in the social political and civil spheres and undermines people's ability to fulfil the public and private obligations of citizenship (1998, p29). She argues that there is a need to distinguish between a person's capacity to be a citizen and to act as a citizen, and that to tackle poverty and exclusion and promote inclusion we need to promote the idea of active citizenship (Lister, 1998). We will return to these arguments later.

While some of these debates may seem to have historical rather than contemporary relevance, it is important to locate current debates around the poor within a continuing negative discourse. For example, a brief glance at discussions of poverty today suggests a number of discourses within public discussions of poverty which seek to blame the poor for being poor. These include:

- **Around young people** – the lower rate of income support for young people under 25, which was introduced because of public concern, fostered by the media and the government that young people were abusing the benefits system.

- **Around single mothers** – the assumption that benefits causes young single mothers to become dependent on the state.

- **Around disability** – the work capability test, which again suggests that people with disabilities are cheating the system.

- **Around food** – *'surely the debate around living standards should start with the immorality of food banks in one of the richest countries in the world'* (Suzanne Moore, Food Banks, *Guardian*, 17/10/13).

- ***Benefits Street*** – a Channel 4 documentary that portrays the poor as undeserving and feckless.

Within these discourses people in poverty are often referred to as 'scroungers', 'feckless', 'spongers', 'idle'. Abigail Scott Paul from the Joseph Rowntree Foundation refers to much of the coverage as *'poverty porn'*. She says, *'we know that the media is partial, and that people in poverty themselves feel victimised, stigmatised and objectified'*, adding:

> When public attitudes are hardening towards people in poverty and when life is getting worse for people at the lowest end of the income scale, is it right that broadcasters commission shows that compound stereotypes by pitting deserving against undeserving poor?

> (JRF blog, 23/08/13)

Novak and Jones (2014) quote Bamfield (2005), who said:

> The size of the gap between between popular conceptions and the reality of life in poverty is...profoundly depressing – and difficult territory to start putting together a compelling public case for tackling poverty.

> (Bamfield, 2005, in Jones and Novak, 2014)

Yet this is precisely what a refocusing of social work on a radical agenda can achieve.

ACTIVITY **2.2**

Look again at the situation that Jane and Tom find themselves in (Activity 2.1). Using Levitas' typology of social exclusion, indicate:

- *how the models of social exclusion can be used to understand the circumstances they find themselves in;*

- *which model of social exclusion a radical social or community worker would use to underpin their intervention with the family.*

Comment

Levitas (2005) categorises social exclusion as being of one of three types: redistributive, social integrationist or moral underclass. Apply these typologies and think about their implications for social or community work practice.

From radical social work to critical social work

Can we legitimately use these insights to construct a transformatory and critical social work? Langan (2002) has suggested that the radicalism that was seen in social work practice in the 1970s became transformed in the 1980s to a top-down process in which a progressive agenda, to the extent it existed, was promoted from above – by academics and managers. While the 1990s saw the promotion of anti-discriminatory/anti-oppressive practice, from both practitioners and the regulatory body, The Central Council for Education and Training in Social Work (CCETSW), she argued that *'the radical commitment to liberation appeared to have been transformed into a mechanism for regulation'* (Langan, 2002, p215).

Healy (2000) argues that critical social work has become marginalised because it has failed to re-evaluate its own practice. In particular, she suggested that critical or radical social work privileges *'certain practice contexts'* over others in a way that fails to take account of the way in which social workers minimise the implications of power relations in their practice; they oversimplify the power differential between workers and users and they devalue some forms of change activity. She says:

> Radical analyses can overlook the emancipatory potential in everyday social work practices by establishing standards that devalue much of the change activity in which social workers are involved. At the same time, the emancipatory potential of other practice contexts is exaggerated because of a failure to acknowledge the extent to which the historical context of social services impacts on the kinds of practices that are possible.

> (Healy, 2000, p5)

This is an important corrective to an overly naive approach to the issue of social change and social transformation and in some ways replicates earlier invocations to work *'in and against the state'* and Mullaly's argument that we should work *'within (and against) the system'* by using social work skills and techniques in such a way that we *'demystify it by discussing its origins, purpose ... and by encouraging service users to ask questions'* (1993, p174 – see Mullaly, 2006 for a more up-to-date account).

Dominelli and Hoogvelt (1996) argued that an emphasis on competence in social work has been part of the process of *'bureaucratisation of quality'* which has afflicted social work and which, in part, is a response to changes in the mixed economy of welfare over the period since 1979. They suggested that

> the breaking up of complex social work tasks which require fine professional judgements be made, reflects an attempt to move the work away from autonomous critical reflective practitioners, for the critical reflective practitioner is a worker who is capable of independent judgement and who wields a certain

degree of power as a professional over the employer and any given client in
defining the task to be done in any particular situation.

(1996, p56)

Social work is therefore currently the site of a battle of ideas: on the one hand, those who are seeking to reduce social work as an activity to a set of professional competencies, and on the other, to a group of people who are seeking to create a form of social work which is based on notions of reflective and critical practice (Gardiner, 2014; Dominelli and Hoogvelt, 1996).

Dominelli (1999) has suggested that social workers have responded to the increased privatisation of social work, an accompanying loss of professional autonomy and a dissipation of their professional role in three ways: through accommodation, escapism or resistance. Accommodation she characterised by the social workers' engagement with the new contracting culture in a naive belief that they will continue to provide a service that is more consistent with a public service ethos and social work's professional ethics (p20). Escapism strategies are pursued by those who feel professionally disempowered and respond by looking for work outside the public sector. Rather than naivety, their position is characterised by a cynicism derived from their view of the system's capacity to respond appropriately to any challenge which is mounted against it (p20). The resisters are also characterised by their feelings of alienation and disaffection from the system. The difference is in their response. They take an activist role in challenging the decisions of the agencies within the system. Dominelli says:

The activities of women, black people, gay men, lesbian women and disabled
people in raising the failure of social services to respond appropriately to their
needs are examples of resisters who have sought to change the situation that
service users face.

(1999, p21)

This schema provides an interesting means of distinguishing the responses of social professionals to the challenges faced by globalisation, privatisation and the dampening down of the radical agenda which was so much at the forefront 20 years ago. However, it oversimplifies a complex reality. Social workers are still, if to a much lesser degree, working within the system to bring about change (Rowbotham et al., 1980; Ferguson and Woodward, 2009). In addition, Dominelli's account is guilty of over-concentrating on the public sector. Many of the changes she describes have been experienced by state social workers. However, a consequence of privatisation has been the expansion of social work into other areas of the mixed economy. NGOs or voluntary sector organisations have to some extent benefited from the disillusion of state workers. Forms of radical and alternative practice are, if not flourishing, at least with strong enough roots to ensure that emancipatory forms of practice can still be found. I would suggest that Dominelli's typology could be expanded to encompass a more diverse range of practices. The typology could therefore be reconstructed as in Table 2.2.

Table 2.2   Models of practice

Type of practice response	State social work (child care)	Anti-racist work	Social/community action
Accommodation	Child protection/court work	Race equality councils	Councils of community service
Escapism	Voluntary sector	Multi-cultural festivals	Non-state service providers
Resistance	Organisations of young people in care	Anti-racist organisations	Social action projects

Dominelli (1998) suggests elsewhere that anti-oppressive practice can provide a way of helping people organise their responses to the questions of equality and social justice posited by the theorists of 'radical', 'structural' or 'critical' social work. It is, she suggests,

> *[i]ntimately bound up with notions of improving the quality of life or wellbeing of individuals, groups and communities. This concern lends it a holistic mantle, which encompasses all aspects of social life – culture, institutions, legal framework, political system, socio-economic infrastructure and interpersonal relationships which both create and are created by social reality ... [this has led people to] look for bonds of solidarity which acknowledge the different starting points held by groups of people working towards a common aim.*

> (Dominelli, 1998, pp5–6)

An example of the way in which social work has sought to address these issues of marginalisation can be seen in the work of the ECSPRESS network – an initiative supported by the European Union which brought together social workers and other social professionals from across Europe who were concerned about the threat of social exclusion (Lorenz, 1998; Barry and Hallett, 1998; Marynowicz-Hetka et al., 1999). The ECSPRESS network symbolised a growing commitment to the development of networks of social professionals and the establishment of training and education initiatives which sought to improve inter-country cooperation. Walter Lorenz, writing in 1997 about the future facing the ECSPRESS network, argued that there were a number of challenges confronting us if we wanted to develop a European perspective in social work, particularly as

> *a broader European perspective relativises the traditional national understanding of the duties and responsibilities of a particular professional group.*

> (Lorenz, 1998, p28)

The challenge this poses has been taken forward by a number of writers more recently (Lavalette and Ferguson, 2007; Hatton 2011, 2013; Henderson and Vercseg, 2010; Gojova, 2011). This need to Europeanise and internationalise our approach to social work is dealt with more extensively in Chapter 7. However, it is worth noting the comments of a group of social work activists, people who use services and academics expressed through the Social Work Action Network (SWAN). They note how *[t]he current degraded status of social work as a profession is inextricably related to the status and standing of those we work with. Social work clients are amongst some of the most vulnerable and impoverished in our society, and have benefited least from New Labour's social welfare reforms. In fact, under New Labour we have witnessed not only greater levels of material inequality, but also an intensified demonisation of asylum seekers, young people and poor families, the very groups that social workers engage with. Too often today social workers are often doing little more than supervising the deterioration of people's lives.*

(SWAN, 2010)

However, despite the recognition of the problems of working within the current configurations of social work, they maintain that it remains possible to develop radical forms of practice which can transform the lives of people using social work services and those working within them.

Conclusion: Promoting inclusion

Where does this leave us? The above analysis suggests that we can learn from the theorists of radical social and community work and apply the lessons learned to the complex problems of poverty and social exclusion, which structure the experience of so many users of welfare services. Our focus should be on inclusion, on how we bring people into society in a way that acknowledges, and tackles, the severe marginalisation and disadvantage they suffer and which recognises that these processes of exclusion are structural to the societies in which we live. Clearly we need to develop a multi-dimensional response to the multi-dimensional problems outlined above. But this is more than just producing joined-up solutions. Joined-up solutions are often more discriminatory than fragmented responses as they enhance the power of the politicians and professionals and further marginalise the excluded.

Any solutions we develop will need to be based on a number of principles, which can be summarised as the 'A–F of inclusion'. These are:

- **Active citizenship** – by and large people are not passive, they merely lack the belief in their own capacity and the knowledge and skills to achieve change.

- **Bringing people in** – overcoming the 'them and us' mentality which so often creates impasses in attempts to revitalise areas; normally people express anger and frustration because they are not being heard, not because they are.

- **Capacity building** – to overcome this passivity people need to be given the resources – physical, material and economic – to change their situation.

- **Doing things for themselves** – this means local authorities, key agencies and voluntary organisations not imposing their agendas but allowing people the opportunity to make their own mistakes and learn from their experiences.

- **Empowering people and promoting equality** – this is more than giving people information or £100 to support their community newsletter. This means really listening to people, hearing what they say and taking action together to bring about change. We can participate in the process of enabling people to become empowered. Equality should be our central concern because that is the only way in which we will overcome the discrimination and oppression that underpins people's experience of exclusion.

- **Fear, or rather, overcoming fear** – partnership and real involvement are challenging but they do work; we all need to lose our fear of the excluded.

Making these principles real can provide a way for us to link together the political and social analysis in 'radical social work' with current concerns about marginalisation and exclusion and provide an agenda for the future direction of social work or the social professions.

C H A P T E R S U M M A R Y

This chapter began by looking at the way the control and management function of social work has become preponderant in current social work discourses and how consequently the more liberatory and empowering elements of social work have become marginalised. In an attempt to redress this imbalance the chapter looked at the histories of radical social and community work and demonstrated the continuities between them. It suggested that debates around poverty and social exclusion provided a way of refocusing the attention of both professions to the wider structural issues with which users of social work services contend. Using Levitas' typology of social exclusion the chapter looked at how social and community work would need to refocus their orientations to a more egalitarian, redistributive approach and thus reclaim the agenda around social justice. Chapter 3 builds on these insights and explores the continuities and differences between social and community work.

FURTHER READING

Ferguson, I. and Woodward, R. (2009) *Radical Social Work in Practice: Making a Difference*. Bristol: Policy Press.

An interesting account of the current state of 'radical social work' looking at neo-liberalism and social work, the constraints and possibilities of state social work, the potential of the 'third sector' and the importance of collective approaches.

Healy, K. (2005) *Social Work Theories in Context*. Basingstoke: Palgrave Macmillan.

A complex but interesting account of the way in which social work theory informs practice. It has a useful chapter on radical and anti-oppressive practice and another chapter on creating frameworks for practice.

Levitas, R. (2005) *The Inclusive Society? Social Exclusion and New Labour*, 2nd edn. Basingstoke: Macmillan.

A good, clear analysis of how discussions around social exclusion are not neutral but have important implications for how we as social or community workers relate to people experiencing exclusion.

Chapter 3

Squaring the circle – from the individual to the collective?

This chapter will help you to develop the following capabilities, to the appropriate level, from the Professional Capabilities Framework:

Professionalism. Identify and behave as a professional social worker, committed to professional development.

Values and ethics. Apply social work ethical principles and values to guide professional practice.

Diversity. Recognise diversity and apply anti-discriminatory and anti-oppressive principles in practice.

Rights, justice and economic wellbeing. Advance human rights and promote social justice and economic wellbeing.

Critical reflection and analysis. Apply critical reflection and analysis to inform and provide a rationale for professional decision making.

Intervention and skills. Use judgement and authority to intervene with individuals, families and communities to promote independence, provide support and prevent harm, neglect and abuse.

Contexts and organisations. Engage with, inform, and adapt to changing contexts that shape practice. Operate effectively within own organisational frameworks and contribute to the development of services and organisations. Operate effectively within multi-agency and inter-professional settings.

Professional leadership. Take responsibility for the professional learning and development of others through supervision, mentoring, assessing, research, teaching, leadership and management.

See Appendix 1 for the Professional Capabilities Framework diagram.

Community Development National Occupational Standards

Key area 1: Core – Understand and practise community development.

Key Area 2: Understand and engage with communities.

Key Area 3: Take a community development approach to group work and collective action.

Key Area 4: Promote and support a community development approach to collaborative and cross-sectoral working.

(Continued)

(Continued)

Key Area 5: Support community learning from shared experiences.

Key Area 6: Provide community development support to organisations.

Key Area 7: Manage and develop community development practice.

(Federation for Community Development Learning, 2009)

Introduction: sharing values – individualism and collectivism

In Chapter 2 we looked at how social and community work shared some common theoretical and policy histories which will allow us to develop in this chapter a clearer overview of the way in which the similarities of both approaches could be systematised. This will enable us to begin to outline a potentially new form of welfare practice that can equip us to operate in the constantly changing welfare environment we are currently experiencing. This chapter will seek to explore these similarities, and differences, and begin to produce a framework for this new practice which will be fully articulated in the conclusion to the chapter.

Such an approach begins by seeking to show how the concern with the individual, which is often held to characterise social work, maps against the concern for the communal or collective, which is often attributed to community work; or to rephrase the dilemma: casework or community work?

A number of writers have suggested that to understand the history of social work we need to see how it developed as an approach to the alleviation of social problems at the end of the nineteenth and beginning of the twentieth centuries and how approaches to social work were defined through the work of agencies such as the Charity Organisation Society and the Settlement Movement. The former was characterised by an approach to social work which focused on the relief of individual distress, which became known as 'casework', and the latter by approaches that stressed the more structural causes of social problems – the community development approach (Pinkney, 1998; Kendall KA, 2000). Such a distinction always seemed slightly nebulous in that for the user of social services 'problems' were always framed by both factors. Often a 'problem' impacted on the user and their family directly, personally and immediately, and the social worker was required to intervene to resolve the 'problem' as it was defined at that particular time. However, many such 'problems' were not resolvable immediately and required a more systematic intervention, which often meant the social worker dealing with other agencies, acquiring additional resources, linking with other social institutions. The 'problem' required, in other words, a structural or at least communal approach if it was to be resolved.

As we saw in the last chapter, writers on social work have understood this dilemma for some time even if it was more commonly associated with the 'radical' traditions within social work. More recently writers from the UK (Dominelli, 2004, 2010; Lavalette and Ferguson, 2007; Hatton, 2013), Canada (Mullaly, 2006; Gil, 1998) and

Australia (Ife, 1997; Healy, 2012) have all sought to demonstrate how the individual experience is mediated through a broad range of social, political and structural factors. They have demonstrated how an individual's circumstances only change, in any lasting and meaningful way, if change also occurs in their wider environment – their housing, living circumstances – but more particularly in their own understanding of how their experience is shaped by wider social forces (Freire, 1972).

Community work has often focused largely on these wider factors, supporting people to take action to change their circumstances and equipping them with the knowledge and skills to make these changes sustainable over time. Community workers have not always been so good at understanding the private, individual side of these campaigns, particularly that community work which has been driven by a broader political agenda and underpinned by a Marxist analysis of change (see Chapter 2). However, it is again important not to oversimplify this analysis, and feminist and anti-racist community workers have often sought to integrate the personal experience into the wider social change perspective (Jones and Mayo, 1974; Dominelli, 1990; Ledwith, 1997; Stepney and Popple, 2008; Hatton, 2015).

These debates are reflected in the Professional Capability Framework (PCF) developed by The College of Social Work and the Community Development National Occupational Standards agreed by the Federation for Community Development Learning (see Table 3.1).

Table 3.1 Comparison of National Occupational Standards across social and community work

Social work (Professional Capability Framework)		Community development (National Occupational Standards)	
Domain 1	Professionalism – Identify and behave as a professional social worker, committed to professional development	Key Area 1	Core – Understand and practise community development
Domain 2	Values and ethics – Apply social work ethical principles and values to guide professional practice	Key Area 2	Understand and engage with communities
Domain 3	Diversity – recognise diversity and apply anti-discriminatory and anti-oppressive principles in practice	Key Area 3	Take a community development approach to group work and collective action
Domain 4	Rights, justice and economic wellbeing – advance human rights and promote social justice and economic wellbeing	Key Area 4	Promote and support a community development approach to collaborative and cross-sectoral working
Domain 5	Critical reflection and analysis – Apply critical reflection and analysis to inform and provide a rationale for professional decision making	Key Area 5	Support community learning from shared experiences
Domain 6	Intervention and skills – Use judgement and authority to intervene with individuals, families and communities to promote independence, provide support and prevent harm, neglect and abuse	Key Area 6	Provide community development support to organisations
Domain 7	Contexts and organisations – Engage with, inform, and adapt to changing contexts that shape practice. Operate effectively within own organisational frameworks and contribute to the development of services and organisations	Key Area 7	Manage and develop community development practice
Domain 8	Operate effectively within multi-agency and inter-professional settings		
Domain 9	Professional leadership – Take responsibility for the professional learning and development of others through supervision, mentoring, assessing, research, teaching, leadership and management		
	PCF – 9 domains		NOS – 7 key areas
	Source: www.tcsw.org.uk/uploadfiles/PCFDomainsNOV.pdf (accessed 24/05/13)		*Source*: www.fcdl.org.uk/nos (accessed 24/05/13)

There are some clear points of similarity, and some differences, between the expectations on social workers and community workers suggested by the outline of the relevant standards presented in Table 3.1. Both domain 1 and key area 1 make clear the responsibility on both professions to understand their role and work in a professional way, although this is probably made more explicit in the community development standards where an engagement with the values of equality and anti-discrimination, social justice, collective action and community empowerment is underpinned by a commitment to recognise and share values, skills, knowledge and experience. The values statement is more akin to the commitments to ethical practice, diversity and rights, justice and economic wellbeing in domains 2, 3 and 4 of the PCF framework. Domain 7 of the PCF clearly maps against the key areas within the NOS of understanding and engaging with communities (2), and working collaboratively and cross-sectorally (4). Similar points of connection can also be seen in domain 8, which refers to the importance of social workers engaging with multi-agency and inter-professional settings.

Domain 5, which stresses the importance of critical reflection and analysis, is also mirrored by key area 5 which emphasises the need to *'promote and develop opportunities of learning from community development practice'*. A difference here is that the emphasis is not just on the way individual practitioners reflect and learn from their own practice, but the additional expectation on the community development worker that such learning should also take place within the communities within which they work. There is some evidence that this approach is becoming more widely adopted within social work, but this is still mainly directed at working with people using social work services and receives insufficient attention within the organisational and practice environment within which social workers engage. Social workers could learn from community workers how to develop organisational change strategies, and this may lead to an improvement in service delivery and the experience of social workers on a day-to-day level (see discussion in Chapter 1).

Finally, both sets of standards place an emphasis on the need for practitioners to work in an ethical way that demonstrates integrity and a clear ethical base. Domains 1 and 9 of the PCF place a particular focus on the need for social workers not only to be professional in their approach to their work, but also to provide leadership for the profession. The focus on the need to understand and practice community development in key area 1 of the community development standards makes a similar point.

At the centre of the difference between these approaches – at least as reflected in the standards, if not always so clearly in practice – is the focus within the social work standards on the need to work within a context where the social worker will need to *'use judgement and authority to intervene … to promote independence, provide support and prevent harm, neglect and abuse'* (domain 6). This emphasis on the 'control' function of social work is important, although it presupposes that all social workers work in statutory environments (see Chapter 4). However, it contrasts sharply with the way the community work standards highlight collective action and community empowerment. Yet even this apparent significant difference has to be seen within the context of the PCF making much stronger comments about diversity and the need to *'advance human rights and promote social justice and economic wellbeing'* (domain 4). The points of contact between the two professional activities may now be becoming clearer. However, before we attempt to conceptualise these distinctions it will be useful to look at what current discourses within social and community work tell us about the professions.

ACTIVITY **3.1**

Jane and Ed live in a two-bedroom flat in the poorest area of Northerndown. Their land-lord requires them to leave their flat because he says he needs it for another tenant. Jane approaches you for assistance. They have family close by and want to stay in the property. Your manager agrees that you should offer them support. Identify which of the key roles you would utilise in your work to support the family, differentiating between the social work and community work roles.

Comment

Return to the PCF and NOS key areas. Use Table 3.1 to help you compare the different roles within social and community work.

The meaning of community

'Community' is one of the most widely used and ill-defined terms in social science. In a similar way to which 'empowerment' is frequently used inappropriately, 'community' is often used indiscriminately to enhance the appeal of policies, which may themselves be unattractive – community policing, community safety, community partnership, community school (particularly when the old Borstals were renamed in this way). Day notes that:

> community signifies something vague and ill-defined, an excuse for not thinking
> hard enough about what exactly it is that people have in common ... 'community'
> is a highly problematic term, alluring in its promise but to be approached with
> extreme care.

> (2006, p2)

What then does it mean? Bauman (2001) sees community as a counterbalance to the atomisation and individualisation of a globalising world and as a way through which we can gain or regain control. He concludes his discussion of community by reflecting that

> [w]e all need to gain control over the conditions under which we struggle with the
> challenges of life – but for most of us such control can be gained only collectively.

> (2001, p149)

This debate around the purpose of community is not new. Ferdinand Tonnies (1955) used the idea of community to describe the transformation in social relation-ships brought on by modernisation. He described two processes, *Gemeinschaft* and *Gesellschaft*. The former he suggested is characterised by *'emotional commitment, loyalty, emphasizing common ties and feelings and a sense of moral interdependence and mutual obligation'*, the latter by *'artificial, impersonal, economic relationships designed and controlled by others'* (cited in Brueggemann, 2006, p126). *Gemeinschaft* is held to characterise pre-industrial social relations and *Gesellschaft* industrial social relations. However, much of today's discourse around community, particularly communitarianism, harks back to these idealisations of community, especially *Gemeinschaft.*

Burns et al. (1994) suggest that it is necessary to distinguish between different conceptions of community. They posit five meanings of community: as *heritage;* as *social relationships;* as *the basis for collective consumption;* as *the basis for the most effective production and provision of local public goods;* and as *the source of influence and power.*

They go on to suggest that within these conceptions it is also useful to see a further distinction between communities of interest and imagined communities or communities of place. They suggest these can be characterised in the following way:

- Communities of interest reflect the common material concerns or characteristics of members and/or the common issues around which they group.

- Imagined communities are formed not on the basis of common interest but of common identities. The basis of social bonds is likeness or similarity.

- Communities of place are particular types of imagined community territorially based and can be mobilised to defend local interests.

They stress, however, that people may have multiple identities and linkages.

Jordan (1996) makes a further distinction between 'communities of fate' and 'communities of choice'. The former reflect the restrictions disadvantaged communities face and the social polarisation that is often characteristic of them; the latter the greater freedom accorded those successful in an increasingly polarised society.

Community therefore can be seen as a highly contested concept which is appropriated by the right and left to support claims of accountability and relevance. As Raymond Williams noted,

> *[c]ommunity can be the warmly persuasive word used to describe an existing set of relationships. What is most important, perhaps, is that unlike all other terms of social organisation (state, society, nation, etc.) it seems never to be used unfavourably and given any opposing term.*

> (1976, p77)

Delanty and Strydom (2003) see community as a new way of understanding kinds of belonging with multiple and overlapping relationships at its centre. The boundaries of community are contested, and community in this sense is more a discourse with a focus on *an imagined condition than a symbolically shaped reality based on fixed reference points* (p188). We can conceptualise community as an alternative to individualistic discourses that atomise people's experience and instead suggests ways in which people can regain control over their lives and build positive relationships, which in turn promotes wellbeing. These dichotomies in the theorisation of community reflect divergences in discourses around community work, which will be examined below.

These different conceptions of community provide us with an important reminder of the complex reality with which we are dealing and, in particular, suggest that when we reflect on the models of community work outlined below we should be aware that the types of intervention or strategy we choose need to take account of these different meanings. For example, our method of intervention may differ if we are seeing community as a site of struggle over the allocation of power or as an imagined community without a physical presence. Equally, if we are to equip people to work for change, we will want to challenge the idea that they are located in a community of fate. We need to help people believe in their potential to change their situation by encouraging them to see themselves as capable of generating alternative futures.

ACTIVITY **3.2**

Which of the conceptions of community outlined above best describe the community in which Jane and Ed live (see Activity 3.1)?

What is community work?

Dominelli suggested community work has constituted a political activity through which ordinary people assert control over their communities and lives (Dominelli, 1990, p1). In line with a number of other writers, she sees the activity of community work as being practised in a wide variety of ways. Popple (1995) has suggested that models of community intervention can range from community care to community action (pp54–73; see below for fuller discussion). The National Occupational Standards for Community Development describe community development as a process *'which aims to address imbalances in power and bring about change founded on social justice, equality and inclusion'* (FCDL, 2009).

Twenty years ago, Alison Gilchrist suggested that community work

> is fundamentally concerned with political processes, recognising that many of the problems experienced by people arise from political decisions about financial priorities and power imbalances. Empowerment might be defined as increasing someone's ability (individually or collectively) to influence decisions which affect their lives ... [the community worker must be prepared to] deal with potential conflicts and resistance to change ... many decisions are ... shrouded in the assumptions and prejudices of the policy makers, and manifest themselves as institutionalised discrimination. These need challenging through raising awareness, equality training and campaigning. The people in power must be re-educated

> *to understand and respect the experiences and perspective of people who are*
> *oppressed. They must be compelled to take these views into account in the*
> *decision-making process. Or they must be replaced by those who can.*

(1994, pp20–1)

Taylor (2003) argued that community work is about releasing community power through interlinked processes of learning and organising; the latter she defines as '*mobilising energies and knowledge, engaging people, building networks and organisations, taking action*' (p142). Ferguson and Woodward (2009) point to the way community development can help us move beyond individual approaches, which they characterise as '*case-ism*'. This is particularly important, they argue, as '*problems of poverty, inequality and stigma affect the lives of service users no less today than they did three decades ago … [suggesting] … that the time is ripe for revisiting the role of collective approaches in social work*' (pp133–4). Jordan makes a similar point when he refers to the way

> *[c]ommunity work addresses those social problems which society feels most*
> *concern (or fear) about but not in a way that identifies and singles out trouble*
> *makers, inadequates, criminals and mad people, and takes them for special*
> *attention. Instead, it deals in the collective features of their social worlds, and the*
> *harms, stigmas and exclusions these generate … community work addresses the*
> *overall workings of the collective and interpersonal economy.*

(2007, p115)

He argues that to achieve this, community workers need to gain the trust of the communities within which they work, recognise some of the paradoxes of those communities and set their goal as '*the transformation of cultures of conflict … [and work through] … collective facilities and through methods which mobilise and activate members in their common interests*' (Jordan, p125).

The challenge such scenarios pose to social work is illustrated in the manifesto produced by the Social Work Action Network, who argue that

> *[t]he current degraded status of social work as a profession is inextricably related*
> *to the status and standing of those we work with. Social work clients are amongst*
> *some of the most vulnerable and impoverished in our society, and have benefited*
> *least from New Labour's social welfare reforms. In fact, under New Labour we*
> *have witnessed not only greater levels of material inequality, but also an intensified*
> *demonisation of asylum seekers, young people and poor families, the very groups*
> *that social workers engage with. Too often today social workers are often doing*
> *little more than supervising the deterioration of people's lives.*

(SWAN, 2010)

Freire, Fanon and Gramsci

Much of the more radical discourse around community work has been built around the work of two key thinkers: Paulo Freire and Antonio Gramsci. Mayo describes Freire as possessing a '*vision of society as characterised by relations of power and domination*' (1999, p59). Among the key ideas we can take from Freire are the concepts of:

- **Agency** – *the ability of people to act in their own interests.*

- **Democratic Education** – *which is based on the idea of promoting education through dialogue, which will overcome the codification of reality which they experience. Central to this is the notion of praxis the linking together of action and reflection.*

- **Conscientizaçao (conscientisation)** – *'education, as an exercise in freedom, is an act of knowing, a critical approach to reality'.*

(Mayo, 1999, p63)

Thompson (2001) also makes links to the Freirian notion of conscientisation, which he says is about:

- deindividualisation – helping people understand the extent to which their position is a reflection of broader cultural and political patterns;

- countering internalised oppression – helping people overcome the feeling that they deserve their unequal position.

This is a similar point to that made by Frantz Fanon (1978), who, writing about the experience of Algerian people under French colonial rule, noted that colonisation impinges on the individuality of the colonised person and people. He argued that the colonised begin to *'suffer from not being a white man [sic] to the degree that the white man [sic] imposes discrimination on me, makes me colonised … robs me of all individuality or worth'* (Fanon, 1971, p98). This happens, he suggests, because the white, as coloniser, seeks to *'frustrate the black, binding him [sic] with prohibitions of all kinds'* (p175). The ruling white elite's political and economic power creates in the colonised black person a feeling of inferiority or *'dependency complex'*, which Fanon suggests is historically specific and related to the act of colonisation. This dependency is not, however, intrinsic, specific to a black identity, pathological. Rather, it is a consequence of relations of domination and power. Remove the domination, and the accompanying psychological and sexual stereotype dependent on it, and the dependency complex will itself be attenuated, removed.

These are important processes if social professional practice is to be an emancipatory project, rather than a reinforcement of existing patterns of discrimination. We need to recognise that what services sometimes interpret as the passivity or lack of engagement of people who use services may be a reflection of the negative dominant power relationships which they experience on a day-to-day level. Replace those relationships of domination with a belief in the capacity of people to change their circumstances and we will see a significant change in the way in which people view their lives and their potential to change their circumstances.

Gramsci was an Italian Marxist who was active in establishing workers' councils in Turin in the period during and after the end of the First World War. He rejected what he believed was a simplistic version of Marxism, which focused only on class relations, and developed a broader conception of politics that drew attention to the struggle for moral and political leadership through a process he called 'hegemony'. He maintained that ruling classes dominate through a mixture of force and consent, where the consent is gained through assuming the political, moral and intellectual leadership in society. He argues that civil society (political parties, churches, cultural, charitable and voluntary groups) are central in maintaining hegemony. Civil society is the place where democratic struggles can be linked together. The ruling class maintains control by making their rule and the legitimacy of state rule appear like 'common sense'. It is then the role of external agents, such as intellectuals, union organisers and community leaders, to challenge this common sense. He believes that an oppressed group needs its own organic intellectuals (those that emerge from within their own ranks) to challenge these dominant ideas. He argues that

> 'everyone' is a philosopher ... it is not a question of introducing from scratch a scientific form of thought into everyone's individual life, but of renovating and making 'critical' an already existing activity.

> (Gramsci, 1971, pp330–1, cited in Allman, 2001, p114)

Allman suggests that this passage should be read as Gramsci encouraging leaders or radical educators to help people question their already existing activity (commonsense thinking) until it becomes 'critical' activity (dialectical thinking) (Allman, 2001, p11). This focus on helping people become aware, to develop a critical understanding of the way their experiences are mediated by a wide range of social and economic factors, is central to Freire, Fanon and Gramsci and can become the key element of a new radical practice. To paraphrase Marx, philosophers may have described the world; the community worker's (and social worker's) role is to change it.

ACTIVITY 3.3

Community work role play

You will need to divide into two groups for this role play. The scenario is based around an issue which has arisen within the local community. A group of people living in a high-rise block in Sanderstown, an area of social housing which scores high on all the indices of social deprivation and disadvantage – high levels of unemployment, low levels of educational attainment, poor health, lack of community facilities – has approached the local community worker at the neighbourhood community centre because they are concerned at the lack of facilities for young people in the area.

They have approached the local schools to ask them to increase their after-school provision, but without any success. They have also approached the local councillor, who has dismissed them as unrepresentative and suggested that if there were any problems in the block he would long ago have resolved them. The local leisure services and youth departments are equally uncooperative.

Group A: As a community worker, how would you deal with this problem? How would you help the local people formulate a strategy to resolve this problem?

Decide who will play the community worker and allocate key roles among the rest of the group. It is likely that you will be asking the local authority to attend a meeting

ACTIVITY **3.3** *continued*

to discuss your concerns. How would you plan for that meeting? Develop an agenda and work out your strategy for dealing with this meeting.

Group B: As representatives for the local authority, you realise that you will have to meet with the residents. You are all confident that you have done everything in your power to sort out this estate's problems. It seems to you that this issue has been sparked by a number of people with their own agenda. How would you prepare for the meeting?

Allocate roles within your group, ensuring that all of the above interests are represented, such as housing management, leisure, youth, education, elected councillors and so on.

For both groups you realise that this issue may not be resolved in one meeting. How do you ensure that your strategy can work over time? How would you ensure that you maximise support for your views?

Comment

This activity is designed to be used within classroom settings. You may, however, adapt it so that it can be undertaken virtually by way of either chat rooms or through the use of virtual learning environments (VLEs). If you are looking at this scenario individually instead of through role play, map the activities of each group across the following matrix.

	Community group	Local authority
Strategy		
Identify key roles		
Organisation of own group		
Agenda		
Desired outcomes		

Within each box identify how each of the key actors – community group and local authority – would prepare for the meeting; organise themselves as a group; and how they would seek to develop their own agenda so that they achieved their desired outcomes. *You may wish to return to this exercise after reading Chapter 5 and see if your analysis changes in the light of the analysis in that chapter.*

Look at the Professional Capability Framework and the National Occupational Standards for Community Work outlined above. It is also worth looking at Marilyn Taylor (2003).

What then of social work?

Lorenz suggested that social work faced many uncertainties but that social work practice interprets and makes manifest the nature of solidarity that prevails in a particular society and the level of citizenship reached (1994, p10). Smale et al. make a similar point when they suggest that *'social work is an integral part of the society within which it is practiced. It is one dimension of the way social problems are managed'* (2000, p19).

Lyons (1999) suggested that social work can be distinguished by its methodology: field casework, group and community work and 'child rescue' services, practices underpinned by concepts of conscientisation and empowerment such as 'radical social work'. To these can be added perspectives around identity or 'social division' such as feminism/gender (Hanmer and Statham, 1999), disability (Sapey and Oliver, 2006; Goodley, 2011) and anti-racism (Ahmad, 1990; Aluffi-Pentini, 1996; Chouan et al., 1996; Dominelli, 2010; Williams et al., 1998). Lorenz pointed to the challenge racism posed for the social professions when he suggested that

> *[r]acism ... represents a challenge to pedagogy as the institution responsible for society's cultural reproduction ... It also provides a challenge to social work with its mainly unexamined notions of 'normality'.*

> (1995, p34)

There have also been renewed calls for attention to be given to the impact and influence of users of services in the struggle to democratise and make relevant services and to reposition the user as a 'subject' (Williams, 1999) or an active agent in the process of social transformation (Beresford et al., 1999). Describing the exclusion of people in poverty from poverty discourse, Beresford and Croft argued that it is only with their involvement that poverty discussion is likely to identify, reflect and advance their needs, concerns, interests (1995, p91). The same can be said to apply to users of welfare services, and it will be a mark of social work's ability to promote social change in how far it can create genuine partnerships with users and their organisations (see Chapter 5 for a fuller discussion of this issue).

One other factor is also worth remembering when we try to account for what social work is. Shardlow and Payne (1998) have argued that we should see social work both nationally and locally. Lyons argues that the best way for social work to contribute is through *'taking a structural perspective and giving an increased emphasis to the concept of empowerment [which] clarifies the need to promote community networks and their interaction with the formal organizations in society'* (1999, p46). Lavalette and Ferguson (2007) noted that social work was increasingly being seen as an international activity.

Giarchi and Lankshear (1998) suggested that social work is a fragmented and diffuse activity that is being increasingly eclipsed by trends in the delivery of welfare which promotes the blurring of professional boundaries and the reduction of professional autonomy. The profession, they suggest, is riven with tensions, to the extent that it is not possible to speak of a 'Eurosocial work'. This appears to miss the point. Social work needs to be located within its own national and cultural contexts. However, that does not imply isolation because equally social work needs to learn from theory and practice in other countries (see Chapters 6 and 7 for an in-depth discussion of these issues).

Lorenz modelled the challenges facing social work as set out in Table 3.2

Table 3.2 The impact of globalisation (Lorenz, 1998, p3)

Risks	Opportunities	
Market–driven competition	Changing professional identities	Increased accountability
Economic dictates suspend democratic policy-making	Sense of powerlessness	New grassroots politics of community action
Populism, politics of self-interest	'End of grand political narratives'	New international lobbies

Dominelli clearly articulates the challenge for social work:

> *Contextualise social work within the state apparatus; understand the dynamics in both covert and overt forms of racism; recognise how racism is legitimated through social processes and institutions outside social work structures; and relate these to everyday routines in social work.*

> *(1997b, p19)*

Humphries points to a further factor that impacts on the practice of social work – its relationship to people in poverty. As she suggests,

> *social work has always had a contradictory function in regulating the poor by both control and support. With growing state intervention in all aspects of social life comes a more direct inspectorial role for social workers ... the tradition of emotional support is marginalized in the social worker's repertoire in a disciplinary society.*

> *(1996, p647)*

Writing about the Irish child care system, Buckley et al. made a similar point when they referred to the way that poor and disadvantaged people figure disproportionately in the child protection system (1997, p31). Barry argued that this is the key issue for social workers, who operate at the interface of, and hence mediate between, advantage and disadvantage, self-determination and dependency, integration and marginalisation (1998, p7). Social work's focus on self-determination and empowerment ensures that, at its best, it develops participatory and inclusive ways of working with those who use services. This would suggest a way of linking together the concerns of both professions. How can this be achieved?

These comments echo the most recent definition of social work produced by the International Federation of Social Workers (2014) which says:

> *The social work profession promotes social change, problem solving in human relationships and the empowerment and liberation of people to enhance well-being. Utilising theories of human behavior and social systems, social work intervenes at the point where people interact with their environments. Principles of human rights and social justice are fundamental to social work.*

> (ifsw.org/get-involved/global-definition-of-social-work
> downloaded on 30/07/15)

In the commentary to the definition it adds, 'social workers are change agents in society and in the lives of the individuals, families and communities they serve' (ifsw.org/policies/definition-of-social-work 12/08/14). These foci on social change, empowerment and liberation and the need to work as change agents demonstrate the clear points of contact between the theory and practice of both social and community work.

Coming together – new professional identities?

Social and community work can now be seen to share some common knowledge, skills and values. These may include those listed in Table 3.3, which illustrates the points of similarity between the two professional activities, while at the same time identifying subtle differences of emphasis which locate the activities of both professions within different elements of the welfare state.

Table 3. 3   Knowledge base of community work and social work

Knowledge	Community work	Social work
Theoretical paradigm	Sociology/politics	Sociology/psychology
Theoretical paradigm	Social policy	Social policy
Practice framework	Law and policy analysis	Law and policy framework
Action perspective	Networking and community action	Networking
Action perspective	Partnership and power	Partnership and cooperation
Primary focus	International/national	National/international

While social and community work share theoretical concerns with sociology and social policy, they in turn look to other theoretical disciplines for their identity. Community work is concerned much more explicitly with challenging power at a political level and so looks to politics to sharpen its understanding of the way social change can be brought about. The concern noted above with the work of Gramsci and Freire is a clear illustration of this process (Ledwith, 1997; Mayo, 1999; Allman, 2001). Social work looks to psychology to reflect its concern with the individual and with the necessity of engaging with internal psychological processes of change (Pinkney, 1998; Kendall, KA 2000).

While both professions work within clearly defined legal frameworks, community work's concern is more with using the law as a tool to challenge the actions of political actors at local and national levels (Bateman, 2006; Stepney and Popple, 2008). Social work is more concerned with the procedural elements of law and to the extent to which the law is used to challenge the decisions of public bodies, it is frequently used to support individual rather than collective rights (Brayne and Carr, 2013).

The action perspective of both professions is also different. Community work's focus is on engaging with networks to secure change at community, neighbourhood or regional levels. Often this will involve pursuing strategies of community action which seek to mobilise people to secure long-term change (Hoggett, 1997; Stepney and Popple, 2008). To social workers, networking often means developing relationships with other professions operating in the same locality. It often infers the need for better coordination of service delivery and closer collaboration between professions working in the same field (Coulshed and Orme, 2012; Quinney, 2006; Fletcher, 2006; Payne, 2014). Finally, while both professions share a commitment to international work, the focus within the community work literature is much more on learning from other countries (*Community Development Journal*, 1990 to present; Craig and Mayo, 1995; Hatton, 2015). Within social work a concern with international issues is increasingly important but is secondary to the focus on practice within the UK (Adams et al., 2005; Hatton, 2013; Lyons and Lawrence, 2006b).

Sharing values

Table 3.4   Common values?

Values	Community work	Social work
Tackling discrimination	ADP/AOP	ADP/AOP
Beyond discrimination	Focus on diversity and equality	Focus on diversity
Tackling change	Empowerment/advocacy	Empowerment/advocacy
Primary value	Collectivisation	Individualisation
New v old?	Organisational innovation	Organisational change

As can be seen in Table 3.4, there are significant points of connection between the values underpinning social and community work. Both have a central concern with discrimination and oppression (Harris, 1994; Gil, 1998; Thompson, 2001) and with developing strategies to overcome them. These strategies may differ slightly, focusing on individual, achievable goals (social work) or longer, more strategic change (community work), but this commitment is central to good practice across both sets of professional activity (see discussion of the Professional Capability Framework and key areas above).

Community work may have a greater focus on the pursuit of equality but both share a concern with developing work in a way which promotes diversity and difference. Both share concerns with empowerment and advocacy (see Chapter 2) and with organisational as well as individual change. Community work's focus may, however, be with promoting new organisational structures which generate participation and control such as collective working, parity and community control (Law Centres Federation, 2001). Social work's focus is more often on effective service delivery, quality enhancement and strategic leadership (Payne, 2014).

The principles shared across the two professions can be most usefully articulated through Table 3.5.

Table 3.5   Principles which are shared by community and social work

Principle	Community work (drawn from Popple 1995; Ife, 1999)	Social work
Confront structural disadvantage	To be consistent with a social justice perspective needs to ensure that it does not reinforce oppression/discrimination, that community worker is aware of own prejudices/assumptions and of the complex way class, race, gender etc., interact	Enhance focus on individual with recognition of way people who use services are impacted upon by wider structural and cultural factors (Thompson 2001, 1998; Gil, 1998; Dalrymple and Burke, 2006)
Human rights	Important in two senses – the negative (protection of human rights) and positive (the promotion of human rights)	Promotes idea of protecting people using services by matching HRs against current policy (Brayne and Carr, 2013)
Empowerment	'Providing people with the resources, opportunities, knowledge and skills to increase the capacity to determine their own future, and to participate in and affect the life of the community' (Ife, 1999, p182)	Challenges power relationships and promotes individual and collective empowerment, but sometimes constrained by regulatory framework (Baistow,1994; Jordan, 2007)
Self-reliance	Community should seek to utilise its own resources rather than relying on external support; this not achievable in total but the aim should be to maximise, e.g. LETS schemes, also has elements of social enterprise – see Chapter 4	Need to avoid danger of pathologising service users/carers and instead promote their self-activity and empowerment (see discussion of community work above)
Immediate goals and ultimate visions	Essential to maintain balance between the immediate and the long term, both indispensable to each other	Focus on crisis intervention can render long-term goals invisible
The pace of development	CD is by its nature a long-term process, change occurs at the community's own pace. The process itself is important in determining the outcome, but need to keep in mind both, and that both are integrated	Replace short-termism such as task-centred social work, brief solution-focused therapy with longer-term perspective which focuses on social change
Community building	'Involves strengthening the social interactions within the community, bringing people together, and helping them communicate with each other in a way that can lead to genuine dialogue, understanding and social action' (Ife, 1999, p191)	Need to de-individualise social problems (Freire, 1972; Healy, 2012) Return to preventative work rather than crisis intervention
Inclusiveness	Based on dialogue, understanding, respect for other person's point of view even if it is different, always be ready to learn from others (Jordan, 2007). Aims to maximise participation while recognising that different people have different skills, broadens participation and values all	Promote greater level of service user involvement – move beyond tokenism – see Chapter 5. Participation should become part of wider strategy which not only involves service users but also leads social workers to question own role in their organisations and seek to democratise those organisations
External expertise	Be deeply distrustful of any solution imposed from outside; external experts need to value the contribution of local communities	Desire for professionalism should not create expectation of social worker as 'expert' whose knowledge and skills become privileged over non-qualified staff and service users and carers

A framework for understanding social and community work

How then can we begin to make sense of the similarities and differences within these two apparently distinct approaches? This section will examine these issues within a framework which draws on theoretical and practical issues from both traditions. To do this it is necessary to conceptualise the debate as representing both a continuum from the individual to the structural and an iterative dialogue between the different levels which represents a properly reflexive account of how the different traditions operate. This may sound overly complex but is in fact a relatively simple process as demonstrated by Figures 3.1 and 3.2 and the discussion below.

Social work   Community work
Individual   Community

Structural change

Figure 3.1   The continuum between social and community work

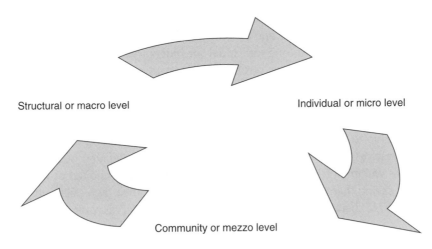

Structural or macro level   Individual or micro level

Community or mezzo level

Figure 3.2   The interaction between social and community work

The individual or micro level

Figures 3.1 and 3.2 provide a way of visualising the connections between social and community work. The continuum reflects the belief that the professional activities are a substantial distance apart. It posits a view of social work as being about individual change and community work as being about structural change. They may share some common concerns within local communities but their foci and rationale are different. The second diagram, however, suggests that the process of interaction between the individual and the structural is much more continuous, reflective and that it constitutes a process in movement. This more clearly reflects the dynamic interplay which, this book suggests, is the basis of good practice.

Clearly neither social nor community work has legitimacy unless their primary focus is seen as improving the life chances of the most marginalised and excluded sections of society. The Global Definition of Social Work was agreed by the International Federation of Social Workers (IFSW) and International Association of Schools of Social Work (IASSW) in July 2014. It says:

Social work is a practice-based profession and an academic discipline that promotes social change and development, social cohesion, and the empowerment and liberation of people. Principles of social justice, human rights, collective responsibility and respect for diversities are central to social work. Social work engages people and structures to address life challenges and enhance wellbeing.

(The above definition may be amplified at national and/or regional levels. Downloaded from ifsw.org/get-involved/global-definition-of-social-work, 08/10/15)

Dominelli (2004) has argued that to understand the service user experience at the local level we need to focus on the power relationship between the service user and worker (Hugman, 1991; Hatton and Nugent, 1993; Adams, 2001). However, following Foucault, Dominelli sees power as not just a zero-sum game (A has power over B, B can only change this by taking power from A) but as an interactional process that *'creates positive environments for communication and action and which can result in win–win situations'* (2004, p41). In this sense no one individual (or indeed group) can be *'either totally powerful or powerless'* (p41). This position allows us to see people as not just objects who are acted upon by external powerful forces but as being capable of resistance and the creation of new realities over which they can exercise control. For social workers this means seeing beyond the service user as someone whose experience is framed only by their relationship to the service they use. It involves seeing them also as active agents of change themselves. For community workers this means not defining people within the communities within which they work as being downtrodden, exploited or marginalised but instead seeing them as the people who can, through their own skills and resourcefulness, generate change themselves (see Chapter 5 for a fuller discussion of power).

The mezzo or group level

Writing about homelessness, Avramov described the mezzo level as being the arena in which we can map the intermediate causes of the problems people face. He suggests that analysis at this level can tell us about

[t]he ways in which families, friends, informal networks, neighbourhoods, peer groups and sub-cultural groups operate and how they may be preventing or exacerbating (housing) exclusion.

(1997, p21)

This may seem a more appropriate level of intervention for community rather than social workers. Community work is largely about building and sustaining networks, relating to peer groups and tackling exclusion (Stepney and Popple, 2008; Hatton, 2013). However, social work must also have a role in what Parton and O'Byrne call the *'art of resistance'*, which is based on the belief that *'people, no matter what their circumstances, have significant resources within and around them … social workers … can help people refocus their resources to assist them best in accomplishing their goals'* (2000, p184). This is a particular challenge for social work because of the way many service users are presented as being responsible for the position they find themselves in. Young people are increasingly criminalised through Anti-Social Behaviour Orders, dispersal orders and the demonisation of elements of youth culture (such as Chavs etc.). Jordan (2000) has pointed to the way social work is asked to buy into a discourse of service users as problematic and being unable to relate to the broader society. The people we work with as social workers or community workers are often pathologised and seen as dysfunctional and a 'threat' to normal society. As he notes:

> Service users react negatively to what they perceive as attempts to blame them for their problems, and to attribute causation to their character, personality, attitudes or motivation, pathologizing their behaviour and locating all their difficulties in themselves ... [they] are expert in rejecting these discourses of stigma and dysfunction and in developing their own narratives of injustice, oppression and exclusion, identifying the external forces in the economy and polity which disadvantage and trap them.
>
> (Jordan, 2000, p216)

Social workers and community workers can therefore both be seen to have a role in promoting these positive models of the individuals and communities with which they work. They can begin to secure changes that challenge the social construction of the service user as dependent and deficient and which are legitimised through 'common sense' understandings of users of services as 'other', 'different' and 'deficient'.

Macro or structural work

This approach is more often associated with community work, although writers such as Thompson (2001), Mullaly (2006), Fook (2002) and Brueggemann (2006) all suggest the importance of social workers looking at the structural or macro level, if they want to secure lasting and sustainable social change. Indeed, both Mullaly and Brueggemann's work focuses heavily on what are often assumed to be community work strategies. Brueggemann describes macro-social work as the practice of helping individuals and groups solve social problems and make social change at the community, organisational, societal and global levels (2006, p7). Pierson suggests that social workers should see their role as a catalyst and change agent regardless of their position in the organisation (2000, p232). Pierson's focus is on tackling social exclusion. Barry made a similar point when she said:

> Social work in its task of meeting human need and developing human potential and resources, must, therefore, inevitably address problems associated with social exclusion and, at least, ensure that the services provided – or the terms on which they are made available – do not further marginalize the already excluded.
>
> (1998, p8)

At a time when levels of social inequality are deepening (UNICEF, 2010; Wilkinson and Pickett, 2006, 2007), community is increasingly being seen as a potential site through which meaningful change can occur. Sometimes this is reflected in the more conservative attempts to reconstitute community such as communitarianism, with its focus on rights and responsibilities (normally the latter – see Tan, 1998 and Jordan, 2000; see also Chapter 4). Jordan suggests a role for social work in the community as being to soften the harshness of the informal code, to uphold the rights of the oppressed within all social units, and to develop more constructive links with the world outside (2000, p200).

To move forward in this way social and community work need a perspective which fuses together advocacy and empowerment. We will look at how this can be achieved in Chapter 4.

ACTIVITY 3.4

Perspectives of Irish women community activists

Below are comments from women the author interviewed during research in Ireland. Their comments reflect some of the dilemmas faced by people active in the community when they try to articulate their desires and aspirations. Answer the following questions.

- *As a social worker, how would you work with these women to support their aspirations for change?*

- *As a community worker, how would you work with these women to support their aspirations for change?*

- *Would there be any differences in the approaches you adopted? If so what would they be?*

> *We are all working-class women, the majority early school leavers, we are all disadvantaged in relation to education and training. We recognised we all have value and all have something to offer and we were all very active before the funding ... in communities, throughout disadvantaged areas. [They designed courses aimed at working-class women who they felt needed a progression route into higher education.]*

> *Women have been treated as second-class citizens, for generations men have been seen to speak more assertively on things ... a lot of poorer women seem to be passive because they have not got the energy for all this fight, they are worrying about the day-to-day survival and the struggles. While I can understand that I feel that if they remain in the victim syndrome things will never change. I'm not a victim, I'm a survivor.*

> *I think Travelling working-class women are doubly marginalised ... because they have to struggle with being working class and poor as well as being a Traveller ... it's harder for them in the society we have today because they are just ostracised completely from communities. They are not allowed to use public houses, cinemas, they are victimised an awful lot.*

> *I'm part of a women's group where we do our own research, we produce our own books, we access our own funding. It's like because we are working class you can't manage monies and yet we get more from our small amount of funding and we are doing more with it for people on the ground than [others] are with [their] millions.*

> (Comments drawn from interviews with women in Cork, Ireland,
> which the author conducted as part of comparative research
> into community work in Ireland, Denmark and the UK)

Comment

These quotations reflect a number of the key issues highlighted in the chapter. Read them carefully and see how they relate to the National Occupational Standards and the values and principles articulated in this chapter.

C H A P T E R   S U M M A R Y

This chapter has looked at the contribution that both social and community work can make to help us become effective and critical practitioners. It suggests continuities in our practice that can allow us to move beyond the dichotomies of 'social work equals individualised' approaches and 'community work provides the more collective, radical alternative'. It demonstrates the connectedness of both forms of practice but also builds on the analysis in Chapter 2 to suggest that we can develop an integrated form of practice which can allow us to intervene at micro, mezzo and macro levels.

FURTHER READING

Bauman, Z. (2001) *Community-seeking Safety in an Insecure World.* Cambridge: Polity Press.

A good discussion of the way in which the concept of community has been used and misused.

Gilchrist, A. (2009) *The Well-connected Community: A Networking Approach to Community Development.* Bristol: Policy Press.

A look at the key importance of networking in community development practice. Reviews the meaning of both and links to complexity theory

Hoggett, P. (ed.) (1997) *Contested Communities: Experiences, Struggles, Policies.* Bristol: Policy Press.

A collection which looks at the way communities have actively sought to resist the impact of negative social and economic changes.

Ife, J. (1999) *Community Development: Creating Community Alternatives – Vision, Analysis and Practice.* Sydney: Longman Pearson.

A clear, well-written account of the principles of community development practice. Ife is an Australian writer but draws on a wide range of material which is relevant to UK social and community work.

WEBSITES

Federation for Community Development Learning: www.fcdl.org.uk

ESRC Research Centre for Analysis of Social Exclusion (CASE): http://sticerd.lse.ac.uk/case/

Joseph Rowntree Foundation Research Findings: www.jrf.org.uk/publications

Chapter 4

The voluntary and independent sectors: Communitarianism, the 'Big Society' and the potential for social action

The chapter will help you to develop the following capabilities, to the appropriate level, from the Professional Capabilities Framework:

Professionalism. Identify and behave as a professional social worker, committed to professional development.

Values and ethics. Apply social work ethical principles and values to guide professional practice.

Diversity. Recognise diversity and apply anti-discriminatory and anti-oppressive principles in practice

Rights, justice and economic wellbeing. Advance human rights and promote social justice and economic wellbeing.

Critical reflection and analysis. Apply critical reflection and analysis to inform and provide a rationale for professional decision making.

Contexts and organisations. Engage with, inform, and adapt to changing contexts that shape practice. Operate effectively within own organisational frameworks and contribute to the development of services and organisations. Operate effectively within multi-agency and inter-professional settings.

Professional leadership. Take responsibility for the professional learning and development of others through supervision, mentoring, assessing, research, teaching, leadership and management.

See Appendix 1 for Professional Capabilities Framework diagram.

Community Development National Occupational Standards

Key area 1: Core – Understand and practise community development.

Key Area 2: Understand and engage with communities.

Key area 4: Promote and support a community development approach to collaborative and cross-sectoral working.

Key Area 5: Support community learning from shared experiences.

Key Area 6: Provide community development support to organisations.

Key Area 7: Manage and develop community development practice.

(Federation for Community Development Learning, 2009)

Introduction: the changing role of the voluntary sector – implications for social work

The more radical discourses around community work featured in earlier chapters not surprisingly differ in style, emphasis and philosophy from those put forward by government, particularly the successive Conservative governments from 1979 to 1997 which placed an emphasis on community responsibility through ideas such as Neighbourhood Watch or 'active citizenship'. Often such conceptions evoked, uncritically, nostalgic notions of the past such as Victorian conceptions of frugality, family responsibility and minimum state intervention. The family was envisioned as the fulcrum of social life.

New Labour when it came to power in 1997 sought to distance itself from such analysis by promoting a more inclusive sense of community. Some writers have seen this attempt to recraft the idea of community as a *'fundamental concept'* in New Labour's ideology (Fremeaux, 2005, p267). Drawing on Gidden's ideas about the 'Third Way' (the alternative to the politics of the left or right), New Labour promoted an idea of community which offered an alternative to centralised and top-down policies and attempted to invoke the capacity of the community to revitalise and regenerate local areas (Fremeaux, 2005).

This approach was exemplified in programmes such as New Deal for Communities, Single Regeneration Partnerships and the compact between the government and the voluntary sector. At the heart of this concern, however, was a process in which the needs of the community and the individual become elided. Community was promoted in an unproblematic and uncritical way so that the interests of the community become the interests of all (see Chapter 3; Jordan, 2000; Fremeaux, 2005). As Fremeaux pointed out, Tony Blair saw the community as the collective ability to further the individual's interests (Blair, 1994, quoted in Fremeaux, 2005, p270). At the heart of this confusion over the nature of community was New Labour's articulation of the philosophy of communitarianism, which is discussed below.

The reconfiguration of welfare that characterised both the Conservative administration between 1979 and 1997 and New Labour from 1997 to 2010 was predicated on the ideological assumption that the state creates dependency, stifles initiative and is intrinsically a poor way of delivering welfare. The result has been the creation, or more accurately the enshrining, of what has been variously known as a *'mixed economy of welfare'* (Johnson, 1999), *'welfare pluralism'* (Gould, 1993) or the establishment of *'quasi–markets in welfare'* (Le Grand, 1991).

The mixed economy of welfare, Johnson (1999) suggests, is defined by the presence of four sectors in the production and delivery of welfare: the state sector; the commercial sector; the voluntary (non-profit or third) sector; the informal sector (family, friends and neighbours). These sectors have, he argues, always been present; the key factor that distinguishes welfare states is the balance between them. This in turn varies along four dimensions: between countries, between historical periods, between services and between one component of a service and another (e.g., the degree of privatisation, role of the voluntary sector) (Johnson, 1999, p22–9).

Gould suggests that these developments can be traced back to the 1980s and argues that

> [t]he more affluent members of the working class were coming to resent the burden of taxation to finance a welfare state from which there seemed to be few marginal gains for them. Employers, coping with recession and the threat of increased competition from the countries of the Pacific Rim, such as Japan, wanted a reduction in the size of the public sectors. Growing sections of the middle class, particularly those employed in the private sector, were also demanding that welfare spending be reduced.

> (1993, p7)

Ginsburg (1992) pointed out how the insecure nature of the welfare state in capitalist societies limits their scope to alleviate or mitigate hardship. As a consequence *'the overall impact of the welfare state under capitalism on the social class distribution of welfare has been to stabilise and thus reinforce the class structure'* (p4). These processes lead to a situation in which the legitimacy of the welfare state is often jeopardised by crises in the economy. This legitimacy can be challenged because it is seen to inhibit productivity, reduce innovation and create dependency. People, it is suggested, will have no motivation for moving beyond their situation because the welfare safety net will ensure that they are always provided for. Indeed, proponents of welfare pluralism from the radical right see the welfare state as being more about the protection of the interests of those who work within it (Stoesz and Midgley, 1991).

A consequence of these trends was, Clarke et al. (2001) assert, the development of a welfare pluralism which has four main features (Yeates, 2014, suggests a formulation based on the state, market, intermediate – national service NGOs and consultancies – community and household):

1. Welfare services have been broken up and/or become fragmented so that rather than a welfare state that reflected a common set of assumptions and concerns we now have a welfare state which is provided through an array of public, private and voluntary sector organisations. Significantly this has led to demands that the voluntary sector should play a more substantial role in welfare provision (see later in this chapter for the way in which this trend has developed).

2. The rise of consumerism – the belief that welfare is best delivered through the market and that the market will ensure the most efficient use of welfare resources.

3. New regimes of inspection and regulation (see Chapter 1) based on a belief that the provider of services should be separated from the purchaser of services to the extent that the 1990s saw a significant expansion of regulatory, inspection and audit agencies, offering new means for control *'at arm's length'* (Clarke et al., 2001, p88). Interestingly, the new forms of neo-liberalism introduced post-2010 by the Coalition government have sought to reduce what is called the 'burden of regulation' by increasing the rate at which responsibility is devolved to the private sector. It is believed that government regulation inhibits the ability of the private sector to innovate and provide cheaper services. Yet one of the paradoxes of the Coalition's concern with regulation is that deregulation attaches primarily to differences in class – the wealthy will have the burden lifted while the poor will become increasingly regulated in all parts of their lives. Hodgkinson and Robbins suggest that the consequences of this deregulation can be seen in the worsening position of social housing tenants whose experience is reframed to tap into the discourse of the deserving and undeserving poor. They suggest that

[w]e are not just witnessing a continuation of neoliberal policies but a radical intensification of their logic wrapped up in a far more overt class politics ... This class warfare only furthers the contradictions in the housing market and explains why the government is so keen to boost the private rental sector by beefing up private property rights, weakening tenants (and squatters) rights and unlocking huge swathes of public land for low risk development.

(2013, pp71–2)

Hepple has noted similar processes in the development of employment law (e.g. restrictions to compensation for unfair dismissal). He notes that *'the constant refrain from politicians on the right is that legislative burdens must be removed'* (2013, p220). Pollock and Price refer to the trend to turn *'the English National Health Service over to the global health care market'* (2011, p294).

4. The transfer of responsibilities from the public to the private realm, particularly the family. Prior to 1997 this was seen as a justifiable attempt to remove the state from interference in the family. Fox Harding linked these arguments to those of the radical right (although she also demonstrated how some on the left also bought into this approach) when she said that

freedom from state control is stressed; the state is seen as threatening, as a force to be kept within bounds; and counterweights to state power are highly valued. The family may be seen as a locus of alternative power. It is also seen as a locus of social responsibility.

(1997, p22)

Since 1997 there has been some recognition that this can lead to gendered forms of care through a focus on the 'costs' of informal care on families. Care UK calculates that there are currently 6.5 million carers in the UK who 'save' the state an estimated £119 billion per year (www.carersuk.org). There has been some recognition over the last 20 years that carers and their families need support (Carers Recognition Act 1995, the Carers (Equal Opportunities) Act 2004, Children and Families Act 2014 – young carers needs assessments, Care Act 2014), but there has also been an attempt to 'problematise' certain families, particularly those suffering exclusion or margin-alisation, through an increased emphasis on anti-social behaviour and inadequate parenting (Jordan and Jordan, 2000).This is exemplified by the Troubled Families Programme introduced in 2011. The Troubled Families Programme claims that

the government will work alongside local authorities to:

- *get children back into school*

- *reduce youth crime and anti-social behaviour*

- *put adults on a path back to work*

- *reduce the high costs these families place on the public sector each year.*

(Department for Communities and Local Government, 2014)

In a report published in 2012, Louise Casey, Head of the Troubled Families Unit in the Department for Communities and Local Government, said:

What came from these families' stories were that they had entrenched, long-term cycles of suffering problems and causing problems. Their problems were cumulative and had gathered together over a long period of time – perhaps over generations. Listening to the families there was a strong sense of them having problems and causing problems for years. The longevity of their relationship with services was also striking. In many cases their problems began with their own parents and their parents' parents, in cycles of childhood abuse, violence and care which are then replayed in their own lives.

Family, and its influence past and present, was the pervading subject of conversation. The overwhelming themes that came out of the interviews were the complexity of these families' lives and the length of time the problems had gone on for – in many cases – from generation to generation

(Casey, 2012, Foreword, p1).

She concluded that

[t]his requires services who work with families to take the long view; of what happened to the parents as children, and of what happened to the children since birth. This may not be a pretty sight, and will lay bare the extent of the dysfunction that is accumulated in the lives of some of these families

(p. 64).

Although Casey claims to be optimistic and suggests that some families have made 'huge leaps forward', it is worth looking at the language underpinning the approach to 'Troubled Families'. In the short sections quoted above there is mention of 'cycles of suffering', 'generations', 'having problems and causing problems' and 'dysfunction'. These are not new discourses and can be traced back to the US War on Poverty in the 1960s, Keith Joseph's 'cycles of poverty' in the 1970s, not to mention the more recent discourses about the 'underclass'.

Charles Murray, an American sociologist, caused considerable controversy in 1989 when, in an article in the *Sunday Times* magazine, he argued that

> Britain does have an underclass, still largely out of sight and still smaller than the one in the United States. But it is growing rapidly. Within the next decade, it will probably become as large (proportionately) as the United States' underclass. It could easily become larger.

> (Murray, 2001, piv)

Returning to the UK 5 years later, Murray produced an updated 'analysis' in which he argued that there was now an emerging consensus that the underclass was growing. He attributed this to rising crime rates, 'illegitimacy' and unemployment. At the centre of his analysis was a belief that the traditional family was in crisis and that there was a consequent breakdown in the moral fabric of society. This he argued produced a *'New Rabble'*, an economic underclass in which

> [i]llegitimacy in the lower classes will continue to rise and, inevitably, life in lower class communities will continue to degenerate – more crime, more widespread drug and alcohol addiction, fewer marriages, more dropout from work, more homelessness, more child neglect, fewer young people pulling themselves out of the slums, more young people tumbling in.

> (Murray, 2001)

The solutions he proposed were equally direct and included the elimination of benefits for unmarried women *'altogether'*. The attempt to attribute such a wide range of social problems to the breakdown of the family and the number of people choosing not to marry clearly fits within neo-liberal discourses around dependency and the withdrawal of the state from social programmes. It ignores the substantial increase in social inequality that had occurred over the previous 15 to 20 years and which, after a small improvement, has continued to increase.

A common theme within these discourses is that they blame people for the situations they find themselves in. They are not part of the wider progressive discourse around poverty and inequality discussed earlier (although they clearly influence the more reactionary discourses around the moral underclass). They see people in the 'troubled circumstances' as needing professional intervention and not as actors or agents in their own right (see earlier discussions). They are part of the wider neo-liberal agenda that sees the market and market forces as essentially beneficent and any problems as located within people's inability to meet the expectations of the market. Again this degree of blame is directed at people in poverty facing marginalisation, not at those who benefit disproportionately from crises in the financial system.

Lowndes and Pratchett (2012) have suggested that the users and providers of public services faced a *'disproportionately high share of the cuts'* (p23). As they note, the Coalition government

> [p]roposed to cut public services fast and deep, with £30bn of spending cuts being announced over a four year period … The subsequent Spending Review … went further, bringing the total value of cuts over four years up to £81bn …
> In total, it targeted a cut of 490,000 public sector jobs, with an average 19 per cent cut over four years to departmental budgets and a further £7bn cut in the welfare budget.

(2012, p23)

This provides the context in which families such as those drawn into the Troubled Families Programme are leading their lives. Blaming people for their poverty and exclusion seems somewhat ironic given the social and economic context within which people are living their lives. As Wilkinson and Pickett (2006) have noted, poor health outcomes are significantly related to levels of social inequality in a society. Among their findings were the following correlations:

- 10x difference in homicide rates between more and less equal countries.

- 6x difference in obesity rates.

- 6x difference in teenage pregnancy rates.

- 4x difference in how much people feel they can trust each other.

- Between 5–10 x difference in imprisonment rates.

- Average rates of hostility and racism greater in more unequal societies.

- There was a significant correlation between income inequality and serious or any mental health problems.

- The large majority of studies reported that more egalitarian societies tend to be healthier.

(2006, p1774)

Wilkinson and Pickett's analysis has been heavily critiqued because the conclusions provide a severe challenge to governments of all political persuasions. However, a recent review of the evidence on health inequality concluded that *'what the new evidence shows is that inequality has an "independent" effect on health that cannot be tackled without narrowing the (inequality) gap'* (Peacock and Bissell, 2011, p26).

As social workers and community workers, we have a clear responsibility/duty to argue for a reversal of discourses (Foucault, 1980) which promote such negative outcomes and the policies underpinning them. This is reflected in PCF domain 5 (Rights, justice and economic wellbeing) and the key value of community empowerment in the Community Development NOS.

Understanding the underpinning theories: communitarianism and the 'Big Society'

Concern about the pathologising of the poor, which lay at the heart of American debates on the underclass, led a group of liberal academics to attempt to restate a social philosophy that recognised the way people's lives were influenced by the network of social arrangements within the locality. Etzioni, a leading proponent of communitarianism, claimed that their agenda was predicated on the need to 'bring about the changes in values, habits and public policy that will allow us to do for society what the environmental movement does for nature; to safeguard and enhance our future' (1993, p3).

The communitarian philosophy was based on the need to rekindle people's sense of social responsibility by correcting the 'imbalance' between citizens' rights and responsibilities. Etzioni argued that this could best be achieved by a four-fold strategy, which included:

- a moratorium on the development of new rights;
- a re-establishment of the link between rights and responsibilities;
- the recognition that 'some responsibilities do not entail rights';
- the adjustment of some rights to changing circumstances.

(1993, pp263–4)

He argued that at the heart of this social philosophy lies the idea of 'reciprocity', the notion that 'each member of society owes something to all the rest, and the community owes something to its members ... members of the community have a responsibility to the greatest extent to provide for themselves and their families' (pp263–4).

This framework suggests a view of people as one in which 'individuals cannot be perceived to exist in a vacuum. Individuals are an inherent part of their community' (Mullard and Spicker, 1998, p200). Mullard and Spicker point to the way in which the apparent inclusiveness of communitarianism can mask potential discrimination in that it can offer

> preference to some people over others. The social relationships of family and community imply that people have special responsibilities to the people they are closest to, responsibilities which go over and above the responsibilities they have to others.

(1989, p95)

Perversely then, communitarianism could further the processes of social exclusion which New Labour sought to tackle through its social policies, particularly through the project teams set up to tackle social exclusion which were initially based in the Cabinet Office and the Office of the Deputy Prime Minister. Before we deal with this argument it is worth noting the important way in which communitarian ideas influenced New Labour's social policy agenda. Commenting on the development of New Labour's social philosophy, Ruth Lister pointed out how

> [w]hen Tony Blair talks the language of citizenship, it is to emphasise obligations and responsibilities. This is reflected in the statement of values that replaced Clause 4 of the party's constitution. This offers the ideal of a 'community ... where the rights we enjoy reflect the duties we owe,' ... Gordon Brown, announcing his 'new deal' on youth unemployment ... promised that 'opportunities and responsibilities' would dominate Labour's modernisation of the welfare state.

> (Lister, 1998, p 49)

Johnson suggested that communitarianism had implications for policy which went well beyond the personal social services and community care, but it has a particular significance in this area (1999, p92). He suggested that it is particularly resonant in debates concerning decentralisation with its implied increased role for local agencies and its emphasis on community as the unit of social organisation. He argued, however, that communitarians, although they would welcome the increased emphasis on self-reliance and mutual aid, would probably baulk at the idea of such groupings becoming campaigning or advocacy organisations. Johnson suggests that New Labour would be supportive of such developments because they have constantly emphasised the empowerment of users and carers (p93) with its focus on the idea of welfare recipients as consumers or even stakeholders in society. This is at best debatable as New Labour was not sympathetic to radical campaigning activity. As Popple and Redmond pointed out,

> [n]ow radical work can be quickly identified and isolated, funding can be withdrawn on the back of regular assessment of project work, and reassigned to 'safe' and often competing projects.

> (2000, p396)

Jordan suggests that an emphasis on choice and the user as consumer typified the way the welfare state was developing. He argued that

> [t]he public infrastructure is redesigned so as to promote choice, giving citizens information (for instance in the form of league tables) about the performance of hospitals, school and care homes, so that they can switch to the best amenities.

> (2006, p142)

However, as he suggested, those without the material resources to make these choices real lose out in this newly marketised form of welfare.

The community may only meet the needs of a section of society, one which buys into the welfare pluralism we have discussed earlier. What then becomes of those who are not part of this grouping – those who are excluded or marginalised – and who are often the focus of social work intervention? It is helpful here to return to the discussion of social exclusion in Chapter 2. Silver noted that by the mid-1980s, social exclusion had come to represent a wider understanding of social problems:

> *The term referred not only to the rise in long-term and recurrent unemployment, but also to the growing instability of social bonds: family instability, single-member households, social isolation, and the decline of class solidarity based on unions, the labour market, and the working-class neighbourhood and social networks. There were not only material but also spiritual and symbolic aspects to this phenomenon.*

(1994, p533)

Spicker suggests that the French concern had been to foster a sense of *mutualité* or solidarity as exemplified by the development of the Revenu Minimum d'Insertion, a benefit established as a safety net for those without other entitlements and which seeks to draw people into defined relationships with the rest of society (1995, p9).

The European Commission's final report of the Poverty 3 programme in 1995 noted that the concept of social exclusion was gradually replacing poverty as the operative concept in member states and at community level. The report said of social exclusion:

> *We are acknowledging that the problem is no longer one of inequity between the top and bottom of the scale (up/down) but also one of the distance within society between those who are active members and those who are forced towards the fringes (in/out). We are also highlighting the effects of the way society is developing and the concomitant risk of social disintegration and, finally we are affirming that for both the persons concerned and society itself, this is a process of change and not a set of fixed and static situations ... there is not only one group – and a small one at that – of people living in permanent poverty and exclusion but a variety of increasingly large groups whose economic and social integration is insecure, who experience periods of sporadic or recurrent poverty and who are threatened by the loss of social ties which accompanies the process of social exclusion.*

(European Commission, 1995, p7)

As we noted earlier, Levitas (2005) suggests three distinct discourses around social exclusion which she characterises as the redistributive discourse, the moral underclass discourse and the social integrationist discourse.

These concepts of the underclass, social exclusion and communitarianism, when related to discourses around the family which engage more with ideas of 'blame' rather than rights, have an important resonance within social work as they characterise the people with whom we work in ways that have direct implications for social work interventions. As Jordan suggests, Labour's distrust and dislike of public services can lead to:

[a] very restricted view of social work's role... suspicion of the public sector, and its top down notions of implementation... social welfare services need to recapture their sense of moral purpose, as transformative agencies that thrive on change and uncertainty, rather than as structural features in a system of regulation and control.

(2002, pp 218–19)

This move from neo-liberalism to communitarianism was predicated on an inter-change of ideological positions between neo-liberal and communitarian ideals which led to a focus on delivering welfare outside of state institutions. Within this conception, communitarianism can be seen as the 'soft' side of neo-liberalism, stressing individual responsibility, providing a 'safety net' for the most disadvantaged but not challenging the overall distribution of material, economic and financial resource.

The 'Big Society', localism and social action

Within current debates around the welfare state, however, communitarianism has been replaced by the Coalition government's ideas on the 'Big Society', with an emphasis on localism, empowerment and social action. These form part of what is claimed to be a focus on decentralising power so that communities can take control of their own affairs. As the architect of the 'Big Society', David Cameron said when launching the policy on 19 July 2010, *'You can call it liberalism. You can call it empowerment, you can call it freedom, you can call it responsibility. I call it the "Big Society"'* (McCabe, 2010). McCabe has suggested that the 'Big Society' may lead to a fragmentation of the voluntary or third sector, particularly as it comes after years in which voluntary/third sector organisations were increasingly expected to compete against each other for scarce resources through processes such as competitive tendering. He asks:

[W]ill community trust in politics be restored if 'Big Society' becomes inexorably linked in the public mind with 'deficit reduction', the delivery of services 'on the cheap' and the rolling back of the welfare state to a residual role where consumers with resources have more access to quality choices whilst services for the poor become poor services?

(2010, p14)

Anna Coote of the New Economics Foundation says of the 'Big Society' that it *'shifts responsibility from the state to individuals and families, and from public services to self-help, charity, local enterprise and global commerce ... It is also a bid to replace paid with unpaid labour on a massive scale'* (2012, n.p.). The reality is that rather than promoting a radical agenda the policy is characterised by the promotion of neo-liberal policies, including increased privatisation of welfare, a rolling back of the state and a reduction in public spending (Jordan, 2011). Indeed, Alcock in his review of the 'Big Society' agenda, argues that it has become more of a *'political slogan than a theoretical departure from existing forms of public action'* (2012, p11).

Implications for social work

This discussion of the way the nature of the welfare state has changed has clear implications for the practice of social work. It suggests that attempts to characterise social work as an activity which takes place in the statutory sector can provide an inaccurate account of the way social work is heading. While qualified social workers still tend to gravitate toward working in local authorities, whether in the children or adult workforce or multi-disciplinary initiatives such as Youth Offending Teams or Community Mental Health Teams, much of the more innovative practice is taking place outside these sectors and can be found in the voluntary and independent sectors. The *Guardian* reported research from the National Council for Voluntary Organisations, which suggests that whatever the challenges it faces there is growth and vibrancy in the voluntary sector. There are approximately 660,00 paid jobs in the sector, a 23 per cent increase over 10 years, which they attribute to the '*expanding role of charities in delivering public services and within this social care work is one of the fastest growing sectors*' (Smethurst, 2010). Dickinson et al. (2012) point to a dearth of quality research and information about the role of social care in the sector and call for more systematic and high-quality research. They note, however, the importance of social care within the voluntary/third sector, particularly around personalisation.

Morison saw evidence of an '*increasing involvement by the voluntary sector in delivering a whole range of services*' (2000, p105). He noted how the voluntary sector had been estimated to account for 1 in 25 of the workforce, with a total contribution to the economy of £25 billion per annum. Clearly the sector is not, therefore, an insignificant part of the welfare environment in the UK. Bateman (2006) has drawn attention to how important the voluntary sector is, for instance, on the development of welfare advice services.

Popple and Redmond (2000) suggested that involvement with the voluntary sector was one way in which New Labour could be seen to distance itself from the policies of the previous Conservative administration. However, as they noted, the motivation for such developments was not always based on altruism but instead was conditioned by the fact that

> [t]he voluntary sector delivers a range of services cheaper than those in the state or provided for by the private sector, not least because such agencies are long used to operating with fewer overheads, in accommodation that is usually cheaper, and of a lower standard than that found in the public sector. Here staff, often female, are paid less and employed on short term contracts.

> (Popple and Redmond, 2000, p397)

Whatever the motivation, it is undoubtedly true that the voluntary sector has been given a pivotal role in delivering social work and welfare services. The compact between the government and the voluntary sector agreed in 1998 gave formal expression to this improved relationship, although to what extent it allowed the voluntary sector to become the lead sector is debatable. The aims of the compact were the creation of a new approach to partnerships between the statutory and voluntary and community sectors – an approach which is of mutual advantage based on shared values and mutual respect (Carrington, 2002, p2). The aim was to make these principles a key part of the local infrastructure and day-to-day activities. This was coupled with a commitment to a more stable funding regime, including the award of three-year contracts instead of the previous one-year contracts. Osborne and McLaughlin suggest that the compact provided

> *potential participative challenges to its concept of representative democracy …*
> *and real dangers to the voluntary sector, which could lead to the negation of its*
> *legitimate societal roles as independent watchdog and voice for the marginalised*
> *and oppressed.*

(2002, p61)

Osborne and McLaughlin suggest that for positive rather than negative outcomes to be achieved, a number of key factors must be in place:

- The partnerships involved should be locally owned rather than centrally imposed.

- Both sides need to develop relationships based on trust.

- The process should be led by the voluntary sector.

- The replacement of hierarchical forms of control with local control.

- Voluntary organisations should be involved in developing policy, not just implementing it.

- The process should embrace the large range of community organisations and community interests, not just the traditional voluntary sector.

Certainly the support successive governments have shown for the voluntary sector centres much more on the services it delivers than any increased capacity to challenge or pursue a radical agenda over the structures and the overall development of services, which it was suggested (in the previous chapter) should be part of any realignment of social work to allow it to pursue a social change agenda.

This increasing role can come at a price. Wyatt (2002) argues that when the state seeks to draw voluntary organisations into partnership the result can be that they become peripheral, particularly where provision is patchy and discontinuous. The result may be that the vibrancy and diversity of the sector may be diminished as local or national government seeks to standardise relationships. As he argues,

> *[t]he importance and strength of voluntary organisations taken together is that*
> *they express the right and willingness of citizens to do what they want, in the way*
> *that they want, for the benefit of themselves and others. The resulting diversity*
> *and non-conformity open up possibilities of change, of challenge, of offering*
> *alternatives, and doing something better. The right to be different is protected but*
> *also increasingly restricted by regulation from the government sphere.*

(Wyatt, 2002, p177)

The result, he suggests, is that voluntary organisations may be sucked further *'into the sphere of government interest'* (p178) and end up being co-opted by the state.

Implications for social and community work

Using the analysis of the three approaches to welfare provision discussed above – the underclass, communitarianism, the 'Big Society' and social exclusion – use the Internet to find three voluntary organisations, one national, one that covers a city/town, and one of a small local organisation. How would you evaluate their activity against the approaches? Has there, in your opinion, been any sign that their activities have been constrained by their relationship with the people who fund them?

Comment

Use the web resources at the end of the chapter as a way of addressing this question. You will need to access the annual reports and mission statements of the organisations. It may also be helpful to email the organisations you choose to research to ask them if they feel their activities are in any way constrained by their funders.

Social enterprise – the way forward?

It has been suggested that one way of resolving the dilemmas outlined above is to embrace these apparently contradictory pressures and utilise the methods of business and enterprise in creating new, more dynamic forms of practice. These would be able to tap into available community resources, material, intellectual, social and cultural capital to create a vision which regenerated marginalised communities and used any surpluses generated to promote local activity. This model, known as 'social enterprise', first rose to prominence in the UK in Bromley by Bow through the creation of a community project that was driven by the energy of a small group of activists and which sought to create, through a mixture of trading and social activity, surpluses that could be used to benefit the local area. They defined social enterprise as

> *a business which trades for a social and/or environmental purpose. Social enterprises will have a clear 'social mission' outlining what difference they are trying to make, who they aim to help, and how they plan to do it. Social enterprises also have clear rules about what they do with their profits, reinvesting these to further their 'social mission'.*

> (www.bbbc.org.uk/what-is-a-social-enterprise-, accessed 3/3/15)

With its classic attempt to find a third way between the state and the market it was a model embraced by New Labour, particularly as it allowed the government to claim that local self-activity could generate profit and thus reduce the burden on the state.

It has been suggested that *'there is no universally accepted definition of social enterprise, their key distinguishing features are their social aims and social ownership, combined with trading viability'* (CEEDR, 2001, p4).

However, Spear suggested that social enterprises have four main characteristics in that they:

- engage continuously in activity aimed at producing goods and/or selling services;
- have a high degree of autonomy – they are governed voluntarily by a group of people without control by an outside agency;
- engender a significant degree of economic risk – they are dependent on their members to generate sufficient income to survive;
- they combine voluntary and paid members but with a minimum amount of paid work.

(2006, p3)

The National Strategy for Neighbourhood Renewal report on enterprise and social exclusion (Policy Action Teams, 1999) suggested that social enterprises were important because they could play a key part in tackling social exclusion. Social enterprises can build *'human and social capital ... [and] strengthen local communities'* (p107). They identified one of the main problems facing social enterprises as sustainability, in as much as there needed to be embedded support mechanisms so that they could draw down finance from various sectors of government, including 'loans' from relevant government agencies. The report notes that they differ from private-sector businesses in that *'they are geared towards social regeneration and help, rather than simply the generation of profits. As such they do not fall within the standard definitions of private or public sector enterprises'* (p105). In 2006, the creation of the Office of the Third Sector (OTS) resulted in responsibility for social enterprise moving to the Cabinet Office, thus putting social enterprises at the heart of government (Teasdale, 2011). Teasdale quotes from the OTS report, *Social Enterprise Action Plan: Scaling New Heights*, which said:

> Social enterprises are part of the 'third sector', which encompasses all
> organisations which are non-governmental, principally reinvest in the community
> or organization and seek to deliver social or environmental benefits.

(OTS, 2006, p10, quoted in Teasdale, 2011, p15)

A core element of the more innovative social enterprise models is the idea of the social entrepreneur, which has been defined as *'people who realise where there is an opportunity to satisfy some unmet need, and who gather together the necessary resources (generally people, often volunteers, money and premises) and use them to "make a difference"* (Thompson et al., 2000, p328). Thompson et al. further point out that there is nothing new in the concept of social entrepreneurship: it was the bedrock of Victorian private hospitals; it is a key feature of charity work; it is clearly evident in the more recent hospice movement (p328). McCabe has noted how elements of the 'Big Society' including social enterprises have *'a long history within right wing political thinking ... (including) ... the search for a "viable private, non-political alternative to the welfare state"'* (2010, p4).

How then can social enterprises contribute to social work's agenda? This may happen in a number of ways. First, they tap into a core belief within social and community work that we should support people to take action to empower themselves and their communities. They appear to provide a third way between the state and private welfare which can allow people to engage with processes of change, take risks, and achieve levels of self-development. To this extent they provide a challenge to the more moribund and procedural focus still found in too much contemporary social work. Gray et al. concluded in their review of the relationship between social enterprises and social work in Australia, Canada, New Zealand, the UK and the US that,

> *[g]iven social worker's historical mission to address social disadvantage, the profession has a vital role to play in current debates on social enterprises, in particular, to participate in the much needed examination of its strengths and limitations for achieving social justice with marginalized individuals and communities*
>
> (2003, p152)

Second, social enterprises relate to the changing structure of welfare in that they are a clear expression that the mixed economy of welfare does not necessarily mean an increase in managerialism or central control but that they can provide a way of allowing local people and communities to generate their own solutions to their problems. Indeed, it has been suggested that social enterprises exist because of the failures of both the state and the market not just in the UK but across Europe. Teasdale (2011) has argued that they exist at the interface of notions of individualism (incorporating social business and the focus on earned income for the non-profit sector) and collectivism (the link between cooperative and community enterprises). As Teasdale has pointed out, the enthusiasm shown for social enterprises by New Labour has continued under the Coalition, although they are noticeably more reticent about what constitutes a social enterprise and how they should be supported.

Third, the focus on the social entrepreneur can at least mirror some of the ideas in the more radical alternatives that postulate the way in which community leaders can emerge organically from the local community (Freire, 1972; Gramsci, 1971).

However, these challenges to current practice need to be contextualised. The creation of social enterprises is clearly a part of successive governments' agendas. While espousing the importance of the voluntary and community sectors, governments are doing so in a situation that seeks to unburden the state from the high levels of social expenditure with which it is deemed to be grappling. Equally it can be seen as an attempt to 'socialise' the market so that as social workers we become even more used to competing for scarce resources against other providers. The discussion then moves from the broader radical agenda we outlined in earlier chapters, in which issues of redistribution, equity and fairness re-enter the social work vocabulary, to arguments over the distribution of diminishing resources within an increasingly inegalitarian society. The 2013 report on Poverty and social exclusion by the Joseph Rowntree Foundation/New Policy Institute, estimated that 13 million people in the UK were in poverty in 2011/12 and that there were a *'further two million with incomes that would have been low enough to count as poverty in 2007/9. This is the effect of the recession and its prolonged aftermath'* (MacInnes et al., 2013, p6).

A more radical interpretation of social enterprise is provided through the experience of mental health service users in Trieste, Italy. Here the community developed a service in which:

- the human and material resources of the hospital are used to benefit the community.

- resources are delivered directly to the consumers.

- collaboration with other providers is promoted.

- … [they created] productive, integrated cooperative societies that combine diversified job opportunities and vocational training with user involvement in the economical and decision making structure of the various enterprises thereby bridging the gap between the labour market and the welfare system, and providing an alternative to the inefficiency, ineffectiveness and unproductivity of welfare services.

(Rotelli et al., n.d., pp1–2)

These discussions parallel concerns within social work about the most effective way of involving users of services and carers in decisions about service development and service delivery. We will address them in Chapter 5 before drawing out the lessons for the future directions of social work in the final chapters.

However, before leaving this discussion about the UK voluntary sector and work in the community it is worth reminding ourselves of the way the community development approach has been recognised across Europe. In March 2004 an international conference brought together policy-makers, community workers, civil society organisations and community groups to look at how community development could contribute to the development of civil society. They agreed a common statement on community development in Europe, which became known as the Budapest Declaration. They defined community development as:

A way of strengthening civil society by prioritizing the actions of communities, and their perspective in the development of social, economic and environmental policy.

(Craig et al., 2004, pp423–9)

The declaration called for all national governments to appoint a minister with responsibility for community development, and linked community development to policies around rural communities, urban regeneration, sustainability, lifelong learning and cultural development, local economic development and tackling racism and discrimination against minorities. Contributing to the debate at the conference, Hautekeur argued that *'community development has most certainly found its place in the European welfare scene and in many European countries it is obtaining a higher profile'* (2005, p397).

The upgrading of communities to become a ministerial responsibility by the Labour government, and the continuation of that policy under the Coalition government with the establishment of the Department for Communities and Local Government, suggested that this message has been heard in the UK. However, the challenge will be to ensure that while contributing to a revitalised welfare agenda, community development and community work more generally are not emasculated. As Powell has noted,

> *[s]upport in the West for the expansion of voluntary organisations was distinctive because of its top-down character and its association with the scaling down of the welfare state. Neo-conservatives were at the forefront of this process.*
>
> (2001, p119)

To achieve its goals, particularly as a form of social work intervention which contributes to the empowerment of the communities, families and individuals with whom we engage, community work needs to retain a radical and campaigning aspect. One of the key ways in which this can occur is through a refocusing of the attention of social and community workers to new forms of participatory practice such as those developed by the service user and carer movement. Chapter 5 looks at the potential of such approaches and at how we can ensure that any such initiatives are not merely tokenistic.

C H A P T E R   S U M M A R Y

This chapter has sought to place the discussions in Chapters 2 and 3 in the wider social policy context. It began by reviewing developments in the UK welfare state and focused particularly on debates around the underclass, communitarianism, the 'Big Society' and social exclusion. It then looked at developments in the voluntary or independent sector and examined the contradictory pressures faced by voluntary and independent sector organisations – initial increased funding and responsibility for the delivery of a wide range of services coupled with an increased level of accountability and control by the state, followed by a process of retrenchment and diminishing resources. The chapter asked if this diminished the sector's capacity to engage with the more radical interventions suggested in Chapters 2 and 4.

It then looked at an area which is receiving increasing support from the government: the promotion of social enterprises and social entrepreneurship. It questioned whether this emphasis masked a commitment to less radical forms of practice as the sector grappled with the need to be financially self-reliant and to reduce dependency on the state. It looked briefly at the experience of social enterprises in Trieste as a possible alternative approach which was more consistent with a social change agenda.

Centre for Enterprise and Economic Development Research (CEEDR) (2001) *Final Report to the Small Business Service.* London: Middlesex University Business School.

A useful account of the development of social enterprises.

Jordan, B. (2006) *Social Policy for the Twenty-first Century*. Cambridge: Polity Press.

An up-to-date account of the way contemporary social work in the UK is developing, which builds on his earlier work.

Policy Action Teams (1999) *National Strategy for Neighbourhood Renewal, Enterprise and Social Exclusion.* London: HM Treasury.

One of a series of reports from the Social Exclusion Unit within the Cabinet Office. It looks specifically at the ways in which social enterprise can be used to regenerate local communities.

The Bromley by Bow Centre: www.bbbc.org.uk

University of Birmingham: www.birmingham.ac.uk/generic/esrc/index.aspx

www.triestesalutementale.it/inglese/allegati/Rehab.pdf

European Community Development Network: www.eucdn.net/organisation. A social enterprise is a business which trades for a social and/or environmental purpose. Social enterprises will have a clear 'social mission' outlining what difference they are trying to make, who they aim to help, and how they plan to do it. Social enterprises also have clear rules about what they do with their profits, reinvesting these to further their 'social mission'.

Chapter 5

Involving, integrating or ignoring? Service users, carers and social work

This chapter will help you to develop the following capabilities, to the appropriate level, from the Professional Capabilities Framework:

Values and ethics. Apply social work ethical principles and values to guide professional practice.

Diversity. Recognise diversity and apply anti-discriminatory and anti-oppressive principles in practice.

Rights, justice and economic wellbeing. Advance human rights and promote social justice and economic wellbeing.

Critical reflection and analysis. Apply critical reflection and analysis to inform and provide a rationale for professional decision making.

Intervention and skills. Use judgement and authority to intervene with individuals, families and communities to promote independence, provide support and prevent harm, neglect and abuse.

Contexts and organisations. Engage with, inform, and adapt to changing contexts that shape practice. Operate effectively within own organisational frameworks and contribute to the development of services and organisations. Operate effectively within multi-agency and inter-professional settings.

See Appendix 1 for the Professional Capabilities Framework diagram.

QAA Benchmarking Statement

The term 'service user' is used ... to cover the wide and diverse set of individuals, groups and organisations who are involved in, or who benefit from, the contribution of social work to the well being of society. ... In providing services, social workers should engage with service users in ways that are characterised by openness, reciprocity, mutual accountability and explicit recognition of the powers of the social worker and the legal context of intervention.

(QAA, 2008, p 5)

Community Development National Occupational Standards

Key Area 1: Core – Understand and practise community development.

Key Area 2: Understand and engage with communities.

(Continued)

(Continued)

Key Area 3: Take a community development approach to group work and collective action.

Key Area 4: Promote and support a community development approach to collaborative and cross-sectoral working.

Key Area 6: Provide community development support to organisations.

(Federation for Community Development Learning, 2009)

Introduction: from tokenism to involvement

The last three chapters have illustrated how social and community work are dynamic activities that possess traditions which can be drawn on to inform current practice. Radical activity now needs to be reframed so that the potential illustrated in Chapters 2 and 3 can be articulated within the changing welfare mix described in Chapter 4. How can we connect these apparently divergent analyses? The concept of inclusion can enable us to see how these historical and contemporary analyses converge. A fully developed concept of inclusion also enables us to locate power as a central part of any analysis of social and community work's potential for change. It particularly helps us to see people who use social work services as active agents in changing their own situation and challenging the perspective of agencies with whom they work.

An insight into the importance of engaging with the people who use services is provided in the writings of Michel Foucault. When asked why he looked at the local rather than structural aspect of political problems, Foucault said:

> [T]he problems which I try to address ... which involve daily life, cannot be easily resolved. It takes many years, decades of work carried out at grass roots level with the people directly involved, and the right to speech and political imagination must be returned to them ... the complexity of the problem will be able to appear in its connection with people's lives ... the object is to proceed a little at a time, to introduce modifications that are capable of, if not finding a solution, then at least changing the givens of a problem.
>
> (1981, pp158–9)

While Foucault was addressing issues of political power in the broad sense, his comments can just as easily be seen as a prime legitimation for social workers' concern with involving people who use social work services. Work with service users and carers is specifically about releasing people's political imagination so that they can envision an alternative experience, a different way of experiencing and delivering welfare and social work services. It is also about focusing on the particular daily experience of those people most directly involved in delivering social work services. It is concerned with changing the way issues are framed so that service users are not seen as 'problems' or 'clients' but rather as active partners in changing the services they directly experience. As Castells argues, we need to *live with the tension, and the contradiction, between what we find and what we would like to happen.* I consider social action and political projects to be essential in the betterment of a society that clearly needs change and hope.

(2000, p389, emphasis added)

This suggest that engaging and creating partnerships with people who use social work services has a change dimension, it is essentially political, which means that when examining service user involvement we need to ask whether the involvement we are discussing is real or tokenistic. This is the focus of this chapter.

Before seeking to integrate Foucault into our analysis we will first focus on: how a concern with service user involvement originated; the legislative and policy context within which it has developed; the increasing involvement of service users in the development and delivery of social work education; and the international context within which debates about service user involvement, which are essentially about the meaning of our welfare system, can be understood. We will then seek to develop a model for evaluating service user involvement which integrates Foucault and other key social and political theory.

The origins of service user involvement

The involvement of service users in service delivery and development is now so firmly embedded in legislation and policy that it is easy to forget that it was not that long ago that the role of service users was seen as a much more marginal one. The idea of empowerment had been central to at least some social work discourses since the 1980s (Dominelli, 1988; Adams, 2008) and arguably since the 'radical social work' movement of the 1970s (Bailey and Brake, 1975, 1980; Corrigan and Leonard, 1978; Ferguson and Woodward, 2009; and can be seen as the key concept which emerged out of the radical social work movement, which:

sought to generate a wider awareness of the power that social workers had by virtue of their access to information and sources that were not readily available to service users. 'Empowerment' was the process of transferring this power into the hands of the people who were systematically denied it within the framework of the Welfare State.

(Langan and Lee, 1989, p9)

The first examples of user involvement come from the users/survivors of the mental health system, which emerged from the anti-psychiatry and civil rights movements in the 1960s (MIND, 2005). However, the idea of involving service users as partners in service delivery did not really take off until the early 1990s when the Social Services Inspectorate reviewing the National Health Service and Community Care Act 1990, argued that the primary motivator for this development was service user empowerment. Equally, the Children Act 1989 was *'peppered with references to the need to inform, consult and involve people who use services'* (Braye, 2000, p13). However, from the beginning the process of user involvement was often poorly articulated and confused in its implementation. As Braye notes, *'the legal mandate for participation and involvement may be criticised as partial, contradictory and ineffectual'* (2000, p15).

An example of this confusion and contradiction can be seen in the development of policies around disability, particularly around community care and direct payments, both of which were supposed to empower and give a voice to people with disabilities. As Priestley argued, *'the first assumption of community care policy is that disabled people are dependent and need "care"'* (1999, p43). Looking at the direct payments legislation, he says *'the administrative and professional dominance over the assessment of "need" remain largely unchallenged'* (p202). Moreover, these discussions remain locked into discourses around the individual/medical model of disability. As Oliver noted when reviewing the development of these policies, *'there was little evidence that disabled people were being involved in the planning and delivery of services in the way that legislation had required'* (2003, p314).

Largely this was because professionals and legislators failed to appreciate the capacity of people with disabilities to make their own choices about the type and quality of service they wished to access. As Hersov suggested,

> the first obstacle towards believing that people with learning difficulties can begin to make real choices and decisions in their lives is our own reluctance to acknowledge the possibility that they might be able to do so. This may be a legacy of viewing this group of people as eternal children who will always need their parents (or other carers) to help them function and cope: it may also reflect our own discomfort when they demonstrate that they don't need us anymore.

> (1992, p286)

The lesson, he suggests, is that people with disabilities should be given choices over decisions that affect their lives, as illustrated by the following case study.

CASE STUDY

Women First

An interesting account of the ways in which women with learning disabilities sought to develop their own methods of self-organisation is provided by Jan Walmsley (1993). She described the Women First Conference, a national conference for women with learning disabilities. She pointed out that the planning and the running of the conference was an exercise in involving women with learning difficulties in a national event which addressed their interest (pB7). She demonstrates the ways in which professionals and carers were not allowed to outnumber women with learning disabilities within the conference. She points out also how although women obviously attended the conference on the basis of a common recognition of their experiences of learning difficulties, it became quite clear that within even the group of women who attended the conference there was a wide diversity in experience and expectation. Discussions in groups emerged around abuse, race, sexuality and HIV/Aids.

Walmsley argues:

> *Women First was an important event, a milestone in delineating the right of women with learning difficulties to have their interests aired, discussed, recorded*

CASE STUDY *continued*

and written about. As an exercise in participation, it deserves recognition, and has some valuable messages for others embarking on a similar enterprise.

(1993, p97)

She pointed to lessons that can be learned from such a conference, particularly about ensuring the real and not tokenistic involvement of people with learning disabilities in such an event.

During the mid-1990s, there was little sign that policy-makers or legislators were acknowledging the importance of people with learning disabilities exerting greater control over their lives. Ramscharan et al. argued that people with learning disabilities should have *'sufficient entitlement to resources to prevent oppression and inequality, and maximise self-determination and participation ... such participation and inclusion ... provide the conditions under which citizens with learning disabilities make choices about their everyday lives'* (1997, p256). It was 2001 before this began to become central to social policy (see discussion on Valuing people in Chapter 1).

Legislative and policy context

Over the last few years this situation has changed. Service users have at last been recognised as having a significant role in the delivery, management and development of welfare services. This is reflected in the attention given to service user involvement in both the legislative and policy contexts. These debates cut across all service boundaries and raise questions about service user representation (Warren, 2007; Stepney and Popple, 2008; Payne, 2014), the efficacy of current initiatives (SCIE, 2004) and the usefulness of the service user perspective across a range of service user areas: young people (Freeman et al., 1996; Hayden et al., 1999; Children's Rights Alliance and National Youth Council of Ireland, 2002); people in poverty (Bennett and Roberts, 2004; Beresford and Hoban, 2005); evaluating community outcomes (Jakes and Cassidy, n.d.; FEANTSA, 2009); and with traditional service user groups such as people with mental health problems, people with disabilities and older people.

The drivers behind these initiatives have often been service users themselves. The role of disability activists in creating the political climate to support anti-discriminatory legislation around disability is well known (Beresford and Campbell, 1994; Campbell and Oliver, 1996; Hughes, 1998), as was their role in ensuring that the Disability Discrimination Act 1995 was amended to give disabled people the right to enforcement action if their entitlements were not met. Equally, the voice of the service user can be seen in the *Valuing People* White Paper (Department of Health, 2001) and subsequent policy developments which grew out of that, including *Valuing People Now* (HM Government, 2009). The White Paper enshrined the concepts of rights, independence, choice, inclusion, and argued that *people with learning disabilities have little control over their lives ... The Government's objective is to enable people with learning disabilities to have as much choice and control as possible over their lives and the services and support they receive.*

(Department of Health, 2001, p4)

It recognised the capacity of people with learning disabilities to take control of their lives and suggested that people should be supported to become self-advocates because

[t]he growth of the self-advocacy movement shows how people with learning disabilities can make a real difference to service development and delivery.

Citizen advocates make a vital contribution to enabling the voices of people with more complex disabilities to be heard.

(Department of Health, 2001, p46)

Valuing People Now reinforces this message when it suggests that

[t]he vision remains as set out in Valuing People in 2001: that all people with a learning disability are people first with the right to lead their lives like any others, with the same opportunities and responsibilities, and to be treated with the same dignity and respect. They and their families and carers are entitled to the same aspirations and life chances as other citizens.

(HM Government, 2009, p10)

Service user involvement has also been built into other policy initiatives. The Green Paper on adult social care, *Independence, Well-being and Choice,* argued that we want to move to a system where adults are able to take greater control of their lives (Department of Health, 2005a, p10). The Green Paper further emphasises this point when it says that we want to give people greater choice and control over how their needs shall be met (p11). Following the Green Paper, the Social Care Institute of Excellence (SCIE) published a report by Wistow (2005), which was based on initial consultations around England with service users. This part of the research, conducted by Shaping Our Lives, an independent user-controlled organisation, reported that service users had strong, well thought-out ideas about the future of social care (2005, p3). The responses to the consultation supported these earlier conclusions and emphasised that part of this greater choice and control should be the desire expressed by many people who use services to have more control over the risks they would choose to take to lead more independent lives (Department of Health, 2005b, p6). The management of risk was an important element in the responses received. As the paper says,

[m]any powerful comments were made about how the approach to managing risk affects people's lives, the choices they make and the independence and well-being they experience.

(Department of Health, 2005b, p19)

This mirrors a central concern in social policy of which it has been said key elements are issues of blame, defensibility and rationing. The social work carried out by local authority

Adult and Children's Services is no longer about collectivist provision to those sections of society deemed to be 'in need', it is a residual service for those both at risk and posing a risk (Kemshall, 2002, p89). In this context we are dealing with a system that seeks to manage risk for reasons of professional control and resource restraint, and there must therefore be concern about how far social work agencies will go in promoting risk when it may result in the generation of extra demands on resources.

Hudson et al. (2004) produced a scoping report which attempted to establish the views of service users about adult social care. They highlighted the concern among service users to *'be in control and make their own decisions about their lives. Ensuring independence ... is arguably the most important outcome for adult social care service users'* (p6). From their reading of the literature they identified ten service principles that service delivery should be based upon. These included a personalised service model, a choice and diversity model and a user empowerment model. They suggested that the latter should be based on a social model of ageing and disability, which places the emphasis on rights as well as needs. This focus on rights would, they argued, *'transform the nature of current debate and social care practice'* (p13). User empowerment could be further facilitated by the development of user-controlled services, similar to the model in Centres for Independent Living, and by *'the promotion of collective user "voices" and of effective service responses to those voices'* (p13).

Recently the development of services incorporating personalisation and co-production have provided an important motor for this enhanced move toward empowering people in the adult social care sector. The seven core principles for self-care promoted by Skills for Care and Skills for Health in 2009 suggested that services should ensure that people are able to make informed choices, communicate their needs effectively, develop skills in self-care, be supported to access other networks and *'support and enable risk management and risk taking to maximize independence and choice'* (Department of Health, 2009, p44). This is supported further by Local Authority Circular/Department of Health which says that personalisation is about *'every person across the spectrum of need, having choice and control over the shape of his or her support, in the most appropriate setting'* (2008, p2).

Such an approach is further developed in the proposals around co-production which places the emphasis on users and user-led organisations. Ramsden (2010) cites the Personal Communications Toolkit, which describes co-production as occurring when

> *[y]ou as an individual influence the support and services you receive, or when groups of people get together to influence the way that services are designed, commissioned and delivered.*

> (Ramsden, 2010; emphasis added)

The Social Care Institute for Excellence (2013) has produced a guide to co-production which, while wary of providing a definitive definition as clearly meanings need to be co-constructed by partners, suggests that it is possible to identify some key features that are present:

- (it) define(s) people who use services as assets with skills
- breaks(s) down the barriers between people who use services and professionals

- build(s) on people's existing capabilities

- include(s) reciprocity (where people get something back for having done something for others) and mutuality (people working together to achieve their shared interests)

- (to) work with peer and personal support networks alongside professional networks

- (to) facilitate services by helping organizations to become part agents for change rather than just being service providers.

(SCIE, 2013, p7)

One of the organisations consulted on the development of the guide *Think Local Act Personal* are quoted as saying:

> Co-production is not just a word, it's not just a concept, it is a meeting of minds coming together to find a shared solution. In practice, it involves people who use services coming together to find a shared solution. In practice it involves people who use services being consulted, included and working together from the start to the end of any project that affects them.

(Ramsden, 2010, p7)

We have highlighted three features of personalisation – design, commission and delivery – as they are critical to our ability to distinguish whether such involvement has any meaning. Equally the key elements of co-production involve promoting people's strengths, reciprocity and mutuality, and the idea of people as change agents. All of these ideas resonate with the key debates in this book and we will return to them in this and the following chapters.

Similar developments can be seen in children's services. The report from the Commission for Social Care Inspection (CSCI), *Making Every Child Matter* (2005), recognised the importance of listening to young people in the public care system in order to get a clear view of the way children's services are developing and of whether they were meeting the needs of young people. They commented in the report that

> [l]ooked after children and young people appear to be increasingly positive about their experiences. Many tell us they are generally treated well, their views sought and their rights explained and that their lives have improved since they became involved with children's services.

(CSCI, 2005, p6)

This picture is not, however, always reflected at local level and members of Care Can Change, a group of young people with experience of the care system in the South East, expressed a more measured and critical attitude towards their experience (Bown, 2004).

Organisations working with the homeless also explored issues around service user involvement with a service user group which is probably more unpredictable and chaotic than most. Shelter supports the CHiP network (Changing Homelessness in Practice), which has produced a guide to service user involvement in homelessness.

Shelter suggested that there are three priorities if we want to make service user involvement work:

- the development of statements and policies to reflect a commitment to service user involvement;
- practical support to engage service users;
- genuine engagement at a strategic planning level.

As they noted,

> it is counter productive to develop the capacity of people affected by homelessness and the organizations and workers who support them, but invest no time, energy or money in ensuring that key decision making bodies are receptive and involved in the process.
>
> (Shelter, 2004, pp6–7)

Similar points are also made by a number of writers in the FEANTSA (the European Federation of Organisations Working with the Homeless) magazine *Homelessness in Europe* (Spring, 2009, pp12–13; see also Hatton, 2013).

The way such debates are now reflected across the welfare spectrum is further illustrated in *Improving Services, Improving Lives,* an interim report from the Social Exclusion Unit within the Office of the Deputy Prime Minister. The report looked at what changes needed to be made in the delivery of public services to meet the needs of disadvantaged people. One of the six key themes identified within the report was the need to build personal capacity. The authors argued that this was important because:

> People are more likely to get what they need from services if they are equipped with confidence and self-esteem, communication skills that enable them to articulate their needs, and knowledge of how the system works. These kinds of capacity have a key role to play in helping to build aspirations and ensuring that people benefit from mechanisms for involving users in public service delivery.
>
> (ODPM, 2005, p7)

This quote illustrates the extent to which the rhetoric of empowerment has now become part of the general welfare discourse in the UK. Indeed, Jordan has suggested that the notion of the 'Big Society' can be seen to be based on ideas of '*localism, mutuality, participation*' (2011, p13). It also included rhetoric around social action, empowerment and the promotion of social enterprises (Hatton, 2013). Increasingly, however, this language of radicalism has been used to mask the outcomes of successive austerity budgets, and localism increasingly means providing low-cost services without state support.

> ### ACTIVITY 5.1
>
> *What are the key issues identified by the researchers/organisations looking into service user involvement? How do these link to the discussion of empowerment and advocacy in earlier chapters?*

Comment

You will need to refer back to discussions in earlier chapters. At this stage it is helpful to focus on the issue of risk and the way in which people who use services and service providers conceptualise risk quite differently.

Service users in social work education

Not surprisingly, given this wide-scale endorsement of the principle of service user/ carer inclusion and participation, there has been a significant increase in the level of service user involvement in social work education. As a workshop contributor to the Living and Learning Together Conference said,

> *We are determined to teach social work students because we do not want anybody to go through what we went through and we want services to be better.*

> (SCIE, 2004a, p36)

This quote illustrates the importance service users attribute to their having a greater role in training and educating social workers. Their concern is not just to highlight issues but to contribute to the development and improvement of services. The decision by the General Social Care Council to provide financial support for service user involvement in social work education in the new degree, from 2003, provided a welcome impetus to service user involvement in social work education. Such an involvement is essential if services are to be able to meet the demands placed on them in the new welfare mix. SCIE have noted the connection between values underpinning service user organisations and social work. They argued:

> *The service user movement emphasises the importance of models of participation that are based on human rights, equalities, inclusion and the social model of disability. Their approaches seek to empower people and counter oppressive and discriminatory practice. There is overlap between the values of service user-controlled organisations and those of social work and social care.*

> (SCIE, 2004b, p11)

SCIE (2004b) suggest that service users should be involved at a strategic and management level with universities. This may include involvement at programme management and partnership levels (although this is an area of collaboration and partnership which remains underdeveloped at present). It is more likely to focus on:

- selecting students;

- teaching and learning provision;

- placement learning opportunities – the opportunity to work with and within service user-controlled organisations (the recently formed Learning Resource Centre Networks are in some cases funding work to develop such placements and to support service user-controlled organisations to offer placements);

- assessment of students;

- quality assurance.

Peter Beresford argues that to achieve such a level of involvement will entail a focus on values – treating service users with honesty, openness, respect, equality and of course commitment, and strategy, which will involve 'a fundamental culture change. We will all need to do things differently and make changes in practice – supporting service user training, developing user-controlled organisations, addressing diversity, research, evaluation and payment' (SCIE, 2004b, pp13–14). The issue of payment is a major one, particularly if we are to demonstrate to service users that we value their involvement at a real rather than tokenistic level. As Levin noted, 'prompt and acceptable payment arrangements are key to the success of recruiting service user and carer trainers and retaining them' (2004, p28). Unfortunately this remains an issue particularly for those service users and carers claiming benefits despite the recent report from SCIE (Turner and Beresford, 2005). Despite a series of meetings between government departments, Healthcare Environment Inspectorates and service user/carer organisations, this matter remains unresolved.

Wilson and Beresford (2000) have warned against a simplistic attempt to suggest that a commitment to anti-oppressive values of itself ensures that service users' views are heard and respected. Instead they argue that

> [s]uch a theory [of anti-oppressive practice] is by definition reliant upon user knowledge and ideas. Social work's adoption of a façade of 'anti-oppressive practice' which in reality appropriates and incorporates the knowledge and experiences of service users, whilst retaining the power to determine just what it is that counts as 'anti-oppressive' is for us the most oppressive aspect of its anti-oppressive stance.
>
> (2000, p565)

They conclude that anti-oppressive practice needs to be re-evaluated to ensure that it properly reflects service users' views and aspirations. One way of ensuring this in the academic environment is, they suggest, to recognise that service user involvement should be across the curriculum and not just in those areas where the service users are deemed to be experts because of their experience of a particular service. Davis and Wainwright (2005) provide a useful reminder that even within the protected environs of academia a focus on social work's potential to change the life chances of the poorest sections of society should not be forgotten. ATD Fourth World pointed to the importance, following the Laming Report and Every Child Matters in 2003, of services developing an 'increased understanding of family poverty across professional disciplines'

(ATD Fourth World, 2005, p8). They report on a joint project between the Family Rights Group, ATD Fourth World and Royal Holloway, University of London, which aimed to:

- bring together the experience of people living in poverty (who are service users) and the experience of academics and social work practitioners;

- build an understanding between families living in poverty and those responsible for training social workers;

- develop a pilot training project.

They concluded that the project demonstrated the importance of involving service users in respect of designing (as well as participating) in its work programme (ATD Fourth World, 2005, p28). This is an important reminder of how service user involvement needs to be mainstreamed rather than regarded as an add-on, even if that is value added, of social work education.

A practical example of what this can mean to a social work programme is presented in the case study that follows.

CASE STUDY

Service User Inclusion Group (SUIG), University of Portsmouth (now the Social Work Inclusion Group SWIG) was formed in June 2004 with support of money provided by the General Social Care Council to secure the involvement of service users in the delivery of social work education. Since its formation the group has been involved in:

- *interviewing and admissions procedures;*

- *teaching – the group was one of the pilot groups chosen by Skills for Care to deliver a training programme to train service users to teach on the Portsmouth social work degree programme;*

- *assessing students 'Readiness for Practice' at the end of Level Four;*

- *assessing student presentations;*

- *assessing presentations by applicants seeking academic positions;*

- *redesigning the curricula;*

- *auditing work placements – the group is currently designing an audit tool to assess whether placement agencies meet students' learning needs;*

- *producing a video, 'What I want from a social worker' and a series of DVDs for Palgrave's Social Work Toolkit;*

- *developing a range of drama and cultural activities for use in social work training, particularly around a CREATE day in which people who use social work services work with*

---

groups of social work and creative arts students to produce a creative artifact such as a photographic exhibition, a piece of drama or film, a poem and so on (for more detail see Hatton, 2013, Ch. 4);

- *small-scale research around homelessness.*

SWIG members attend, and contribute to, course validation and other events (see www. swig.uk.net).

SWIG's experience can help illustrate the point made by Foucault at the beginning of this chapter about the pace at which we are seeking to secure meaningful change. He speaks of the need to proceed a little at a time. Yet many agencies, in the desire to be seen to be ticking all the right boxes, treat service user involvement as if it is an immediate imperative and the service user should sublimate their own needs to achieve it. In 2005, SUIG, (the precursor of SWIG), along with a number of other service user organisations, were commissioned by the Training Organisation for the Personal Social Services (TOPSS; now Skills for Care) to undertake training of service users to enable them to teach on the new social work degree. After successfully tendering for the contract, SUIG was encouraged to pilot a training programme in two cities in the South.

This involved recruiting service users for the programmes and supposedly would include piloting training material developed by TOPSS. When the agreed start date for the training arrived, TOPSS had not produced the relevant training material and the group needed to develop their own. TOPSS appeared to think that training could be easily rescheduled. They had no conception that service users were themselves extremely busy people with their own schedules, and they also appeared to be unaware that SUIG members had their own expectations and aspirations, which they had invested in the programme (SUIG, 2005). The hard copies of the training material arrived only after the project had finished. This further illustrates the point made by Wilson and Beresford (2000) when they spoke of how there was a real danger that service users' views and aspirations could be appropriated by larger, more powerful, professional or sectoral organisations.

ACTIVITY **5.2**

Consider how students and/or lecturers on social work programmes can ensure greater service user involvement. Which of those levels of involvement discussed in the above case study apply in your university/college? How can you increase the degree of service user involvement?

Comment

Look at the SCIE website and read their papers on service user involvement. Use their analysis to supplement the above discussion.

International dimensions to service user involvement

Evers (2004) has suggested that we can distinguish between five discourses around user involvement in Europe, raising an important point: service user involvement is not a particularly UK phenomenon. Writing as part of the Expert Group on Service User Involvement for the Council of Europe, he argued that in Europe we can see five models of service user involvement (see also Council of Europe, 2004). These models are:

- *welfarism* – characterised by a top-down approach to participation;

- *professionalism* – identified as indicating that the welfare professional does things for rather than in partnership with the service user;

- *consumerism* – predicated on the idea of the market and the belief that the service user can be given choice and exit options through which their preferences can be gauged;

- *managerialism* – an approach which puts the provider rather than the user at the centre and focuses on managerial imperatives such as effectiveness and efficiency;

- *participationism* – of which Evers said *'the specific point of participationism ... is the belief that people should engage personally in the shaping of services'* (2004, p7).

Participationism, Evers suggested, emphasises localism and diversity and can be seen to be a bottom-up approach to participation, which may only have a small impact on complex mainstream services such as hospitals or the labour market. It does pose a challenge as it is based *'on a very demanding concept of the user as co-producer'* (2004, p7). As such, this model would appear to be much closer to the partnership approach this chapter attempts to develop and which is discussed below.

A range of service user initiatives have also been seen in other European countries (Wirth and Schulze, 1996; Schulze and Wirth, 1996). Heikkila and Julkunen (2003) produced a report for the Council of Europe which documented the barriers to service user involvement across Europe. Their research was an outcome of the work of the Group of Specialists on User Involvement in Social Services and Integrated Service Delivery commissioned by the European Committee for Social Cohesion (CDCS). This research identified a number of key principles for service user involvement in social services that should be applied across all countries (Council of Europe, 2004, p5). These were:

- involvement as a right and responsibility – there should be a democratic right for service users to be involved;

- the centrality of service user involvement in agencies' mission statements;

- access to services – the provision of services in sufficient quantity and quality;

- the importance of evidence – through relevant research;

- a culture of user involvement – a consistent commitment from different service sectors;

- users as recipients and actors – service users are not passive recipients but should play a full role in social care;

- the need to take account of users' networks – the need to recognise the key people involved with service users to maximise their involvement.

As part of this research Heikkila and Julkunen (2003) identified a number of examples of good practice, which are outlined in Table 5.1.

Table 5.1   Examples of good practice across Europe

Country	General comment	Practice exemplar	Outcomes
Netherlands	'A culture of client and user participation' (p7)	Prevention and combating of Poverty and Social Exclusion Act 1997	Created statutory right to client participation
Denmark	Welfare state moved from central planning to decentralisation	Bikva – model based on an idea that the concept of quality is problematised and evaluated from user perspective	At end-1990s Ministry of Social Affairs established project to make service users more active in quality development
Norway	Pioneer of voluntary centres – integrated cooperation between municipalities and voluntary organisations	Fattighuset – a client organisation addressing political issues around poverty	'A good example of a country which has exceptionally active client organisation that addresses poverty issues' (p7)
Sweden	Country with strong legislative structures for user involvement	Long tradition of advocates, *'gode man'* representing people in vulnerable groups	Social Services Act is 'considered to be based on an empowerment model'; 'services should be delivered so as they empower users' (p8)

Source: adapted from Heikkila and Julkunen, 2003, p7

The analysis of Heikkila and Julkunen (2003) demonstrates that the UK is not alone in seeing involvement and inclusion as key elements of social work practice. They drew attention to the way in which the Scandinavian countries have a particular commitment to working with service users. Sweden enshrines the approach in a clear legislative structure and Norway has a strong tradition of partnership between municipalities (local authorities) and voluntary organisations which underpins their commitment to service user involvement.

ACTIVITY **5.3**

Using the above analysis, think about the organisation you are currently working in (or in which you are undertaking your practice or work placement). Plot along the matrix below how you see your organisation scores in respect of these issues.

ACTIVITY **5.3** *continued*

Indicator of good practice	Very good Score 5	Good Score 4	Satisfactory Score 3	Poor Score 2	Very poor Score 1
SU/Carers have right to involvement					
Included in mission statement					
Service users/carers needs met					
Consistent commitment to involvement across organisation					
SUs/carers actively involved					
Relates to SU/carer network					

Key: Maximum level of Service User Involvement 30, minimum 6

Task:

- *How does your organisation score on the above matrix?*

- *What factors account for that score?*

- *How could the score be increased, or maximised?*

Heikkila and Julkunen (2003) identified a number of barriers to effective service user involvement. These are shown in Table 5.2.

Table 5.2 Barriers to good practice

Potential barriers	Cause
Political/legal	Lack of clear legislative rights, existence of some legislation which mitigates against involvement
Administrative	Lack of clear goals and knowledge of good practice
Professional	Social workers not used to ceding control, 'activation of service users can be seen and felt as an extra burden for hard working professionals' (p9)
Language	Both in sense of service users and social workers speaking different languages but also in sense of them coming from different viewpoints
Personal	Different attitudes and views on involvement – service users' focus may be financial independence and decent living conditions, social workers may focus on self-activity and self-reliance

Source: adapted from Heikkila and Julkunen, 2003, p9

Heikkila and Julkunen concluded that better involvement could be achieved by:

- Greater service user and NGO involvement in social services.

- The development of effective strategies for service user involvement including financial support and the development of user boards.

- Learning systematically from current experience.

- Putting in place proper support frameworks.

- Use of a variety of approaches.

(2003, pp9–10)

The barriers they identify relate to issues of professional power and accountability as well as those of organisational culture and tradition. Getting professionals to cede power to people who use services is extremely difficult and cuts across the trends towards creating professional expertise and knowledge which are currently a significant part of debates within social work in the UK. These issues will be dealt with in greater detail in the next chapter.

ACTIVITY 5.4

Using the matrix below, evaluate how your organisation can overcome the barriers to good practice identified in this research.

Potential barriers	Cause	Solution
Political/ legal		
Administrative		
Professional		
Language		
Personal		

Applying this analysis to your organisation (or practice or work placement), how would these factors improve the way it related to service users?

Comment

It is worth looking in detail at the articles by Heikkila and Julkunen and by Evers. Also look at the SCIE website and the author's discussion of power and pedagogy (Hatton, 2013).

Making service user involvement effective

How then can we utilise this understanding of both the barriers to involvement and good practice around involvement to construct a model of service user participation and involvement? This presents a major challenge for social work – people who work in and use social work services, policy-makers and academics – in the changing welfare environment. How can we make service user involvement effective, real and sustainable and avoid the problems of agency inertia, organisational blockage and tokenistic response? How do we measure the effectiveness of service user involvement? How do we ensure that agencies involve service users not just as lay consultants but as real, active and equal participants in all aspects of social work?

A number of ways of evaluating service user involvement can be seen in the literature and a possible model for evaluating service user involvement can be constructed which draws on the best of these initiatives.

109

Developing an evaluative framework

Debates around participation and involvement are not new and can be traced back to earlier discussions around radical social work and community action (see Chapters 2 and 3). However, there has been limited research into the impact of service user participation and involvement on service provision (Carr, 2004). Carr has suggested that *'the principal barriers identified in the literature are the power differentials and dynamics between service users and professionals'* (2004, p14). Indeed, she argues that

> [e]xclusionary structures, institutional practices and attitudes can still affect the extent to which service users can influence change. It appears that power sharing can be difficult within established mainstream structures, formal consultation mechanisms and traditional ideologies.

> (2004, p14)

How then can we evaluate the way these processes operate? Is it possible to produce an evaluative framework which can allow us to make explicit the way these processes operate? One of the earliest attempts to provide a framework for evaluating participation is provided by Sherry Arnstein, who developed her 'Ladder of citizen participation' in 1969.

Arnstein suggested that

> there is a real difference between going through the empty ritual of participation and having the real power needed to affect the outcome of the process.

> (1969, p215)

She argued that a central concern is the redistribution of power *'that enables the have-not citizens, presently excluded from the political and economic processes, to be deliberately included in the future'* (p214).

Arnstein's model suggests that participation can be evaluated along a typology of eight levels of participation (see Figure 5.1). *Therapy* and *manipulation* constitute levels of non-participation in which those with power seek to cure or educate those seeking power. *Informing* and *consulting* are characteristic where people are encouraged to articulate their views but lack the power to have them implemented. With *placation* these elements are characterised by tokenism in which *'the ground rules allow the have-nots to advise, but retain for the powerholders the continued right to decide'* (Arnstein, 1969, p216). The final three levels illustrate increasing levels of influence and power until at the level of *'citizen control, have-not citizens obtain the majority of decision-making seats or full managerial power'* (p216). This, she argues, is where citizen control rests.

The language used is similar to that used by other 'radical liberals' such as Alinsky, who equally couches his analysis in the rather simplistic language of 'haves' and 'have nots' (Alinsky, 1971). However, the analysis does point to the dangers of accepting at face value agencies' and institutions' claims that they are seeking to increase levels of participation, promote involvement and empowerment and work in partnership with service users. Such claims can, through this model and those discussed below, at least be subjected to analysis and argumentation.

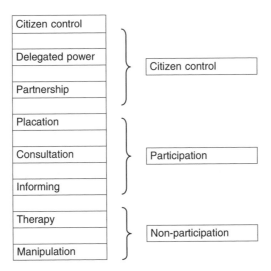

Figure 5.1 Arnstein's ladder of participation

This model has been taken on and developed by others to suggest a more complex way of mapping involvement. Burns et al. (1994) applied the model to local authority participation strategies in London and suggested that Arnstein's ladder could be expanded to include 12 factors. Retaining the distinction between citizen control, citizen participation and citizen non-participation, they suggest that a ladder of citizen empowerment might be impacted upon by the nature of the decision-making process (see discussion of street-level bureaucracy in Chapter 1). On one level they see decisions being mediated by the behaviour and performance of staff (operational practices), the way money is spent (operational decisions) and by the strategic objectives of a particular service (policymaking) (1994, p160). On another level the major factor may be what Hirschman (1970) has called 'exit' and 'voice'. 'Exit' is defined as the withdrawal of support for a service from those using it. 'Voice' is where dissatisfaction is more actively articulated through protest or action (Burns et al., 1994, pp162–3).

ACTIVITY 5.5

- *Think about a service user involvement process you have been involved in.*
- *Where would you place that example of service user involvement on this participation ladder?*
- *What were the key factors that led you to this decision?*
- *Would you describe that process as one of exit or choice?*

Comment

You should by now be undertaking your practice placement. Use the organisation within which you are placed as the reference point for this activity.

At this stage it is worth highlighting another factor: the role people play in participation strategies. Simmons and Birchall (2005) suggest that levels of participation are affected by the type of activist who was participating. They distinguished between five types of activists:

- campaigners – very active and confident in participation, seeking change rather than the status quo;

- foot soldiers – quite committed but at different level, often undertook group's support functions;

- thinkers rather than doers – more likely to be educationally qualified and interested in participation as a learning experience;

- habitual participants – guided by internalised norms, part of a regular programme of involvement;

- marginal participants – less active and motivated, *relatively uncommitted*.

Simmons and Birchall (2005) suggested that to make participation effective it was necessary to recognise that participation is an activity mediated by a variety of factors: time, resources, skills, motivation. They suggest that it is possible to construct a 'participation chain' to explain levels of participation. This may consist of a number of key factors, including motivation, resources and the level at which people mobilise to become involved.

They found that income levels did not impact on involvement and that time was a resource barrier that could be surmounted. However, skills (indicated by educational qualification, previous experiences and training) appeared to be *'very important for service users both in getting started and in supporting higher levels of participation'* (Simmons and Birchall, 2005, p272). Mobilisation was strongly impacted upon, they suggested, by 'catalysing issues', which, in relation to public services, included

> *negative relationships with authorities ('authorities are not listening to people like me', 'authorities cannot be trusted to make decisions on behalf of people like me'), a sense of relative deprivation ('my community is worse off than other similar communities') and a desire for change ('change is not happening quickly enough'.*

> (2005, pp272–3)

Their research led them to suggest a fourth factor governing people's involvement, what they term the *'dynamics of participation'*, which they suggest is impacted upon by cultural and institutional factors.

Quoting DETR research, Simmons and Birchall argue that people often hold a positive view of their experience of participation. This may lead to the affirmation of participants' key motivations and to the development over time of a commitment to participate (DETR, 1998, p273). These factors are in turn impacted upon by the group of which they are a member in so far as the group can play an important role in the transformation of individuals' motivations over time. This may involve the promotion of collectivistic motivations to a primary position in people's *'motivational hierarchy'* (p275).

Developing an evaluative framework integrating theory and practice

This discussion suggests that the research evidence, theoretical frameworks and participation models that emerge can start to provide us with a way of integrating the theory and practice of participation and involvement. What these models lack, however, is the systematic analysis of power that Carr (2004) suggested was central to current initiatives around participation and involvement.

Lukes (1975) has suggested that power needs to be understood in three ways: as the capacity to act (A having the power to make B do something against their wishes); as the management of dissent by the prevention of issues being placed on the public agenda; and by the lack of recognition on the part of powerless groups that their interests are being threatened (Lukes, 1975, 2004; Hindess, 1996).

While this discussion takes us further than the rather simplistic analyses of power put forward by Arnstein and Alinsky, there is still a danger that we produce an analysis which appears to suggest that service users are passive in the face of the institutional power of large social work or professional agencies. How do we assert the capacity of service users to take action to gain power rather than have power handed to them (which must in any case be an unlikely scenario)? We can do this by seeing service users as people with the capacity to bring about change not only in their own, individual circumstances, but in the broader institutions and structures against which they struggle. In this sense we can see empowerment as essentially a strategy to bring about personal and political change.

To make involvement and participation real, we need to look not just at how power can be exercised but also at how it can be resisted. How can we develop strategies to promote meaningful change? Giddens' analysis of agency and structure can provide some pointers as to how this may occur. He refers to power as 'the transformative capacity of human action' (Cassell, 1993, p109). This, Giddens (1977) suggests, following Marx, is the key element in the notion of praxis. The creation of a radical practice, based on notions of overcoming oppression, tackling discrimination/oppression and the creation of new cooperative social relationships, is at the heart of any theory of social action. Similar ideas can also be seen in the writings of Gramsci and Freire and particularly in the former's idea of the 'organic intellectual', someone with an understanding of the need for change which derives from their own experience, and the latter's idea of 'conscientisation', the notion that when the person becomes aware of the way their oppression is determined they develop the capacity to take action to change their situation (Gramsci, 1971; Freire, 1972; Burr, 1995; Mayo, 1999).

Foucault (1980) points to the way in which power is *'localised, dispersed, heteromorphous and accompanied by numerous phenomena, of inertia, displacement and resistance, so that, one should not assume a massive and primal condition of domination, a binary structure with "dominators" on the one side and "dominated" on the other'* (p142). In fact, power should be viewed as a dynamic concept in which individuals *'are always in the position of simultaneously undergoing and exercising ... power [they] are the vehicles of power, not its application'* (p98). Foucault suggests that *'the mechanisms of power [need to be analysed] on the basis of daily struggles at grass roots level, among those whose fight was located in the fine meshes of the web of power'* (p116). This is the agency that we, as social workers, academics and users/carers, are looking for, the sense that service users can resist and reframe their experience in a way that can change the way services are delivered. However, it is necessary to avoid an outcome in which the organisation benefits more than the service user. As Jordan noted, outcomes can be seen in significantly different ways:

> the agencies' goal is to get target groups to bear as much of the costs of
> social care as possible, without sacrifice of professional power or significant
> material resources; the groups' to gain relevant resources and influence
> policy.

> (1996, p185)

A similar point is made by Ellis (2007) when she discusses the way social workers exercise discretion over direct payments. She suggests that there is a powerful imperative for informal rationing because of the process in which front-line workers are encouraged to generate take-up yet manage scarce time and resources. This occurs, she argues, partly because of the discretionary gap which allows social workers to choose not to introduce direct payments, which they regard as *'illegitimate challenges to their decision-making power'* (p418). This is compounded by the restriction on resources, making it more difficult to keep up with expressed need.

Can we therefore integrate these understandings into a framework for evaluating involvement and participation which reflects the complex power dynamics in current welfare practice? The above models and theories can, taken together, begin to provide a framework that we can use to evaluate the real extent of service user involvement in the newly aligned services we have discussed in earlier chapters. An outline of how this may look is provided in Table 5.3.

This still has the danger of presenting us with a static, rather than dynamic, understanding of how service users can exercise power to challenge and change the current configuration of welfare services. We therefore need to superimpose a further matrix on that present in Table 5.3. This would show Lukes' dimensions of power overlaying the left-hand column with the first dimension mirroring citizen control, the second participation and the third non-participation. This would allow us to argue that service users need to generate the capacity to make agencies and institutions react favourably to them (citizen control/capacity to act). Participation would occur where agencies were no longer able to manage dissent but had to put issues on their agenda (citizen participation/management of dissent). Non-participation would be overcome where service users recognised their interest and acted to have them met (non-participation/ignorance of own wants).

Table 5.3   Measuring service user involvement

Level of control/ strength of participation	Motivation	Resources	Degree of mobilisation	Dynamics of participation	Type of activist
Citizen control	Very strong	Managed	Strong catalysts	Collective identity	Campaigner
Citizen participation	Strong	No drain on resources	Dependent on issue	Weaker collective identity, more individualistic	Foot soldier Thinker rather than doer
Citizen non- participation	Weak	Not significant factor	Weak	Follower rather than leader	Habitual participant Marginal participant

Equally there is a need to identify why people act or fail to act to redress any disadvantage they experience. One way of understanding this is by returning to Giddens' concept of agency, or what Fook has characterised as a *'sense of responsibility, of agency, an appreciation of how each player can act upon it to influence a situation'* (1999, p200). Central to this, Fook suggests, is the development of a consciousness, which can imagine another different way of doing things, a point similar to that attributed to Foucault at the beginning of the chapter (Foucault, 1981) and is also reflected in Vygotsky's idea of the 'creative imagination' which occurs *'whenever a person imagines, combines, alters and creates something new'* (2004, p11). This will involve setting agendas for change, not just responding to the agenda of those with power (Campbell and Oliver, 1996) and developing new participatory organisations and practices which signify real and lasting change (Hardcastle, 2004). This would clearly illustrate Foucault's point about individuals simultaneously undergoing and exercising power and would help us understand the way power operates (Foucault, 1980).

This change in perspective could then suggest a multi-dimensional model of involvement (see Table 5.4).

This model would provide us with a way of measuring activity and recognising the capacity of service users to generate change at all levels. Foucault's discourse can remind us to see power as a fragmented rather than monolithic process and therefore one amenable to influence and control at a grass-roots as well as a structural level. This may help us as welfare professionals to recognise that change is possible and may lift the sense of anxiety many welfare professionals express about their own lack of social and political power. We will return to these debates in later chapters.

Table 5.4 Power, participation and involvement

Level of control/ strength of participation	Degree of power: Lukes	Degree of agency: Giddens, Foucault, Gramsci, Freire	Motivation	Resources	Degree of mobilisation	Dynamics of participation	Type of activist
Citizen control	Capacity to act	Strong ↑	Very strong ↑	Managed	Strong catalysts	Collective identity ↑	Campaigner
Citizen participation	Management of dissent	Medium ↑	Strong ↓	No drain on resources	Dependent on issue ←→	Weaker collective identity, more individualistic	Foot soldier Thinker rather than doer
Citizen non-participation	Lack of awareness	↓ Weak	↓ Weak	Not significant factor	↓ Weak	Follower rather than leader	Habitual participant Marginal participant

ACTIVITY 5.6

Jo and Karen have lived together for the last ten years. Jo was a manager in an IT firm until he was forced to give up work because he began suffering from severe reactive depression. Karen uses a wheelchair following a road accident and she is paralysed from the waist down. They both attend the local community centre.

Karen has been approached by her social worker to become a member of the local Disability Information Forum. This meets monthly with professionals from social services, health, the Department of Work and Pensions and the university. The group makes representations to the local services about how disability services are run. There are two service users with disabilities and two carers represented on the committee. The other 12 places are made up of local professionals. They want Karen to replace a service user representative who is standing down. She will not receive any expenses but will have travel provided. Jo was also interested but there is only one place available.

This is a chance for Karen to influence how services are developed and she is keen to be involved. Karen is considering joining the Forum.

- *What issues should she bear in mind when making her decision?*
- *Are there any barriers to her involvement?*
- *If so, how could they be overcome?*
- *Using Arnstein's ladder of participation, how would you evaluate Karen's involvement?*
- *Can Karen ensure that her voice is heard; if so, how?*

Comment

The material provided above should allow you to assess the efficacy of Karen's involvement and the likelihood that she can make an effective contribution to the organisation.

C H A P T E R   S U M M A R Y

This chapter has looked at the way in which the involvement of service users/carers has become part of mainstream policy development within UK social work. It traced the development of service user involvement and demonstrated how it has come to play a central role in current policy development. It pointed to the way recent policies from *Valuing People* (and *Valuing People Now*) to *Independence, Wellbeing and Choice,* and more recent debates around personalisation and co-production have placed a greater emphasis on service user/carer involvement. In most current policy discourse the focus is on issues such as choice, independence and dignity and new forms of practice that incorporate these principles (see the discussion of social pedagogy in the following chapters).

The chapter asked whether this sense of involvement was real or tokenistic, merely a platitude or evidence of real commitment to make services that people use accountable and responsive to people's needs. Using as a starting point Arnstein's ladder of citizen participation, the chapter then went on to develop a model for evaluating service user/carers' involvement which integrated notions of power and empowerment within a framework which explicitly evaluated the quality and impact of such involvement strategies. Drawing on European research around involvement, it concluded that a multi-dimensional model of involvement should be constructed. The chapter ended by suggesting a model of participation that acknowledged the importance of power relationships and reflected a commitment to developing an approach which placed service users at the heart of any participatory framework.

FURTHER READING

Arnstein, S. (1969) 'A ladder of citizen participation', *Journal of the American Institute of Planners,* 35 (4), 214–24.

Classic text which outlines a model of citizen involvement that has been hugely influential since its publication almost 40 years ago.

Evers, A. (2004) *Current Strands in Debating User Involvement in Social Services in Munday, B User Involvement in Social Services, University of Kent with the assistance of the Group of Specialists on User Involvement in Social Services (CS-US),* Strasbourg: Council of Europe.

Report of research commissioned by the Council of Europe into trends in service user involvement in Europe.

Foucault, M. (1980) *Power/knowledge: Selected Interviews and Other Writings.* Brighton: Harvester Wheatsheaf.

Most accessible collection of writings of Michel Foucault, organised into key themes and including some of his most influential writing on power.

Heikkila, M. and Julkunen, I. (2003) *Obstacles to an Increased User Involvement in Social Services.* Strasbourg: Council of Europe.

Looks at the possibilities and constraints on service user involvement, drawing on a wide range of European examples.

WEBSITES

http://scie–socialcareonline.uk

Social Work Inclusion Group: www.swig.uk.net

Chapter 6

Developing new forms of practice: Professionalism, partnerships and social pedagogy

This chapter will help you to develop the following capabilities, to the appropriate level, from the Professional Capabilities Framework:

Professionalism. Identify and behave as a professional social worker, committed to professional development.

Values and ethics. Apply social work ethical principles and values to guide professional practice.

Diversity. Recognise diversity and apply anti-discriminatory and anti-oppressive principles in practice.

Rights, justice and economic wellbeing. Advance human rights and promote social justice and economic wellbeing.

Knowledge. Apply knowledge of social sciences, law and social work practice theory.

Critical reflection and analysis. Apply critical reflection and analysis to inform and provide a rationale for professional decision making.

Intervention and skills. Use judgement and authority to intervene with individuals, families and communities to promote independence, provide support and prevent harm, neglect and abuse.

Contexts and organisations. Engage with, inform, and adapt to changing contexts that shape practice. Operate effectively within own organisational frameworks and contribute to the development of services and organisations. Operate effectively within multi-agency and inter-professional settings.

Professional leadership. Take responsibility for the professional learning and development of others through supervision, mentoring, assessing, research, teaching, leadership and management.

See Appendix 1 for the Professional Capabilities Framework diagram.

QAA Benchmarking Statement

1.10 Contemporary social work commonly takes place in an inter-agency context, and social workers habitually work collaboratively with others towards inter-disciplinary and cross-professional objectives … degree programmes should, therefore, be designed to help equip students with accurate knowledge about the respective responsibilities of social welfare agencies and acquire skills in effective collaborative practice between these.

(QAA, 2008)

Community Development National Occupational Standards

Key area 1: Core – Understand and practise community development.

Key Area 2: Understand and engage with communities.

Key Area 3: Take a community development approach to group work and collective action.

Key area 4: Promote and support a community development approach to collaborative and cross-sectoral working.

Key Area 5: Support community learning from shared experiences.

Key Area 6: Provide community development support to organisations.

Key Area 7: Manage and develop community development practice.

(Federation for Community Development Learning, 2009)

Introduction: professionalism, partnership and power

The last chapter illustrated how inclusion has become a key element of social work practice. This chapter looks at the other dimensions of the model outlined in the introduction to this book – inter-professionalism and internationalism. It draws attention to the centrality of power to discussions about the future of social work. It builds on earlier analyses by extending the discussion to encompass debates about professionalism and partnership. It describes a number of models of partnership and how partnership can be facilitated and enhanced by utilising European models of social care and particularly social pedagogy.

Professionalism and power

A starting point is provided by some well established debates around issues of professionalism and power. Abbott and Wallace (1990) noted how the term 'professional' in modern society has generally been used as a term of approval and one that implies payment for special skills and proficiency. To claim to be a professional was to suggest independence, autonomy and control over work. Typically, until fairly recently, social work has not been seen in this way. It has struggled on the margins of the professional project and social workers have often been seen at best as 'semi-professionals', defined by Toren as *'occupying that place where theoretical study is replaced by the acquisition of technical skill. Technical practice and knowledge is the basis of semi-professions such as ... social work'* (1969, p143).

However, critical and particularly feminist sociologists have pointed to how the existing professions are often structured by social division along gender and race. Hugman (1991) recognised how difficult it was for women to overcome gender division in the professions because of the way their experience was often individualised. Witz pointed to the source of this gender division when she noted how *'strategies of occupational closure aim for an occupational monopoly over the provision of certain skills and competencies'* (1992, p68). The result was that people seeking to enter professions were subject to processes of *'exclusion'*, where the profession sought to deny membership through the imposition of forms of rule and control; *'demarcationary strategies'*, where a hierarchy of professions was established and access to a 'higher' level profession was often denied to 'lower' level professions, and *'dual closure strategies'* could be present, which prevented both upward and downward mobility.

Abbott and Wallace warned about the way the idea of professionalism is used to

> *police the actions of those who lay claim to professional status, certain standards*
> *of performance and behaviour are expected of them, standards set in essence*
> *from outside the control of the profession itself. Groups who aspire to professional*
> *status are laying themselves open to be controlled by externally defined standards.*

> (1990, p10)

Writers such as Witz (1992) and Hugman (1998, 2005) showed how these standards are often inimical to participative forms of practice and that professions often establish barriers to exclude people from their particular professional practice. Often these barriers reinforce processes of discrimination and oppression.

Where does this leave social work? Social workers have often complained about the lack of professional credibility they receive from other professions and the difficulty they have in being heard in inter-professional debates. Is this because of their perceived semi-professional status? Lord Laming was critical of social workers' lack of critical practice in his report on the Climbié case. Introducing his report into the death of Victoria Climbié, he commented:

> *In the months which followed [her becoming known to services] Victoria*
> *was known to no fewer than four social services departments, three housing*
> *departments, two specialist child protection teams of the Metropolitan Police.*
> *Furthermore, she was admitted to two different hospitals because of concerns that*
> *she was being deliberately harmed and was referred to a specialist Children and*
> *Families Centre managed by the NSPCC. All of this between 26th April 1999 and*
> *25th February 2000.*

> *What transpired during this period can only be described as a catalogue of administrative, managerial and professional failure by the services charged with her safety...[He goes on to say]...the training of social workers must equip them with the confidence to question the opinion of professionals in other agencies when conducting their own assessment of the need of the child*
>
> (2003, Recommendation 37, page 3764)

As a consequence, one of his major recommendations was that social workers should be prepared to be more critical of other professionals and be able to challenge decision making which is unclear and lacking in focus. Can an increase in social workers' professional power redress this imbalance and secure for social work the professional identity some within it crave, or will it result in us replicating the power imbalances identified by writers such as Witz? Will we end up erecting our own exclusionary and demarcationary strategies, and if so, what are the implications of such developments for the anti-discriminatory/anti-oppressive practices that are at the centre of our core values?

Arguably since the first edition of this book was published in 2008 some progress has been made in this area. The second Laming report into the death of Peter Connelly (Haringey Local Safeguarding Children Board, 2010), the Munro Report into child protection (2011) and the outcomes of the Social Work Task Force (2009) and Social Work Reform Board (2011) have put social work on the government's agenda (both Labour and the Coalition). There is now an increased emphasis on the professionalism of social work and greater emphasis on regulation of the profession (a process which began in 2003 with the introduction of degree-level qualifications) and through the Professional Capability Framework an emphasis on the key domains in which social workers should demonstrate their ability. However, as Munro demonstrated so clearly, there is still a focus on the managerial and procedural elements of social work. As Lymbery (2004) has suggested, this has had the effect of weakening social works' claim to professional status, particularly if, as he suggests, we assess social work along Jamous and Peloille's (1970) technicality/indeterminacy ratio. This he describes as:

> *The claim that professions must be able to maintain a balance between technical aspects of the work (... rules and procedures), and indeterminate areas that require the exercise of professional judgement. The balance between the two elements is critical.*
>
> (Lymbery, 2004, p52)

Despite the progress made since 2009, it is not clear that social work as a profession has resolved this dilemma. The Professional Capability Framework, particularly domains 1, 2, 3, 4 and 9, suggest a possible pathway out of this dilemma, but equally developments such as the Narey report (2014), if as seems possible it gains government support, suggest an increased technicalisation of social work and reduction of professional autonomy or the indeterminacy Jamous and Peloille refer to.

As we saw in Chapter 5, Foucault (1980) can help provide an insight into how the issue of power and professionalism can be resolved. He conceived of power being about the *'structure of actions'* which bear on those who are free. Often power is unstable and reversible. He says that

> the exercise of power demands a degree of freedom among those being governed, it need not imply the removal of liberty. Where there is no possibility of resistance there can be no exercise of power. Power is of necessity fragmented and diffuse, but is no less important for that.

> (1980, p130)

What he means here is that power is never so all-embracing that it cannot be fought against. For us that must suggest that the negative outcomes of the struggle for professionalism identified above are not inevitable but can be resisted and potential alternative relationships between trained and untrained people, professionals and service users can be developed.

Bauman (2001) suggests that such conflicts may be the outcome of the uncertainty we experience in a post-modern society. Professionalism may be a product of the kind of hierarchical certainties which were prevalent in an earlier era where identity was more fixed and sustainable, while the demands of service users may reflect a break-down in that certainty and the opening-up of new possibilities for people to assert their identity. The disparity between professionalism and service user demands for their needs to be met may signal the beginning of different types of relationship. Seen in this context, we need to be aware of the potential for inter-professional activity to become a means of 'fixing' these professional uncertainties in such a way that professional power becomes re-centralised in the hands of professionals rather than de-centralised to those who use services.

To explore some of these dilemmas around professionalism it is useful to look at current debates around partnership and social pedagogy, each of which suggests some fruitful ways of taking the debate forward.

Partnership

Partnership has been suggested as a way of ensuring the better coordination of services since the modernisation agenda was introduced in 1998 (Department of Health, 1998). Often it is portrayed as being a partnership of unequals, with the more powerful sector, normally the statutory sector (or in the case of health and social care, the former), being seen as dominant. It is assumed that partnership is desirable because it can:

- improve effectiveness;
- see service users and carers as a source of knowledge and understanding;

- ensure that the rights of service users and carers are central to decision making;

- be part of the process of empowerment by breaking down the power imbalances and enshrining as a core principle the idea that equality should be central to our practice.

Thompson sees partnership as meaning

> *working with clients, rather than doing things to or for them. It involves moving away from the outmoded view of social work as a form of 'social medicine' in which the expert social worker diagnoses the problem and prescribes a cure or treatment programme. This medical model is gradually being replaced by a partnership based approach.*

(2005, p123)

This partnership approach, he suggests, is characterised by:

- assessment being carried out in close cooperation with the individual;

- intervention involving parties working together to resolve or minimise problems;

- the situation being jointly reviewed and evaluated.

As an approach, partnership is characteristic of social work in a multitude of contexts, professional and national. For example, moves toward partnership models can be seen in Ireland (Ferguson and Powell, 2002, p93), Northern Ireland (Campbell and McColgan, 2002, p115), Wales (Doel and Williams, 2002) and England (Children Act 1989; Health and Social Care Act, 2004; Department of Health, 2006; Social Work Reform Board, 2011). The National Strategic Partnership Forum (a group bringing together 35 voluntary sector organisations, campaigning charities and primary care trusts) produced a paper in 2006 indicating how the third sector (see Chapter 4) could take forward the commitment to partnership contained in *Our Health, Our Care, Our Say* (Department of Health, 2006). It concluded that joint working could benefit all sectors by ensuring that partnership arrangements include:

- Strong user and care involvement.

- Community engagement.

- Access to hard-to-reach groups.

- Innovation.

(National Strategic Partnership Forum, 2006, p17)

Often the idea of partnership is linked with other concerns about collaborative working, joint working or working together. Quinney points out how, while collaborative working is not new to the social work agenda, it has *been widely promoted as a solution for addressing shortcomings and failures in public services, including the social work, health, education, youth work and housing services. There is now a focus on modern, seamless and personalised public services... that seek to meet the increasingly complex needs of service users and carers though a rethinking of the policies, structures and professionals involved.*

(2006, p22; emphasis in original)

Quinney quotes Whittington (2003), who suggests that working in partnership can mean:

- Working together to ensure 'joined up' services.
- Meeting service user needs through providing services through more than one organisation.
- The nature of the relationships between service provider and service user.

(Quinney, 2006, p11)

Quinney then suggests the following definition, again quoting Whittington:

[P]artnership is a state of relationships, at organisational, group, professional or inter-professional level, to be achieved, maintained and reviewed; and collaboration is an active process of partnership in action.

(Whittington, 2003, p16)

Partnership or collaborative working can therefore take many forms.

- **Multi-disciplinary teams** – teams that comprise a range of professionals from different disciplines or specialisms, for example community mental health teams.
- **Inter-agency working** – situations in which different agencies participate to achieve a particular goal but which do not necessarily involve ongoing joint work or the relative dissolution of professional boundaries.
- **Inter-professional collaboration** – those occasions on which two or more professionals from different disciplines or specialisms work together to achieve a joint goal. This may not necessarily involve inter-agency collaboration but may involve intra-agency collaboration in which, for example, social workers and teachers employed by the same children's trust may work together on a common project.
- **Common learning** – the process through which professionals or trainee professionals from a diverse range of backgrounds come together to share learning in a common learning environment.
- **Networks of organisations** – those situations in which organisations come together in a formal network to achieve a common purpose, for example the Law Centres Federation, Councils of Community Service, homelessness forums and so on.
- **Participatory relationships between professionals and service users** – those situations where service users/carers work in an open and accountable way with

professionals so that they have an equal relationship and through which the service user/carer is able to freely express their views and aspirations.

- **Networks of service users/carers** – formal or informal networks that are typically service user-led and which seek to advance the role of service users within a participatory framework which promotes democratic decision making and engagement.

Power is a key determining factor in assessing the degree of partnership professions engage with. The above list provides a descending order of involvement and real partnerships. The partnerships at the top of the list are functions of improvements in service delivery and could be said to be consistent with Laming's requirement that agencies work together more closely. However, that does not disturb the power imbalance identified by Beresford (2013) in the inter-professional agenda – where do service users/carers feature in this integrated environment?

As we noted earlier, Lukes (1975) suggested that power has three ways of manifesting itself. All three elements of power relationships are evident in debates around professionalism. The professional/service user relationship is often characterised (or constrained?) by the statutory power vested in social workers, particularly around child protection and work with people in mental distress. In itself this raises issues of whether social workers' primary responsibility is to control or empower service users (Hatton and Nugent, 1993; Baistow, 1994). Equally, while many situations require service user/family/carer input, often these interventions (case reviews, child protection conferences, mental health reviews) are structured by the professional, and the service user's input is to comment on rather than set the agenda. Finally, professional ideology invests in the professional an expert status which values their views while marginalising those of the service user. This process seeks to encourage people using services to believe that decisions made are in their interests, while masking the power relationships between provider and user. To some extent good anti-oppressive practice should minimise or reduce these power imbalances, yet there is a danger that the full development of social work's professional identity will push us back toward the idea of controlling the behaviour of the people with whom we work rather than reasserting the commitment to empowerment which the more radical social work traditions discussed in earlier chapters would suggest is the way forward.

Making partnerships relevant and meaningful is therefore dependent on a number of factors, including:

- ensuring that partnerships are real and not tokenistic;
- building-in appropriate evaluation strategies to ensure that this is true;
- learning from the experience of people pursuing different approaches, sometimes in other countries.

Beresford (2013, p198) suggests that effective service user involvement can enhance and improve inter-agency working. The key elements to achieving this, he suggests, are:

- Building on service users ideas, models and values.
- Being rights based.

- Drawing on user-led education and co-learning.

- Valuing service user experience and knowledge.

- Ensuring access and inclusion.

However, focusing on the role of carers in inter-professional working, Byers and Creating Links argue that *'carer participation and involvement with the interprofessional teams is still limited'* partly, they suggest, because of *'a lack of effective communication and information-sharing'* (2013a, p212). This is compounded, they argue, by issues of power and control and the way agencies set the agenda. They suggest that among a range of solutions:

- Carers should be seen as part of the care team and their expertise respected.

- Carers should be offered more involvement in care planning and decision making.

- Carers should have more control over their situations and trust from practitioners.

(Byers and Creating Links, 2013b, p222)

A number of these issues are addressed more fully throughout the book.

ACTIVITY **6.1**

- *What does the definition of power presented in this and earlier chapters tell us about partnership?*

- *Can it suggest something about the way service providers and service users work together?*

- *Which model of partnership makes the issue of power clearer?*

Comment

To undertake this exercise see the sections on Lukes and Foucault in this chapter and Chapter 5. You will also need to look at the implications of the Laming enquiries and the recommendations in the Munro report.

Partnerships in practice

It may help clarify the above issues if we examine some ways in which partnership can be observed in practice settings. The first example is taken from the New Generation Project, a collaboration between the Universities of Portsmouth and Southampton to deliver inter-professional teaching to students. The second looks at a practice-based partnership between agencies and educational institutions to deliver training and education to the social care workforce (SHIP/SWEN – see below).

New Generation Project (NGP) – Universities of Portsmouth and Southampton

This was an inter-professional common learning project, funded by the Department of Health and jointly provided by the Universities of Portsmouth and Southampton, initially with support from the Hampshire and Isle of Wight Workforce Development Confederation. It sought to provide common learning for pre-qualifying professionals in a range of disciplines – social work, nursing, diagnostic and therapeutic radiography, pharmacy, audiology, podiatry, medicine, physiotherapy and occupational therapy – through problem-based learning in small inter-professional learning groups. These groups were facilitated by academic staff at the two universities and the project sought to provide focused learning for students from across the professions.

Integration into Curricula

The two universities sought to make the most of their involvement in the NGP to facilitate and enhance the quality of the students' learning experience by arranging additional teaching support for the programme. This involved:

- *a designated member of staff carrying out preparatory teaching around NGP prior to the students undertaking the Inter-Professional Learning (IPL) units at levels 1, 2 and 3;*

- *an introduction to the way ILP impacts on the students' learning experience while on work placement at levels 2 and 3.*

Students also used these sessions to raise issues directly with the lecturer taking the session.

The staff and student group were committed to inter-professional and collaborative working. Both universities sought to deal openly with its student group, to listen to and value their comments and where appropriate to raise issues either with the NGP or within the university. The student experience was at the centre of this initiative, thus ensuring that students experienced a high-quality programme.

The syllabus

The topics covered in the unit included: adult learning; collaborative learning; communication; giving and receiving feedback; group dynamics; health and social care teams; health and social care trends and issues; learning styles (Honey and Mumford, 1995); professional roles and stereotypes; reflection; strategies for effective team working; team roles; analysis and selection of health and social care information.

An example of an inter-professional learning opportunity was the first exercise the students undertook. This introduced the concept and practice of collaborative learning and team working and involved the students:

CASE STUDY *continued*

- *participating in a discovery trail set in a geographical area of Portsmouth or Southampton;*
- *exploring effective team working;*
- *considering the process of reflection;*
- *researching their health and social care professions.*

This was followed by a further week in which students explored collaborative learning online through exploring a scenario and reviewing the different professions' contributions to the client(s)/patient(s) in the scenario and identifying where inter-professional teamwork would improve the client/patient experience.

O'Halloran et al. (2006) argued that the model of learning within the NGP was based on collaborative inter-professional learning and consisted of three pedagogies: guided discovery learning, collaborative learning and inter-professional learning. These pedagogies they defined as follows:

- **Guided discovery learning** – they describe as 'learning how to learn' through the *'process of discovery and the exploration of knowledge coupled with the responsibility to master the content needed for understanding'* (2006, p18). Learning is achieved here through encouraging students to develop a learning portfolio.

- **Collaborative learning** – quoting Koehn (2001, p160), they describe as an *'intellectual endeavour in which individuals act jointly with others to become knowledgeable on some particular subject matter'* (quoted in O'Halloran et al., 2006, p180). Central to this is cooperation among the student group to achieve joint learning objectives.

- **inter-professional** – learning they characterised by processes of learning with and about one another.

The interaction of these three pedagogies, it was anticipated, would help students achieve a degree of mutual understanding and respect which uni-professional education was unlikely to be able to replicate. The authors pointed to the success of the programme in achieving *'attitudinal and knowledge change in students over the duration of common learning and into practice'* (O'Halloran et al., 2006, p26). Reports from students on the programme suggested that levels of mutual understanding and respect among the professions undertaking the programme increased exponentially throughout the programme. By level 3 students were talking much more clearly about the advantages and potential pitfalls in inter-professional working. The primary aim was to ensure that social work, and other, students become the kind of critical professionals envisaged by Laming while providing a possible model for future professional development.

Professional networks

The second type of partnership refers to the way social work agencies and educational institutions are working together to improve the experience for qualifying social workers. The initial mechanism for achieving this, when the first edition of the book was written, was through the development of Learning Resource Networks (LRNs). These were established in the first instance to support the development of practice learning opportunities (work placements) for the new degree in social work which was introduced in 2003. The degree was seen as an attempt to improve the professional standing of social work vis-à-vis other similar professions such as nursing and teaching by introducing an extended period of training (from two to three years) and regulating and credentialising the profession. This involved the establishment of a new regulatory body, the General Social Care Council (GSCC), to oversee the change and to introduce procedures for registration of all professionals wishing to use the title 'social worker' (see Horner, 2006, pp117–20). These changes moved social work toward a more established professional identity and raised within them some of the key issues discussed above. A fuller discussion of these developments, the replacement of the GSCC by the Health and Care Professions Council (HCPC) and the development of The College of Social Work is provided in Chapter 1.

More recently such professional networks can be seen to have developed with the support of Skills for Care (SfC) and the Children's Workforce Development Confederation (CWDC). Both organisations have provided support to enable the development of professional networks across local authorities and the third sector and between these sectors and Higher Education. In the Hampshire and Isle of Wight area some such activities are coordinated through the Social Work Education Network (SWEN), which describes itself as follows:

> Southampton, Hampshire, Isle of Wight and Portsmouth (SHIP) Social Work Education Network (SWEN) comprises approximately 12 partners, including local authorities (LAs), independent sector organisations and Higher Education Institutions (HEIs). We meet on a quarterly basis and have a structured agenda and processes. The partnership has existed for over six years and we have a co-operative partnership agreement which we all observe.
>
> (www.skillsforcare.org.uk/document-library/social-work/qa-practice-examples/
> swen-partnership.pdf, accessed 4/3/15)

Recently the focus of their work has been on supporting newly qualified social workers (NQSWs) on their entry into practice, more recently through the Assessed and Supported Year in Employment.

Central to the changes introduced following the work of the Social Work Task Force and the Social Work Reform Board was the development of a new framework for assessing social workers – the Professional Capability Framework (PCF) endorsed by the newly established College of Social Work – and a new regulator with the General Social Care Council being replaced with the Health and Care Professions Council. This new framework was also developed to support NQSWs and provided the framework for the ASYE.

Research on the initial NQSW programme by the University of Portsmouth in 2008/9 suggested that the programme:

> *met a need which was and still is, not currently being met. Many local authorities have induction processes but the feedback would appear to indicate a need for a more formalised method of supporting newly qualified social workers ... Given the strength of partnership arrangements in this sub region (Hants/IOW) there is a strong base on which to build.*

> *However ... there is also a need for caution. The enthusiasm of the students is clearly evident, as is the commitment of the partners, and their staff, to delivering such a programme ... the issue of resourcing presents a significant challenge. Agencies and HEIs all operate within funding systems which are tightly stretched. If this very worthwhile initiative is to be developed and sustained CWDC and Skills for Care will need to ensure that adequate funding streams are available for this work to continue. The development of the pilot programmes for NQSW appears to be welcome evidence that this is beginning to happen.*

(University of Portsmouth, 2009)

Subsequently the NQSW programme was replaced with the Assessed and Supported Year in Employment (ASYE) programme. The University of Portsmouth has recently completed a piece of research around the efficacy of the ASYE programme in Hants/IOW. The report has not yet been published but appears to support the findings of earlier research undertaken by academics from the universities of Bristol, Salford and King's College, London, subsequently published by the Department for Education in 2012, evaluating the Newly Qualified Social Worker programme. The report was commissioned under the previous government (Department for Children, Schools and Families – DCSF) and was an examination of the precursor to the ASYE. The report looked at the experience of people undertaking the NQSW programme between 2008 and 2011. It is worth looking at some of the conclusions reached by this earlier research. The key findings and conclusions are outlined below:

- Initial barriers to implementation decreased over the three years of the programme.

- The number of participating local authorities (and voluntary organisations) increased from 90 to 152, including 95 per cent of local authorities with social services responsibilities in England.

- Over 5,000 NQSWs undertook the programme with a completion rate of 78 per cent.

- '[A]lmost all senior managers were generally satisfied with the way in which it has been implemented' (DfE, 2012, pvii) with the most valued elements being high quality supervision and extra funding.

- Workload management, particularly to achieve the 10 per cent reduction in workload, was 'problematic' (pviii).

The report looked specifically at the experience of the programme of participating NQSWs and found that:

- Satisfaction rates increased from 59 per cent to 73 per cent by the end of the programme (2011).
- The NQSWs valued regular and structured supervision and those receiving supervision to the required level increased from just over half in 2008 to just over three-quarters in 2011.

For the purposes of this analysis the detail of the findings is less important than what it says about the importance of employers working together to support their own staff and those of other employers, and by doing so improving outcomes not only for NQSWs but also for other agencies with whom they work and perhaps more significantly for those who use their services.

The question of which partnership model we seek to adopt will then be of more than academic interest and could well impact on the future direction social work takes and in particular its ability to maintain its commitment to humanistic and anti-oppressive principles. In the first edition of this book the author suggested that the Department of Health's agenda fits much more closely with those that support the enhancement of professional power than with those seeking to promote service user empowerment. This may still be the case today, although, as discussed below, this process is not necessarily inevitable.

Other types of partnership

As we have seen, partnership is an elastic concept which can encompass a wide variety of relationships. Other examples, for instance, could include partnerships in research and international partnerships.

Partnerships in research

An example of partnerships in research is the Homelessness Action Research Team, which was a partnership formed to identify the needs of the street homeless, who do not access current services, and comprised:

- local homelessness agencies;
- ex-street homeless;
- police;
- a local hospital's accident and emergency department;
- a university. (Homelessness Action Research Team, 2006)

The group produced a piece of action research, 'Nowhere to go', which highlighted the need for new types of services for street homeless people within the Portsmouth area. The research design was participative. People who had previously lived on the streets themselves were trained to undertake the research as the group knew how difficult it was to engage with hard-to-reach street homeless people and felt that they were more likely to engage with people who had similar experiences to themselves. Consequently the following research design was agreed. The research was split into two elements:

- **The culture of the street homeless** – This research was conducted by at least 2 researchers; 1 ex-service user; 1 social worker/student.

- **Accessing services which are suitable/available** – This research was conducted by ex-service users.

Initially the research findings – primarily that there was a need for a wet shelter to meet the needs of people who would not access dry shelters (where they were unable to drink) – were met with resistance from the local authority. However, one of the participating voluntary organisations introduced wet provision into their existing provision, suggesting that the presence of homeless people in the research process (design and implementation) had been worthwhile.

International partnerships
International parnerships may take a variety of different forms, including:

- Issue-driven partnerships – FEANTSA (European Observatory on Homelessness, partly funded by the European Union, Disabled People's International).

- Politically driven – anti-globalisation movement and globalisation from below.

- Educationally driven – between universities to deliver collaborative programmes which develop programmes across specialisms, for example, European Masters' programmes which bring together universities from across Europe.

- Cross-disciplinary – the author has over the last two years participated in conferences in Paris (of social workers, community workers, educators and youth workers) and in Berlin (of radical social pedagogues – ConCrit). This suggests the need to look beyond our own professional boundaries and to explore the commonalities in our practice between ourselves as social workers and other professional grouping (see Chapters 2, 3 and 7; and Hatton, 2013).

The future development of these approaches seems assured. The *Options for Excellence* review (DHES/DfE, 2006), which grew out of the discussions following *Our Health, Our Care, Our Say* (Department of Health, 2006) and *Every Child Matters* (HM Government, 2003) (see Chapter 1), suggested that one of the ways in which the workforce can be modelled around new ways of working lay in the establishment of common standards for inter-agency working. These standards reflect changes in the delivery of social work services within the UK, but we will also need to consider how we can learn from the experience of European colleagues who have been using social pedagogic and other approaches to deliver a highly qualified and flexible workforce.

Social pedagogy

In the first edition of this book the author described pedagogy as an alternative way of understanding social interventions. It has become clear over the last few years that this is inadequate to describe this complex set of theories and practices. Pedagogy is often understood as a way of teaching and learning more normally associated with the classroom. I have therefore used the phrase 'social pedagogy', which refers not only to the way people learn but also to how they interact with other individuals, communities and the broader social structures that govern their lives and with which they interact (Hatton, 2013). Hamalainen (2003) points to the different ways in which the concept is used across Europe. These include:

> As a translation of thought and action in which social and pedagogical points of view are combined ... (in ways which) ... are interconnected.
>
> (quoted in AIEJI, 2010, p17)

Social pedagogy can therefore be seen as a European social work tradition which, although referenced by writers as early as the 1980s (Davies, 1984) or more particularly the 1990s (Berry et al., 1992; Lorenz, 1994), has only recently begun achieving attention within the UK, specifically as a way of meeting the training needs of that part of the social care workforce in residential settings (more specifically children's residential services) where the levels of qualification remain below those found in Europe (Petrie, 2001, 2004; Cameron et al., 2011).

The Social Pedagogy Development Network define social pedagogy as an

> academic discipline that draws on core theories from various related disciplines, such as education, sociology, psychology and philosophy. In essence, it is concerned with well-being, learning and growth. This is underpinned by humanistic values and principles which view people as active and resourceful agents, highlight the importance of including them into the wider community, and aim to tackle or prevent social problems and inequality.
>
> (www.thempra.org.uk/social_pedagogy.htm, accessed 4/3/15)

Petrie (2003) has written about how 'pedagogy' can be rendered invisible through the process of translation, as its most obvious translation is as education, and pedagogues therefore appear as teachers. While there is undoubtedly an element of education in pedagogy, it seems more useful to see the concept as one that can inform the practice of social professionals. As Petrie notes,

> the whole domain of social responsibility for children, for their well being, learning and competence ... the use of the term pedagogy allows for a discourse that can arise above differences based on for example, the age of those who use services or a service's immediate goals; it permits any particular provision to be located in the context of a wider social policy towards children.
>
> (2003, p13)

Hamalainen (2003) says that social pedagogy has a wide range of uses as an approach in social work because it

> [c]oncentrates on questions of the integration of the individual in society, both in theory and in practice. It aims to alleviate social exclusion. It deals with the processes of human growth that tie people to the systems, institutions and communities that are important to their well-being and life management. The basic idea of social pedagogy is to promote people's social functioning, inclusion, participation, social identity and social competence as members of society.
>
> (2003, p76)

Elsewhere Petrie describes pedagogy as person-centred – 'head, hands and heart – all three being essential for the work of pedagogy' (2004, p4). She suggests that pedagogic training could usefully be incorporated into UK work with children, particularly looked-after children (Petrie, 2004; Boddy et al., 2003).

The author has argued previously that

> [c]entral to the concept of Social pedagogy ... is the idea of creativity. Creativity is envisaged as an active process in which the social pedagogue/social professional works with the person using their service in a way which seeks to maximise their potential, increase their ability to make decisions and improve their life chances. The idea of creative activity is ... central to social pedagogy in Europe.
>
> (Hatton, 2013, p30)

As can be seen from the above, social pedagogy has many elements to it and can be said to be influenced by a diverse range of theories from Kierkegaard to Freire to social constructionism (Burr, 1995; Hatton, 2001, 2013). Higham suggested that pedagogy is rooted in humanistic principles, arguing that 'social pedagogy promotes wellbeing through broadly based educational activities ... [and] prevents social problems by empowering people with knowledge and skills to manage their lives' (2001, p25). Clearly such an approach draws on Freirian ideas about 'conscientisation' (Freire, 1972; Popple, 1995; Mayo, 1999; Hatton, 2013), particularly where Freire talks about the need for dialogue, deindividualisation and critical thinking (1972; see also Chapter 3).

What then is social pedagogy? Lorenz says of the development of social pedagogy in Germany:

> The pedagogical emphasis on socialisation into a community ... informed theories of social intervention promoting social skills and 'integration' ... the radical critique of total institutions diverted pedagogical activities away from traditional settings (schools, homes, the family) and towards the complexity of everyday situations. Social learning and change can only occur through open communication and with full participation of the 'client' or 'learner', not under 'artificial' conditions controlled by the social worker or the agency.
>
> (1994, p96)

This suggests an approach which is much more grounded in the needs and aspirations of the people we work with and is in some way antithetical to any attempt to impose a new managerialism (Ferguson and Woodward, 2009; Dominelli, 2010) into the relationship between people who use services and those who provide them. Can a focus on social pedagogy allow us to reclaim some of the person-centred and humanistic approaches which have got lost in the new professional culture we are being asked to develop? It may also emphasise the elements of indeterminacy that should characterise professional activity and professional judgement (Jamous and Peloille, 1970).

Reference to pedagogic approaches being pursued in Denmark may help answer the question. Two key ideas stand out from the pedagogic traditions adopted by colleagues in Copenhagen: the idea of the 'common third' and problem-based project work.

'Common third'

The 'common third' is an idea which had not been widely explored in debates around the work of the social professions, certainly in the UK, but which is used fairly widely within Danish pedagogy (Hatton, 2006, 2013). Aabro (2004, n.p.) describes the 'common third' as a descriptive project or ambition within the pedagogical tradition of relations in social work in which there is a *'deliberate focus on the object as something outside the subject'*, the object being a *'common thing'* which *'both parts in the relation'* can connect with. Husen describes this process as:

> To be sharing something, to have something in common, implies in principle to be equal, to be two (or more) individuals on equal terms, with equal rights and dignity (subject–subject relation). In a community you don't use or exploit the other (subject–object relation).

> (1996, p231, translated by Aabro, 2004)

At the core of this relationship are notions of equality and respect and the eradication of unequal power relations. As Aabro suggests,

> through a common or joint activity the users and the social workers enter a subject–subject relation … [in which] the professional is meant to 'forget himself' and the things around him – and devote himself entirely to the process and activity … the pedagogical challenge is to be able to realise activities which don't reflect the interests and needs of only one part, but instead seek to establish a common and productive activity.

> (Aabro, n.p., emphasis in original)

Lihme (2004) suggests that this relationship defines the social pedagogical approach as special because in the work with the child, unlike therapy, it is the perspective of 'action', better known as the 'common third', where social workers and children/young adults meet through a common potential of learning, on a basis of activity and action (Lihme, 2004, p181, in Ritchie, 2004 –translation by Aabro, 2004). Storo suggests that practical social pedagogic work is about creating change in people's lives and quotes Madsen, a key Danish theorist of social pedagogy, who argues that *'social pedagogic practice is based on visible interventions in other people's lives in order to create development, participation and learning'* (2013, p7). Storo argues that the idea of diverse intervention is critical within social pedagogy and that it influences the values and theory underpinning such work. He suggests that it is linked to a *'focus on processes in society to do with inclusion, exclusion and marginality. To the extent that this theory focuses on the individual, it is the individual as a participant in a group and community'* (2013, p17).

Borghill, a student on the BA in European Social Work at Portsmouth during the academic year 2003/4, describes this process eloquently:

> *The method involves pedagogues and service users concentrating on an activity together, e.g. sports, repairing a car, or making a film, virtually anything. The point is that both the pedagogue and the service users have to be genuinely interested in the activity. This way their relation is moved to the background and does not seem important anymore. They are working towards a common goal, which is meaningful to all participants.*

> *The activity has to be seen as a whole process where the service users are involved as equals in all phases, which are: choosing the activity, planning how to carry it out, actually doing it and in the end appreciating the result and evaluating the process. The young people must be given responsibility and the possibility to use their potential. According to Husen this should strengthen the young person's self-confidence and identity and at the same time working together with other people requires social and communicative abilities such as understanding, cooperation and respect for the opinions of others and these skills will be developed.*

> (Borghill, 2004)

Problem-based project work

Problem-based project work has been a key element of pedagogical education in Denmark since the 1980s. Drawing on the work of critical theorists from within the Frankfurt School, the liberation pedagogy of Freire and the experiential-based learning of Piaget, a model known as the 'RUC model' was shaped as a combination of political and critical intentions and a learning theory that argued for the importance of student activity as opposed to blackboard activity (Prins, 2004). Berthelsen et al. define this approach as a

> *pedagogical mode of study, where students – in cooperation with teachers and sometimes others – explore and deal with one or several problems closely related to the way in which the problems appear. This implies that the project work is to provide an ever stronger experience, more profound knowledge and a broadened perspective; that the problems are confronted and dealt with from different angles, free from the traditional subject borders, and that the choice of theories,*

methodologies and tools are linked directly to the choice of a problem. The role of the teacher is no longer only to provide knowledge, but also in solidarity with the students to work as inspirator, facilitator, supervisor, and consultant. The project work is concluded in a product which can be a report/paper, or be expressed through other medias or concrete actions.

(Berthelsen et al., 1996, p23, translation by Prins, 2004)

Prins (2004, n.p.) argues that this is consistent with the educational principles at Frobelseminariat (now University College Copenhagen – the pedagogic institution at which she teaches) which focus on *'how to enable students to engage in empowering professional relations and thereby facilitate development in other people's lives. The ideal is self-reliant responsible social workers that are able to question their reality in a critical way and search for knowledge, understanding and solutions'.* Prins is a child pedagogue so naturally her focus is child-centred, in common with much of the recent focus within the UK on the efficacy of a social pedagogic approach.

In a recent lecture Prins (2013) has echoed Storo in arguing that social pedagogy has a dual focus on *'including the excluded'* and *'preventing exclusion'.* Central to her concept of social pedagogy is the notion of agency which is *'politically inspired',* based on *'children's own experiences'* and is aimed at *'integration'.* She suggests that *'the pedagogue, as a practitioner, sees her/himself as a person in relationship with the child as a whole person supporting the child's development'.* In a presentation to the NICE/SCIE Programme Development Meeting in 2013 she said:

Creative activities and the common third are common methods stemming from the idea that children develop self-esteem, competences and potentially good relations creative activities...the common third , where the caretaker and the child engage in something that is neither the child nor the adult but something they can share as equals – is seen as a very important method.

(Prins, 2013)

Chambers has argued that creative arts can encourage *'communication and help children and carers to develop a language for talking about feelings'* that can encourage 'personal inclusion' (2004, p2).

A writer who has influenced the development of social pedagogy is the Russian psychologist Vygotsky. While his work on child development is well known, his focus on the development of the *'creative imagination'* has received less attention. This link between creativity, the 'common third' and 'inclusion' is an important one, and will be explored more fully later in the chapter. An extract from the author's book on social pedagogy (Hatton, 2013) illustrates this point. Hatton suggests that Vygotsky argues:

The basis of all creative activity, ... an important component of all aspects of cultural life, enabling artistic, scientific, and technical creation alike ... whenever a person imagines, combines, alters and creates something new.

(Hatton, 2013, p11)

Vygotsky suggests that central to the development of creative imagination is the need for the child (or adult) to have rich experiences, *'the richer a person's experience, the richer is the material his imagination has access to'* (Vygotsky in Hatton, 2013, p15). He further suggests that there are within the development of creativity intellectual and emotional components, and that they involve links between a person's internal and external worlds. As he says:

> *Imagination is portrayed as an exclusively internal activity, one that does not depend on external conditions…The process of imagination per se, its direction, at first glance, appears to be guided only from within, by the feelings and needs of the individual and thus to be wholly subjective and not based on objective factors. In actuality this is not true. Psychology long ago established a law according to which the drive to create is always inversely proportional to the simplicity of the environment.*

(Vygotsky, 2004, p30).

Vygotsky sees this creative process as being dependent on both current environmental context and previous historical development. Creative developments then can be linked to processes of structural and class oppression. To free the creative imagination is to challenge the organisation of the society in which we live and to improve the life chances of the people we work with (Hatton, 2013, pp30–31; see also Chapters 3 and 4 of this book).

Cameron, reviewing the implications of pedagogy for the UK, argued that pedagogy can be characterised as being about dialogue, relationships and the permission to take risks. Reviewing practice in residential care in Germany and Denmark, she suggested that it demands attention because of its focus on *'the individuality of each resident and their circumstances'* (2004, p143).

Cameron drew attention to the way pedagogy uses the heart, brains and hands in combination. Here 'heart' refers to the way pedagogues deal with the emotional demands of the job, *'the need for warmth and compassion when doing … pedagogic or care work'* (2004, p145).

'Brains' refers to *'an intuitive and a systematic synthesis of information, emotions and, critically, knowledge gained from study'* (2004, p145). While this undoubtedly accords with the pedagogic principles enunciated above, Cameron goes too far in asserting that pedagogy rejects universalist solutions in favour of a diversity of perspectives. Certainly in Denmark there is a tendency to place universalist principles at the core of social work/pedagogic interventions in a way that minimises difference (Hatton, 2001). However, Cameron does suggest the importance of intuition in pedagogic practice, an approach which contrasts with the more managerial and outcome-based approaches discussed earlier. The 'hands' she suggested are represented through arts-and-crafts types of activities, although again this may be taken to infer a lower-key approach to that represented by those writers advocating the common third.

This is consistent with the argument in earlier chapters (and the Conclusion) for an approach which emphasises creativity as a central concern of innovative practice. This can be seen in the development of creative partnerships within the youth service that encourage *'new ways of thinking about learning that ha[ve] the relationship between individual learners, their local communities and creative practitioners at heart'* (Miles, 2007, p274). The work of Eichstellar and Raper points to the connection between this approach and pedagogy, particularly when they refer to the way *'pedagogy brings youth work back to its roots ... pedagogy will force us to think about our respective roles and practices outside of our existing silos, and to share and combine our efforts'* (2006, pp7–8).

The attention afforded social pedagogy in *Care Matters, Youth Matters* and output from the Department for Education and Skills and the Department of Health (Boddy et al., 2005 – for which Cameron and colleagues in the Thomas Coram Unit must take a lot of credit) suggests that the principles underpinning pedagogy have been taken on board and are likely to provide significant challenges to the future direction of children's services in the UK. This research has resulted in calls for a new qualification built on pedagogic principles (Cameron et al., 2007).

A review of youth services in a city in the south of England also mentions pedagogy on a number of occasions, welcoming *'the likely future move towards* a *pedagogy-led approach'* (Portsmouth City Council, 2007, section 5:27).

A report from the Regional Youth Work Unit North East and the University of Sunderland (2010) outlined the conclusions of a six-month review of the implications of social pedagogy for youth work. The unit interviewed professionals, young people and collated information from local authorities carrying out social pedagogy pilot programmes.

The report is notable for its focus on the views of young people themselves. It points out that young people suggested to the researchers that social pedagogy courses could be beneficial to services in the UK. The report suggested that social pedagogy was beneficial in building positive informal relationships, that it enabled professionals to see people in a holistic manner and that it could contribute positively to basic training of all professionals involved with young people (2010, pp47–8).

Vaisanen develops this theme when he talks about the way social pedagogy's main focus is on the integration of displaced young people into society. This can be achieved, he argues, through dialogue which *'implies an equal role of young people and adults in interactions aimed to solve problems of commitment to education ... Paying respect to subjectivity and the rights of self-determination of young people leads to helping them to identify and clarify their own targets'* (2010, p28).

Clearly there are points of connection between the theories, principles and values underpinning both Danish and UK social work. The focus on equality, respect and student-centred learning is central to both traditions. It provides a means of focusing or refocusing social work on its humanist goals rather than the technocratic welfarism currently being promoted in the UK (Narey, 2014; Dominelli and Hoogvelt, 1996).

We can learn from these different theoretical approaches so that, as has been argued elsewhere, we can meet the challenge to *'remain "rooted" in our own understandings but be prepared to shift sufficiently ... [so that] each other's contributions are respected while retaining a belief in the validity of our own contribution'* (Hatton, 2001, p277). The author has suggested elsewhere that the key ideas within social pedagogy can be summarised as:

- A commitment to improve the lives of people through creating positive pedagogical environments.

- A belief that people's lives need to be seen in the whole.

- A belief that people learn best through reflecting on their actions.

- An emphasis on the use of physical activities to promote development.

- An emphasis on social justice and social change, particularly in the context of securing real improvements in people's lives.

- In all the above, an emphasis on the importance of creativity and imagination in promoting human development.

- A view that people are autonomous beings but they only become complete when they take action to change their circumstances. Understanding without action renders the person incomplete.

(Hatton, 2013, p29)

The points of connection between social pedagogy and social work, as exemplified by a comparison of practice in Denmark and the UK, are highlighted in Table 6.1.

Table 6.1   Learning from each other

Country	Theory	Practice	Values
Denmark	Pedagogy	Empowering	Equality
	Common third	Promoting equality	Respect
	Project-based project work	Risk promoting	Dignity
	Social constructionism	Sharing/enabling	Solidarity humanism
		Creativity	Person-centred
UK (recognising the diversity of the UK particularly following devolution).	Person-centred, case management, residual progressive work in community, focus on social inclusion	From individualistic, risk-minimisation casework to community development	Anti-discriminatory
			Promotion of difference
		Active promotion of service user/carer involvement	Empowering humanism
			Radical practice even if remains minority activity

The three key ways in which we can learn from pedagogic traditions are summarised below.

Theory

Social pedagogy reminds us of the need to focus on individual need, while providing a reference point to more collective models of service provision, particularly as found in many parts of Europe. It reminds us of the importance of intuitive and not just evidence-based practice, and its emphasis on individual agency and understanding of broader social structures suggests a way of reconnecting social work to its more radical traditions (see Chapters 2 and 3). The UK emphasis on anti-oppressive/anti-discriminatory practice can, when integrated with this approach, provide a coherent theoretical approach which links together to provide a strategy for social change.

Practice

The trend toward managerialist approaches to social work has left many social workers in the UK feeling as if their training has been rendered irrelevant as the skills they are called on to use, at least in statutory settings, are much more pro-cedural and instrumental than they would desire. Pedagogy and other European traditions can remind us of the importance of relationship work and of the need to promote rather than minimise risk (see Chapter 1). Ideas of empowerment, even if expressed differently, put the focus back on service users and provide an anti-dote to the perceived limitations in the care-management approach. The focus on collaborative working across professional settings can also promote the ideas of partnership and participation suggested in this chapter.

Values

A recognition of the importance of non-Anglo Saxon approaches to social work can also allow us to explore common ethical principles between our European partners and ourselves and can itself promote improvements in inter-cultural understanding and communication. Inter-cultural communication can promote the autonomy of dif-ferent cultures within a framework which respects the way each culture is articulated and in turn can lead to inter-cultural action during which we can form intercultural relationships through which we can *ensure the need for common ground with the need to recognise difference'* (Young, 1996, p209; Hatton, 2001). This in turn can improve our inter-cultural competence (Berry et al., 2002). As social workers this will allow us to be receptive to the differing needs and aspirations of the people with whom we work, and by bringing us into contact with people from other countries ensures a freshness in our approach to our own practice and the possibility that we can learn from each other in a way that respects each other's traditions. As suggested elsewhere, it

> may allow us to see the similarities as well as the differences between us, to recognize that truth does not reside in one set of culturally specific values but that ways of understanding, methods of working and commitments to social justice are often shared.

> (Hatton, 2001, p276)

This approach suggests the possibility of recapturing the focus of social work toward 'relationship' (Ruch et al., 2010) or 'preventative work' (Healy, 2012) which have to some extent become marginalised in the UK, as evidenced by the discussions in Chapters 2 and 3. The focus on the 'common third' and 'problem-based' social work also suggests possible ways of forging partnerships that are more open, accountable and equal than those focused on eligibility criteria and 'risk minimisation' discussed earlier in the book.

Social pedagogy and social work education

The University of Portsmouth ran a BA (Hons) European Social Work degree with a pedagogic seminarium in Copenhagen between 1992 and 2008 (Horncastle and Brobeck, 1995; Hatton, 2006). It would have been easy for the university to impose a UK-centric approach to learning and to minimise the importance of pedagogic and androgogic traditions in other countries. In effect they could have been guilty of what Cornwell (1994) has called *'cultural colonisation'* in that their methods were seen as intrinsically *'better'* or more systematic than those found in other countries.

The University attempted to overcome this problem by developing a joint curriculum and ensuring that the Danish approach to education was as fully reflected in the curriculum as the UK/US approaches. Consequently, the international group-work and reflective review (based on the principles outlined above) in Copenhagen were given the same weighting as the more traditional academic approaches adopted in Portsmouth. The programme was taught in English, and this meant that the responsibility for assessment lay disproportionately with the UK teaching team, although as much assessment as possible was conducted jointly: for instance, UK tutors travelled to Denmark for the international group-work presentations (Social Pedagogy and Social Care in Europe) and Danish tutors travelled to the UK for the individual oral presentations (Frameworks of Comparison). This at least goes some way to meet the requirement that the programme has the

> flexibility to incorporate each culture's (and subculture's) own methodologies of support ... to focus on individual strengths and the structural (organizational, community, political) changes which can support and mobilize these strengths ... [which] can be particularly useful for social work in an international context by virtue of its concentration on people's capacity to live in the face of seemingly overwhelming adversity.
>
> (Taylor, 1999, p317)

One of the key challenges faced when establishing the BA European Social Work was that while the UK academics were all extremely well versed in the methodology, knowledge base and values underpinning UK social work, their knowledge of European traditions was much less developed. This was particularly true of social pedagogy, a tradition which had received little exposure in the UK other than through the work of Hadyn Davies Jones (and initially this was available in Danish rather than English; Courtiox and Davies Jones, 1984). It is easy to underestimate the lack of contact between UK and European traditions in social work, especially since the concept of pedagogy has become more widely known over the last few years (Higham, 2001; Boddy et al., 2003; Petrie, 2004).

The experience on the Portsmouth programme was that pedagogy was used much more widely than in a purely narrow, child-centred approach. In Denmark pedagogues are employed to work in residential and day-care settings, as part of multi-disciplinary teams (often with psychologists, social advisers and health workers;

Harder, 1997) and in initiatives such as the SSP projects (social services, school and police, e.g. the Blæksprutten Project in Copenhagen; Langager, 2009). However, it is undoubtedly true that pedagogy can make a real difference to current UK thinking about social work, both in terms of values and the theories underpinning practice (Hatton, 2001, 2013).

Where does this leave us? We need to critically review our practice so that we are aware that:

- partnership is a complex term which can hide a wide variety of practice;
- professionalism, while providing us with status and recognition, can inhibit collaboration and be detrimental to service users/carers;
- social pedagogy can remind us of the need to focus on relationship work and be less managerial in our practice;
- involvement is the key factor and this must be real, not tokenistic;
- an integration of social pedagogic and social work theory and practice can provide a model of how individuals (children and adults) can be viewed in the whole and account taken of their relationships with, and within, their communities and the social structures within which they operate.

ACTIVITY **6.2**

Consider how the notion of partnership operates in either your placement agency or your employing agency.

- *Where does power lie?*

- *How involved are service users/experts by experience in decision making?*

- *If the agency works with more than one profession, which partnership model best describes it?*

- *Does the involvement of more than one agency change the power relationships?*

- *Would the introduction of pedagogy have any impact on the agency? If so, what impact?*

- *How would a focus on intuition and relationship building change the practice you are currently involved with?*

Comment

This exercise is designed to enable you to think critically about the agency you work with. It focuses particularly on allowing you the opportunity to critically examine what partnership means. Many government publications from the *Modernisation*

White Paper (Department of Health, 1998) onwards and even before through initiatives such as *Working Together* (HM Government, 2013) have enjoined social workers to work in partnership. Often this is seen as a good thing in itself, without any thought being given to the power imbalances at the heart of much partnership work. This is not to suggest that we should not work collaboratively; just that we should seek to understand the relationships underpinning such partnerships.

C H A P T E R   S U M M A R Y

This chapter has focused on new forms of practice and has, in particular, developed two of the book's key themes; inter-professionalism and internationalism. It began by looking at how social work has moved towards securing for itself professional status through enhanced levels of training, registration and a commitment to continuous professional development. It then looked at how notions of partnership and collaborative working could enhance the practice of social workers by ensuring that the interventions of social workers and other professional groupings were more focused and relevant to contemporary challenges. It explored the examples of an inter-professional education initiative, supported by the Department of Health, the New Generation Project, and an initiative to improve collaboration between educational and workforce providers, the Social Work Education Network.

Finally the chapter looked at how European models of care were coming to influence current practice. It outlined the key elements of an approach common in continental Europe: social pedagogy. It identified the common principles underpinning such an approach – the common third and problem-based groupwork – and examined the way in which such an approach calls on a range of skills from the heart, brain and hands to achieve its goals. The chapter ends with a brief discussion as to how the goals of social pedagogy link to the theory, practice and value of social work. It suggests that there are clear points of connection between social pedagogy and UK social work and suggests some ways in which discussions around pedagogy could be taken forward. The next chapter will look at some practical examples of how European social work can influence UK practice.

FURTHER READING

Cameron, C. (2004) 'Social pedagogy and care: Danish and German practice in young people's residential care', *Journal of Social Work*, 4 (2): 133–51.

An early article from one of the key researchers at the Thomas Coram Research Unit. The article looks at the experience of pedagogy in Denmark and Germany and at the possible implications for UK residential services.

Cameron, C., Petrie, P., Wigfall, V., Kleipoedszus, S. and Jasper, A. (2011) *Final report of the Social Pedagogy Pilot Project: Development and Implementation*. London: Thomas Coram research Unit/Institute of Education, University of London.

This is the final report of the pilot project into social pedagogy in children's residential services commissioned by the Department for Children and Families. It needs to be read in conjunction with:

Berridge, D. Biehal, N., Lutman, L. and Palamores, M. (2011) *Raising the Bar? Evaluation of the Social Pedgogy Pilot Programme in Residential Children's Homes*, Research Report DFE-RR 148. London: Department of Education.

Hatton, K. (2013) *Social Pedagogy in the UK: Theory and Practice.* Lyme Regis: Russell House.

An overview of the key ideas in European social pedagogy, with reference to Latin America and their application to residential children's services, youth work, adult services and community development

Quinney, A. (2006) *Collaborative Social Work Practice.* Exeter: Learning Matters.

A useful introduction to the principles underpinning collaborative work.

Storo, J. (2013) *Practical Social Pedagogy: Theories, Values and Tools for Working With Children and Young People.* Bristol: Policy Press.

A translation of a book by a Norwegian social pedagogue and academic which outlines the key principles of social pedagogic practice with children and young people. Provides a clear Scandinavian perspective. Focus primarily on practice rather than theory.

Chapter 7

International social work: European and international reflections on the challenges to social work in selected European countries

Key Area 3: Take a community development approach to group work and collective action.

Key Area 5: Support community learning from shared experiences.

Key Area 6: Provide community development support to organisations.

(Federation for Community Development Learning, 2009)

Introduction: learning from others

The key themes of this book have now emerged. Concerns around inclusion, inter-professionalism and internationalism were clearly at the heart of discourses on social work practice when the first edition of the book came out in 2008. They remain central to debates today. Taking its cue from social work, the Health and Care Professions Council (HCPC), the new regulator for social work following the disbandment of the General Social Care Council, has produced a new set of standards for education and training for *Service User and Carer Involvement in Education and Training Programmes* (Health and Care Professions Council, 2013). The National Occupational Standards for Community Development express a clear commitment to 'community empowerment'.

In the previous chapter we drew attention to the way European and/or international discourses of social work can throw a different light on UK practice and suggested a way in which we can integrate these approaches into our work. Chapter 4 concluded with a brief discussion of the importance of community development across Europe. This chapter concentrates on these developments, and looks in more detail at specific examples of the social work or social pedagogic experience. The chapter suggests, through a review of social work/social pedagogic projects in Ireland, the Czech Republic and Denmark, issues about our current practice that will allow us to test and perhaps implement forms of practice which are consistent with social work's traditional concerns around prevention and empowerment.

UK and European social work

Lymbery et al. suggested that UK social work was much more prescriptive and regulated than social work in other European countries, although these countries may be moving closer to the UK model. They argued that

> *most nations have resisted the reductive power of the competence model and insisted on a broader definition of social work expertise … it is not beyond the bounds of possibility that similar forms of regulation will start to take shape elsewhere. In that sense Britain could yet serve as an unwelcome model for the rest of Europe.*

(2000, p279)

There is certainly some evidence that this development of a more regulated approach is happening internationally. Research by Nett and Spratt (2012) points to the way child protection systems in Australia, Germany, Finland, Sweden and the UK are converging in their approaches to intervention in crisis situations and the identification of the risks children face. However, before looking at social work in Ireland, the Czech Republic and Denmark it is necessary to establish whether there is any such activity as a 'European' or indeed international social work. Lorenz suggested that *'regardless of the particular model of welfare state within which social work operates there are great similarities in the daily practice of social workers'* (1994, p28). He declined to define social work, arguing that *'social work has a history of uncertainty and constantly changing identities'* (p14). Munday described social work as a *'notoriously difficult term to define, with significant variations across Europe in what constitutes a "social worker"'* (1996, p7).

Marynowicz–Hetka et al. suggest that

> *the category of social professions includes both professionals, that is persons specially trained to work with specific types of persons, families, social groups and communities at high social risk, [and] persons who conduct this type of work as volunteers and have no professional training.*

> (1999, p23)

For the purpose of this discussion, we can define social work across Europe as a form of social professional activity which engages with people in a way that promotes their empowerment and aims to achieve a fair and more equitable society. It is beyond the scope of the book to develop a full comparative framework for evaluating social work across different countries and the reader is referred to other works that deal with these issues in far greater depth (Hokenstad and Midgley, 1997; Lyons, 1999; Adams et al., 2001; Lawrence et al., 2009; Hugman, 2010; Yeates, 2014). Within this context social professional activity should itself be seen in terms of the contribution we can make as change agents to igniting processes of social transformation. As such, social work shares professional concerns and dilemmas with a range of occupational groupings, including:

- social pedagogues;
- social and special educators;
- agogues (community leaders);
- *animateurs* (a French profession focusing on young people's leisure activities);
- social workers;
- youth and community workers.

> (Lorenz et al., 1996)

Lyons argues that a *'comparative approach can assist with the identification of common problems and provide encouragement for innovative practices'* (Lyons, 1999, p159). She suggests that involvement with other social professionals can be an enriching experience and that it can raise awareness of the commonality of some basic human needs and problems, and of the cultural differences that influence their expression and the forms of societal and social responses. Erath et al. suggest that comparative approaches to social work can

> [o]ffer a medium through which social work may be reconnected with its primary concern in the alleviation of poverty, alienation and oppression and the promotion of human potential for developing both individual capacities and social environments.

> (2001, p3)

Williams and Simpson argue that as social workers or social professionals

> [w]e belong to a profession which concerns itself with international questions such as ecological disasters, civil war and economic deprivation. Such events trigger the mass movement of people and the international trade in people ... the impact of these events becomes the responsibility of more than one nation state.

> (2009, p5)

This suggests that examining social work in other countries can reconnect us with the central themes of radical social and community work identified in Chapters 2 and 3. This analysis would suggest that social work in the UK, Europe and internationally shares common concerns, which while not exclusive to social work are central to the practice of most social workers and the experience of most people who use social services.

What are these common problems? It is possible to identify a number of significant dilemmas facing social workers across the globe, including:

- racism;

- exclusion, marginalisation and poverty;

- managerialism (see Chapter 1);

- demands from service users (see Chapter 5);

- Europeanisation and internationalisation (see below).

Hugman suggests that *'social work can be seen as the professionalization of responses to those aspects of our societies that are seen as problems of human well-being'* (2010, p158). As such he suggests that *'understanding international social work is crucial for the ways in which we can understand social work as a richly varied set of theories and practices'* (p.159). This challenge of seeing the multi-faceted nature of social work and the variety of responses we can provide is the focus of this book and particularly the remainder of this chapter.

Racism

We noted in Chapter 3 how Lorenz pointed to the challenge that racism posed for the social professions if we see it as part of the process through which dominant discourses are reproduced around power (see discussion of Foucault in Chapter 5). Lorenz suggested that racism was a major challenge for social work and that we need to demonstrate how discussions of racism are not just commonsense understandings of the world around us (it's natural to see people as different) but are the outcome of a discourse that promotes the aspirations of the minority population in a negative and demeaning way.

Speaking at the Ostrava Conference of the European Consortium of Social Professions with Educational and Social Studies (ECSPRESS) in 1998, Lorenz argued that *'the role of the social professions in relation to the growing danger of exclusion and racism remains crucial for the achievement of a social Europe'* (1998, p5). He pointed to the way ECSPRESS was seeking to ensure that European integration *'does not cause greater fragmentation and new forms of exclusion'* (p3).

Despite this emphasis on a more politically active form of practice, social work in the UK is increasingly seen as a residual service meeting the needs of the poor and disadvantaged (Buckley et al., 1997; Davis and Wainwright, 2005). We saw in earlier chapters how social work can adapt to this kind of challenge because of its connection to the experience of people who use services and the commitment to accountability and inclusiveness that are at the centre of good social work practice. It has become increasingly important for social work to resist 'essentialising' people facing oppression. By 'essentialising' we mean the attribution of common characteristics to groups in a way which denies the differences in their experience, for example, the creation of categories such as women, race, disability which fail to take into account that the experiences of all women, people from other races or disabled people cannot be assumed to be the same. For the purpose of our analyses the notion of 'intersectionality' seems more appropriate. Goodley describes this in relation to disability when he says:

> A body or mind that is disabled is also one that is raced, gendered, trans/nationally sited, aged, sexualized and classed. Disability is imbricated with other categories of difference, experiences of marginality and forms of political activism ... This ... is a plea to remain mindful of the complexity of disability, particularly when it intersects with other markers of identity and oppression.

> (2011, p33)

Poverty, exclusion and marginalisation

We noted in earlier chapters how the particular discourses around poverty and exclusion can impact on practice. This remains important in any discussion of European and international social work. Poverty is an important issue across Europe (Gordon and Townsend, 2000; OECD, 2014) and as such impacts significantly on the people with whom social workers engage. Lister sees poverty as spelling *'exclusion from the full rights of citizenship in the social and civil spheres'* (1998, p29). This exclusion is compounded by the way neo-liberal policies increasingly blame people in poverty for their circumstances and attempt to push social workers towards an individualised response to what is a structural problem (Dominelli, 2004; see also discussion in Chapter 1). Writers such as Dominelli, Powell (2001) and Ferguson and Woodward (2009) argue that this leads to a focus on managerialist responses to the problems facing service users, and can result in the marginalisation of the concerns of the people using services in the face of an over-concern with managerial imperatives such as budgetary control, the development of restrictive criteria to govern eligibility for services, and a focus on professional concerns rather than social change perspectives. As a consequence, some of the more innovative and radical approaches described earlier in the book can become marginalised (Penna et al., 2000; Powell, 2001; Dominelli, 2004). This can lead to:

- the individualisation of service users' experience;

- a focus on crisis intervention rather than preventative work;

- social work being evaluated through measurable outcomes and the associated problem of prioritisation by eligibility criteria;

- social work becoming risk averse (see Introduction and Chapters 1, 5 and 6).

How can the negative connotations of such approaches be overcome? This may be achieved, for example, by:

- **Increasing accountability** – we have argued for greater service user involvement in service delivery and education, more democratic structures, and anti-discrimination (Chapter 5).

- **New grassroots organisations** – of Roma/Gypsies/Travellers, organisations of young people from BME groups, disability activists, social action projects. These are about reclaiming social work's radical roots (see Chapters 2 and 3).

- **The development of new international lobbies** – new organisations to replace ECSPRESS, IASSW and IFSW.

- **Confronting the neo-liberal agenda** – and putting social work forward as an agency of change.

ACTIVITY 7.1

Either individually or in groups, consider the following:

- *In what way does poverty impact on people who use social work services in the UK?*

- *How can social workers engage with people experiencing racism?*

- *What implications do these issues have for current social work practice?*

Comment

Use the material in this and earlier chapters to look at what poverty means and how it structures the lives of many people using social services within the UK (see Dominelli, 2004, pp34–9). For many people the experience of poverty is further exacerbated by the racism they experience within the UK (Mac an Ghaill, 1999; Barnard and Turner, 2011). Use the Professional Capability Framework and the National Occupational Standards for community work to look at which key roles a social worker would need to use to undertake practice that could incorporate a concern with poverty and racism.

Learning from a social pedagogic approach

We noted in the first edition and the previous chapter the way the European concept of pedagogy had begun to attract attention in the UK. In 2006 the conference 'What is pedagogy?', organised by the Thomas Coram Research Unit, brought together speakers and delegates from a number of European countries to look at how pedagogy could be introduced into social work in the UK. The author (Hatton, 2006) suggested that pedagogy could remind us of the need to focus on relationship work and be less managerial in our practice. In Chapter 6, it was suggested that we can learn from pedagogic traditions in three key ways: theory, practice and values.

RESEARCH SUMMARY

Reviewing the use of pedagogy in residential child care services in Europe, the Thomas Coram Research Unit identified the following key principles of pedagogic practice:

- *A focus on the child as a whole person, and support for the child's overall development.*

- *The practitioner seeing herself/himself as a person, in relationship with the child or young person.*

- *While they are together, children and staff are seen as inhabiting the same life space, not as existing in separate, hierarchical domains.*

- *As professionals, pedagogues are encouraged to constantly reflect on their practice and to apply both theoretical understandings and self-knowledge to their work and the sometimes challenging demands with which they are confronted.*

- *Pedagogues are also practical; their training prepares them to share in many aspects of children's daily lives, such as preparing meals and snacks, or making music and building kites.*

- *When working in group settings, children's associative life is seen as an important resource: workers should foster and make use of the group.*

- *Pedagogy builds on an understanding of children's rights that is not limited to procedural matters or legislated requirements.*

- *An emphasis on team work and on valuing the contributions of others in the task of 'bringing up' children: other professionals, members of the local community and, especially, parents.*

> **RESEARCH SUMMARY** *continued*
>
> - *Pedagogic theory is especially about relationships; child rearing to the pedagogue is essentially personal.*
>
> - *'It is a job where every day you must ask questions about yourself and your practice right to the end of your professional life' (French pedagogue working in a residential home, interviewed as part of TCRU's Social Pedagogy Study).*
>
> (Petrie et al., 2009)

> **ACTIVITY 7.2**
>
> *In what way could pedagogy be used to change practice in the UK? Using the material in this chapter and in Chapter 6, suggest three ways in which pedagogy could be utilised to improve social work practice with one of the key groups of service users.*

Comment

You may wish to look at some of the more recent policy drivers which have included mention of pedagogy, including *Care Matters* and *Youth Matters*. The impetus for these developments has been concern at the poor experience of many young people in the looked-after system. How do the comments outlined above compare with the Professional Capability Framework and the National Occupational Standards for community work?

Experiencing social and community work: reflections from Europe

The above discussion, and that in Chapter 6, provides a context for this section. Here we look in more detail at the experience of social and community work of particular people in three European countries. In Ireland and the Czech Republic we look at the experience of a similar group: in Ireland, Travellers, and in the Czech Republic, the Roma. These groups have been specifically chosen because the work with which they engage touches on two of the book's key themes: inclusion and internationalism. However, they also throw light on the potential for people within these communities to discover solutions to their own problems and through this develop their own indigenous leadership. They therefore also allow us to reflect on the issues raised in Chapters 2 and 3.

The final discussion is more specifically about the experience of young people in Denmark and the way racism impacts on their lives. It looks at how social pedagogues and social workers can work in a way that enables young people to overcome the racism they face. The remainder of this chapter draws on the author's experience teaching and researching in Ireland, the Czech Republic and Denmark. It looks specifically at projects that work with people excluded because of their race/ethnicity, because given our commitment in the UK to anti-oppressive/anti-discriminatory practice it will allow us to focus on some of the lessons we can learn from attempts by excluded populations and the social workers/social pedagogues with whom they work to develop their own solutions to the problems they face. Each section will provide a short overview of social work in that country before examining one project in greater detail.

Ireland and Irish Travellers

Background

Gilligan (1991) and Buckley et al. (1997) pointed to the way in which the priorities for social work in Ireland were largely determined by the state's response to disclosures of child abuse, particularly the Kilkenny Case. Ferguson (1996) suggests that, in the 1980s, the emergent childcare policy had largely been contained within the 'expert system', which ensured that *'knowledge about child deaths and other organisational "failures" continued to be institutionally repressed'* (1996, p25). This has been replaced more recently by a situation in which childcare discourse and practice has become politicised. Ferguson suggests that the debate on child protection has been reconstituted in two distinct ways. The role of the state has been more clearly articulated by a series of child abuse scandals and enquiries and Ferguson suggested that this has shown that *'the safety of children cannot even be guaranteed by removing them from high risk home situations'* (Ferguson, 1996, p27).

Skehill pointed to the contradictions between this regulatory and controlling framework and the attempts within the areas of community development and community action to engage with ideas of *'participation, empowerment and partnership'* (Skehill, 1999, p177). In a more optimistic vein, Powell (1998) suggested that *'the concept[s] of empowerment and user rights ... are seen as offering a new legitimacy to embattled welfare bureaucracies and professionals. The suggestion is that social workers, offering the quintessentially personal social services, can be pathfinders in this regard* (1998, pp326–7). Elsewhere Powell (2001) has suggested the future of social work may well depend on how well it responds to such problems.

As we have seen earlier, this debate over the potential for social work to engage with processes of change is critical if we are to clearly map the way social work develops in the future. A good example of how people can engage with change processes is provided by looking at the experience of Travellers in Ireland.

Travellers have over the last 20 years begun to articulate their own demands for equality within the Irish state. The social and economic progress witnessed in Ireland during this period put the focus firmly on the way Ireland has failed to address the substantial levels of social inequality in Irish society (Callan and Nolan, 1994; Callan et al., 1996; Healy and Reynolds, 1998). The success of the 'Celtic tiger' (the economy of the Republic of Ireland during 1995–2000) resulted in growth rates of 7.5 per cent (among the highest in the world). The low inflation and interest rates and increases in real living standards meant the economy became almost equal to EU averages

(Sweeney, 1998). A national anti-poverty strategy (NAPS) was developed and the government introduced equality legislation prohibiting discrimination on the grounds of *'gender, marital status, family status, sexual orientation, religion, age, disability, race and membership of the traveller community'* (Irish Government, 1999; emphasis added).

Unfortunately the fiscal crisis of 2007/8 changed the picture considerably and an Institute for the Study of Labor paper (Verick, 2009) suggests that Ireland was one of a group of five countries (Lithuania, Latvia, Estonia, Spain and Ireland) most affected by the crisis, with young men and women experiencing increases of *'up to 20 percentage points'* in unemployment rates as a consequence of the crisis (2009, p17).

Featherstone notes how the fiscal crisis was caused through severe weaknesses in the banking system exacerbated by government policy, with the result that *'the Irish recession has been longer and deeper than almost any other in the industrialised world'* (2011, p20). She points to the way the neo-liberal policies pursued in Ireland have increased levels of inequality, particularly health inequality, gender inequality and poverty. Her focus is on the challenge these developments pose to social work (which she points out is more narrowly defined in Ireland than most of Europe, e.g. youth work, community development and social care are not defined as social work in Ireland (p24)). She points to the debate between Powell (1998) and Skehill (1999), mentioned earlier, as representing alternative discourse around social work in Ireland, Powell positing an optimism about the future and noting the ending of Catholic hegemony over social welfare, and Skehill's focus on the way social work individualises people's experience and if not rejecting at least minimises social justice perspectives. Featherstone noted the involvement of social workers, if not their representative organisations, in protests, including one in October 2010, which she says would

> bring together a wide variety of people from the trade union movement, academics, environmental groups, community groups, migrant worker organisations, women's organisations and others to stimulate the emergence of a cross sectoral community of interest for a more equal, inclusive and sustainable Ireland.
>
> (2011, p27)

Travellers have long been identified as one of the groups in Ireland facing the discrimination, disadvantage and marginalisation. This recognition of the need to tackle the disadvantage and discrimination facing Travellers was partly the outcome of a number of national commissions which focused on the needs of Travellers (Irish Government, Commission on Itineracy, 1963; Irish Government, Task Force on Travellers, 1995), partly the outcome of work generated by the Combat Poverty Agency, a government-sponsored anti-poverty agency, and partly due to the growth of an *'ethnic intelligentsia'* among Travellers (MacLaughlin, 1995). MacLaughlin argues that this was the outcome of developments within the Traveller movement but is also a response to a *'virulent anti-Traveller Racism and the gradual internalisation of feelings of social inferiority among travellers themselves'* (1995, pp2–3). He suggested that the new leadership within the Travelling community faced up to and struggled against this process of devaluing Traveller culture and life and has *'politicised and radicalised Traveller issues'* (pp82–3).

Ireland's history as effectively a British colony for much of the last 600 years encouraged a belief that racism is something that happens to Irish people rather than a part of the experience of people within Ireland. Yet the experience of minority groups within Ireland, particularly the day-to-day experience of Travellers, provides substantial evidence that racism is deeply embedded in Irish social relations.

Aniagolu (1997) has argued that both the Irish people themselves and minority peoples within Ireland are guilty of *misrepresenting Ireland as a country free from racial prejudice. Indeed most Irish people still argue that the Irish are not racist'* (1997, p44). He suggests that on the contrary, Irish people were themselves implicated in racist oppression in many countries of the British Empire: *'substantial numbers of Irish and Anglo-Irish people engaged in the slave trade and were actively involved in projects of colonial expansion'* (p45). He points to the way in which racism in Ireland is constructed through people's own internalisation and replication of racist attitudes which they acquired from their colonisers through the process of colonisation.

Kensika Monshengwo of the Association of Refugees and Asylum Seekers in Ireland described how leaflets have been distributed in streets in the North Inner City and the West of Dublin inciting racial hatred, and that these have been accompanied by physical attacks. He noted that *'the physical abuse is directed almost exclusively towards blacks'.* Pat Guerin (2002) of the Anti-Racist Campaign says *'there is a perception among some local people that refugees are getting preferential treatment with regards to accommodation ... a racially motivated murder is only a matter of time away'.* Christie points to the negative way in which social work with asylum seekers is constructed in Ireland and argues that *'the profession will need to be proactive in developing policies and practices that promote anti-racism and "strong" multi-culturalism'* (2003, p230). He notes the particular problems associated with the accommodation of asylum seekers (and unaccompanied children). Breen (2008) suggests that the experience of asylum seekers in respect of accommodation *'provides numerous examples of Ireland's failure to protect the human rights of asylum seekers'* (2008, p623).

The tension exemplified by the above typifies debates in Ireland concerning asylum-seekers. Cullen (2000) noted that in Ireland, *'official neglect of asylum seekers over the past decade has wasted years of people's lives'* (2000, p.53). He pointed out particularly, and ironically given the history of Travellers in Ireland, that *'when people complain in generalized terms about asylum-seekers, they are frequently talking about Roma'* (p53).

MacLaughlin argued that the development of modern Ireland saw the creation of a politics of exclusion and a geography of closure which *'sought to exclude the foreigner from "Fortress Ireland" and "foreign practices" from Catholic nationalist Ireland'* (1995, p69). However, on the positive side, the recommendations of the 1995 Task Force on Travellers prioritises Travellers' concerns and suggests a state commitment to tackling the discrimination they face. Perhaps more significantly this period *'saw the emergence of an ethnic intelligentsia among the Travellers ... [which] has contributed to the growth of an articulate leadership capable of voicing Traveller concerns and capable of raising the political consciousness of travelling people'* (pp2–3).

Speaking at an international women's conference organised in Cork in 1993, a Traveller focused on the gendered inequalities faced by Travellers. She describes eloquently the hatred and discrimination which was both the historical legacy and current experience of Travellers and suggests that it is hardly surprising that younger Travellers react with anger to the discrimination they face. She said:

> It is as if we are not as human as everybody else. We are seen as dirty, smelly, 'knackers'. It seems that the state can do what it likes with Travellers. This is because we are a minority. We are a small group on our own with no education. We know what we want but all we can use are our voices and our minds. This doesn't seem to have done us much good so far.

> (Hyde, in Ward, 1995, p64)

She concluded by arguing that Travellers need to organise themselves; they cannot or should not any longer rely on others to speak out for them: Travellers need to stand up for themselves (Hyde, 1995, p63).

Helleiner argues that anti-Traveller ideologies and actions are linked to gendered constructions of Travellers (p275). She suggests that:

> the construction of domesticated Irish women in need of protection from a paternalistic state had implications for representations of Traveller women. However, this domesticisation of Travelling women and the gendered social relations incumbent on it was also reinforced within Traveller households. While Traveller women were important contributors to the household economy and possessed as a result a degree of autonomy other Irish women lacked, cultural practices such as restrictions on female sexuality before marriage and arranged marriages reduced their autonomy. Amongst Irish Travellers, as amongst the British Traveller-Gypsies, a controlled female sexuality was central to the ethnic self-definition while the settled women were attributed with uncontrolled sexuality.

> (1997, p282)

Travellers have begun, as MacLaughlin suggests, to challenge these stereotypes. In earlier research carried out by the author (Hatton, 2001), one Travelling woman said, *'Travelling women have been very involved in community development because they have been involved in the issues'*. Another said, *'When we started off we were seen as troublemakers. I should have been home looking after my children. Corporations [local councils] saw us as frightening, not just as Travellers, we were women'* (interviews with Travelling women 1998–2000).

Frazer (2001) has argued that community development has a key role in tackling racism in Ireland. The development of an autonomous Traveller movement with its own ethnic leadership will go a long way to creating the underpinnings for an equality agenda. The Gypsy/Roma community across Europe is developing much closer links and is also developing alliances with mainstream organisations within national and international contexts, including at a European level (McCann et al. 1994, pp174–6; see also the work of the European Roma Rights Centre, www.errc.org/).

Traveller Visibility Group

The new leadership is further exemplified by the Traveller Visibility Group (TVG), a Cork–based community development organisation that brings together Travellers and settled people in solidarity to facilitate community development work with the Travelling community. The TVG recognises Travellers as a *'nomadic ethnic group with its own distinct culture and lifestyles'* (Annual Report, **2007**). Formed in 1992, the mission, key principles and aims of the TVG are as below.

Mission

To work with Travellers in Cork towards achieving real change and improvement in their lives

Principles of the TVG

- Anti-racist and anti-sexist work practices be implemented in all programmes.
- Participation, partnership and empowerment – the core elements of community development.
- Starting from where the Travellers are at and passing on skills.
- Seeing the value of working through a development process with people being as important as completing the task.

Aims of the TVG

1. Continue to promote Travellers as a nomadic ethnic group, with its own distinctive culture and lifestyles.

2. Continue to promote Traveller self-determination and empowerment (enabling Travellers to make decisions and work in a collective way to bring about real change in their lives).

3. Continue to work for real change and improvement in Travellers' lives including the areas of education, accommodation, health, and employment/work and rights.

4. To challenge discrimination and racism against Travellers.

5. Continue to ensure the inclusion of Traveller issues and resource the real participation of Travellers in policy decisions and practices that affect their lives.

6. Develop a suitable, well-resourced Travellers' Centre and Crèche.

7. Develop the TVG's management, administrative and staff structures and procedures.

8. Promote mutual understanding, acceptance and support between Travellers and others in Irish Society.

9. Network links locally, regionally and nationally.

10. Carry out research on the circumstances of Travellers in Cork and contribute to national research which will inform the TVG's work.

The TVG adopts a proactive approach in its work. One of the women in the project described how they began to tackle the discrimination they faced as Travellers:

TVG is in many ways unique. Previously work with Travellers had a very charitable approach. Charities were set up in all the counties. Some were very genuine but more were doing it for the power. In Cork a committee to help Travellers was set up but was not very effective. TVG started in late '92.

We've run on a shoestring. We didn't have any funds. People were concerned about the conditions we lived in but they could not accept the conditions we lived in were caused by the political agendas going around us. We couldn't accept this, we split off. Travellers needed to be visible, that's why we call ourselves TVG. We look at the media and see how Travellers are visualised.

We want to be visible in a positive way for positive reasons, to give Travellers something to celebrate. This community has faced oppression and marginalisation. It has inevitably become very isolated. We want to change that.

This comment and the above discussion illustrate the way even the most marginalised and disaffected groups of people have the capacity and ability to challenge discriminatory and oppressive legal and social processes. It clearly lends weight to the analysis in Chapters 2 and 3 of the potential people have to engage in progressive forms of practice. In particular it demonstrates the way that people can organise to form and control their own organisations and develop their leadership from within their communities. (See http://tvgcork.ie/site/ (accessed 4/3/15) and Annual Report 2007).

Czech Republic: Integration or discrimination?

Background
Before 1989 the Czech Republic (then Czechoslovakia) was a centrally planned economy, with full employment and comprehensive social welfare for its citizens. After the Velvet Revolution (a relatively peaceful transfer of power from the old regime to a new government) in 1989 a number of key social policies were introduced to protect citizens from poverty. These included the development of the Existential Minimum (a social benefit introduced in 1991 to secure a basic minimum income for those without access to other resources), a minimum wage, and a shift from social security (which was viewed as paternalistic) to social protection (which focused on individual need). Central to this new approach was the development of a 'social surviving net', a three-fold system involving social insurance, state social support and social assistance. This was established in 1993 after the separation of the Czech Republic from Slovakia. The split with Slovakia led initially to a combination of a decrease in GDP, high rates of inflation, a fall in real household incomes, a drop in real wages, an increase in rental costs, cost of energy and travel costs (Chytil, 1998, pp48–9). Chytil suggests that the most significant factors characterising the new social arrangements were poverty, unemployment and crime.

- **Poverty** was previously related to family life cycle, but now a new form of poverty emerged characterised by unemployment, discrimination, the freeing of the labour market which made employment less secure, and the development of whole areas suffering poverty which impacted mainly on families with children. In the Czech Republic the percentage of all households with the lowest incomes was 20 per cent but this figure rose to 51 per cent for couples with three or more children (Ferge, 2000, p277). Ferge also noted that for the Czech Republic and other Central European states the figures were not entirely reliable as the Roma population was often missing from the analysis.

- **Unemployment**, which was virtually unknown before 1989, increased substantially from 2 to 4 per cent in 1992, 4.3 per cent in 1996, 5.8 per cent in January 1998 to 6.4 per cent in August 1998.

- There also appeared to be an increase in **crime**. In 1989, 71,069 crimes were committed, while in 1995, 114,791 crimes were committed. An analysis of this phenomenon argued that criminological investigations indicate an increase in brutality of all types of criminal activity among children and teenagers (Chytil, 1998, p49).

Social work in the Czech Republic is delivered through a diversity of providers at the state, regional and municipal levels and through church and other non-governmental organisations (NGOs). Most services are provided by NGOs and church organisations such as the Silesians, Caritas, Diakony. Chytil suggests that there was basically no change in social work after 1989. Social workers continued to work with the same client groups and *'the majority of social workers were employed by the municipal councils and as state employees at district offices'* (Chytil, 1998, p50). Social work was still primarily based on the medical model (Chytil, 1998), psycho-educational models (Krakesova, 1973, in Chytil, 1998) and on the client as consumer (Johnson, 1999). There is some evidence that social work developments have been influenced by social work practice in the UK, particularly in so far as they have relatively early in their social work development adopted quality-assurance processes which mirror UK developments. There was an attempt to regularise social work services at end of the 1990s with the relocation of decision making to localities. It was believed that the focus on quality assurance would *'show organisations are efficient; if they are they will get accreditation and be entitled to long-term financial support. The quality standards have been developed by the Ministry of Work and Social Matters along with the DoH in the UK'* (lecture by Head of Jabok College, Charles University, Prague, 2003).

The legal structure governing the delivery of social work has been in a process of evolution. The 1998 Amendment to Law Concerning Families no.91/1998 defined the rights of children to *'healthy development, proper upbringing and education and the protection of their justified interests'* (Pridhova, 1999, p44). There have been proposals for a new law about social services to set out the circumstances in which people in difficult situations receive social work support. More recently a new unifying opinion (Cpjn 202/2010) of the Czech Supreme Court issued in January 2011 stated that *'family's poverty and poor housing circumstances cannot be the sole basis for removing children from the home and placing them in state care'*.

Also in 2010, the Czech Constitutional Court ruled against the unnecessary break-up of families in cases where it is not absolutely necessary (II.ÚS 485/2010) (see also www. sos-childrensvillages.org/where-we-help/europe/czech-republic, accessed 4/3/15).

Work with the Roma

It is within this developing framework that social work intervention with the Roma can be gauged. The mobility of the Roma had been restricted by the Communist regime prior to 1989. The development of the new state did not necessarily address this problem. As Bancroft noted, *'in Central and Eastern Europe Roma are often simply being excluded from civil society altogether… the Czech citizenship law of 1993 … excluded many Czech Roma from citizenship, pushing many further to the margins of society'* (2005, p155). Official statistics suggested that there were 11,000–12,000 Roma in the Czech Republic. However, it is now accepted that the real figure is closer to between 200,000 and 300,000. The Roma do not constitute a homogenous group but are made up of a number of different ethnic groupings, including Slovakian Roma (largest group), Hungarian, Moravian and Sinti Roma (only a couple of hundred). While the largest population concentrations are in Prague, many live outside Prague in smaller cities such as Brno, Ostrava and Teplice (Office of the Government of the Czech Republic, 2003). Some key characteristics of the Roma experience are as follows:

- **Genocide** – it is often forgotten that the Roma were the focus of an attempted genocide by the Nazis during the 1930s/1940s. It became known as the Roma Holocaust, in which very significant numbers died, and is remembered every April.

- **Education** – a disproportionate number of Roma children attend special schools.

- **Housing** – Roma often live in the worst housing.

- **Unemployment** – there are much higher levels of unemployment among the Roma than in the general population, reaching 80–90 per cent in some areas.

Crowe (2008) has pointed out that,

> well before the collapse of communism, there were hints in Czechoslovakia of a particular virulent hatred of the Roma. In 1972, fear of the dramatic rise in Roma population statistics vis-à-vis the economic and social problems associated with such growth prompted the Czechoslovak government to adopt a program of forced sterilization of Roma women to reduce Roma births.
>
> (2008, p522)

The problem continued for another 30 years until in 2005:

> [T]he Ombudsman issued a report that concluded that the forced sterilization of Czech women continued to be a problem in the Czech Republic. He recommended changes in the country's health care laws better to protect women

from forced sterilization, including the publication of a handbook on sterilization written for the layperson. He also suggested better training for health care professionals on the legal rights of patients regarding sterilization and suggested the government set up some mechanism for giving reparations to women forcibly or ignorantly sterilized.

(2008, p524)

Czech Roma women also experience premature births, newborns were shorter and their birth weight lower than non-Roma (Rambouskova et al., 2009). Across Central and South-Eastern Europe, Roma have higher levels of communicable and non-communicable diseases and exhibit *'a persistent picture of worse health and substantially lower life expectancy than the majority populations'* (Festis et al., 2012, p26).

In an effort to improve the social circumstances of the Roma, the Czech Republic introduced the Roma Integration Project in 2003. This sought to bring the Roma into decision-making bodies and led to the establishment of the Council for National Minorities and the Council for the Roma Minority in Prague (through which 12 deputies and 12 Roma representatives met every two months in the Parliament building) (Council of Europe, 2003).

Social exclusion remains the key experience of the Roma. This is recognised within the integration policy, which suggests that integration means:

the full incorporation of the Roma into society while preserving most of the cultural features and differences that characterise them and that they want to preserve provided that these differences are not against the laws of the Czech Republic Government of the Czech Republic.

(Government of the Czech Republic, 2003; emphasis added)

This led among other things to the appointment of specialist advisers, particularly at ministry, regional and district levels and the implementation of anti-discrimination measures, and affirmative action at all levels, particularly in education. However, there remained substantial problems, including:

- a lack of awareness of cultural difference;
- insufficient knowledge of Roma language and culture;
- the problem of special schools;
- inadequate social and health care.

The integration policy acknowledges this when it says that,

Compared to the majority of society, the Roma community is far more exposed to all the danger factors quoted by the European Social Programme, e.g. long-term unemployment, long-term low or inadequate incomes, low level of education and qualification, early school-leaving, disability, ill-health, unsatisfactory housing, sex inequality, discrimination, racism, family break-up, living in greatly disadvantaged localities, alcohol and drug addiction.

(Government of the Czech Republic, 2003, p25)

A report to the United Nations Human Rights Committee by The European Roma Rights Centre, the organisation Vzajemme Souziti, the Peace work Development Fund and the Centre on Housing Rights and Evictions in Europe suggested that, if anything, the discrimination against the Roma had worsened. Anti-discriminatory legislation such as the Roma Integration Policy was not working, segregation in schools was still a major problem, Roma continued to find it difficult to access the labour market and racism was prevalent. The report argued that

[r]egular and systematic human rights abuse of Roma in the Czech Republic is aggravated by the fact that anti-Romani hate speech is a regular part of public discourse ... Anti-Romani statements are a standard and often unquestioned part of public life in the Czech Republic.

(European Roma Rights Centre, Vzajemme Souziti, Peacework Development Fund and the Centre on Housing Rights and Evictions in Europe, 2006).

RESEARCH SUMMARY

Reviewing the experience of Roma children in the education system, the European Roma Rights Centre said in 1999 that the

disproportionate allocation to schools for the mentally handicapped affects the current and future prospects of at least 25,000 Romani children presently in primary schools in the Czech Republic, as well as numerous other Roma whose lives have been ruined by the school system ... it is clear that many educators in practice regard remedial schools as schools for Roma.

(ERRC, 1999, Section 3:1)

They add:

Numerous Romani parents with their children in basic schools reported to the ERRC that schooling authorities had tried to pressure them into placing their children in special schools ... no Romani parents ... had been told in detail the consequences of putting their child into remedial schools ... none had been told that following an education in a remedial/special school their children would have almost no chance of lucrative employment.

(Section 4:1)

They conclude:

Often Roma are blamed for their situation. Blame is often formulated as 'linguistic handicap' or 'sociocultural disadvantage', a rhetorical device which generalises the discrimination faced by Roma away from them by portraying them as somehow inevitably located on the lower margins of an otherwise dynamic society. This permits the most insidious presentations of the school as a missionary outpost for Czech civilisation, desperately trying to save children from their barbarian families.

(Section 12)

However, some of these more positive developments are now being undermined. The move toward decentralisation allowed each municipality to decide its own attitude toward implementing the integration policy. This has resulted in inconsistency and lack of coverage across Czech municipalities. Local authorities are not bound by the Roma Integration Policy and so they can decide not to implement it. For example, the Mayor of Teplice has abolished the system of Roma deputies previously in place.

What is the European Roma Rights Centre?

The European Roma Rights Centre (ERRC) is an international public interest law organisation engaging in a range of activities aimed at combating anti-Romani racism and human rights abuse of Roma. The approach of the ERRC involves, in particular, strategic litigation, international advocacy, research and policy development, and human rights training of Romani activists. Since its establishment in 1996, the ERRC has endeavoured to give Roma the tools necessary to combat discrimination and win equal access to government, education, employment, health care, housing and public services. The ERRC works to combat prejudice and discrimination against Roma, and to promote genuine equality of treatment and equality of respect.

(European Roma Rights Centre, www.errc.org/, accessed 4/3/15)

Since the first edition of this book was published, an important case has come before the Czech courts which the ERRC reported in its 2008. They noted in their journal that the

ruling that the segregation of Romani students in special remedial schools is a form of unlawful discrimination. This momentous decision for Roma across Europe was made in the case D.H. and Others v. the Czech Republic (also known as the 'Ostrava Case').

The Court ruled that the disproportionate placement of Romani children in special remedial schools breaches Article 14 of the European Convention (prohibition of discrimination), taken together with Article 2 of Protocol No. 1 (right to education). The case was launched in 1998 by the European Roma Rights Centre on behalf of 18 Romani children from the industrial Czech city of Ostrava, in the Czech Republic.

(Roma Right Journal, November 2008, downloaded from www.errc.org/ roma-rights-journal/roma-rights-1-2008)

Local research

The research underpinning this discussion took place in Prague and Teplice during 2005/6 and was based on over 30 interviews and group discussions with social workers and the Roma. The initial outcomes included the following:

- There is a disparity between integration policy and social work professionals' views of Roma. There is some initial evidence that the professionals working with the Roma have a negative view of the potential of the Roma, which results in a pathologisation of the Roma that has striking similarities to that outlined above.

- Discrimination in the education system is still prevalent and may be getting worse. (ERRC et al., 2006, p37).

- High levels of unemployment remain.

- There is a gap between policy and practice. The reality for Roma is closer to notions of assimilation than integration.

However, in a similar way to Ireland, there are also clear signs of positive developments within the Roma community. For example, the Roma have established their own non-governmental organisation (Romodrom) that seeks to represent their interests in discussion with state and regional government bodies. Roma have also established their own internet radio station, Sdružení Dženo, and the Evangelická akademie Prague has been established, which trains Roma as pedagogues. From the interviews conducted with Roma it is clear that there is a definite commitment of individual Roma to change their and their families' circumstances. It appears that links with other Roma, through ERRC, will empower Roma internationally and a new indigenous leadership is growing, similar to the Travellers' movement in Ireland (see the discussion of Gramsci's notion of organic intellectuals in Chapter 3; Gramsci, 1971; and MacLaughlin's discussion of 'ethnic intelligentsia' above).

These developments suggest that there is significant scope, even within situations where discrimination may have been institutionalised for a considerable period, for people to engage with the processes of social change we described in earlier chapters. It is important to see marginalised peoples' struggle as an anti-racist one, not just a struggle for integration. However, the lessons of the Roma in the Czech Republic suggest that as social workers we need to move beyond approaches which pathologise people to recognise the potential of even the most marginalised people to initiate change.

Denmark

Background

The social work task in Denmark differs from the British and Irish experience in that *social ardgivers* (social advisers) carry a responsibility for 'gatekeeping' the financial needs of service users (Melhbye, 1993; Pringle, 1998). The Danish government has also, through its social development programme, put a great emphasis on prevention strategies (Ministry of Health, 1994). The *National Report on Strategies for Social Protection and Social Inclusion 2008–10* reported that *'a steadily greater share of the ... people in the low-income group have moved upwards in the income distribution and, therefore, withdrawn from the low-income group'* (Ministry of Social Welfare/Ministry of Health and Prevention, 2008, p8). It also argues that the governments' aim is to provide *'a strong foundation for an active civil society as a third sector which ... can contribute solutions to the challenges of the welfare society'* (p11).

As consequence of a focus on prevention, there has been a *'significant reduction in the number of children being removed from home over the past few decades'* (Harder, 1997; Pringle, 1998, p103). However, in those cases where a decision is made to compulsorily remove a child under the provisions of the Social Assistance Act, that decision is made by a social committee in each locality, consisting of three municipal politicians, one judge and one psychologist. This decision is only made when *'the child's welfare is at risk [and where] care outside their home [in a residential home or in family care], the offer of their own flat or enrolment in a continuation school etc., can be the most appropriate solution'* (Ministry of Social Affairs, 1995b, pp18–19). This contrasts sharply with the British and Irish systems, where the decision is made by the courts (Pringle, 1998). In fact, in contrast to the experience in Ireland and the Czech Republic, *'it remains a guiding principle that preventative social measures in Denmark be directed towards supporting the family, in such a way as to provide optimum conditions for the child's growth and development'* (Ministry of Social Affairs, 1995a, p66). However, the financial crisis also impacts on the Danish state. As the most recent national report on strategies for prevention says, any such strategy *'requires innovation and creativity in the public sector to make it possible to find an approach between citizen's expectations for the welfare society and the fact that recruiting more nurses, doctors, childhood educators and home help providers is not a viable option'* (Ministry of Social Welfare/Ministry of health and Prevention, 2008, p11).

Fridberg argued that in Denmark, *'during the 1990's children's issues have gradually become more visible in public discussions and a policy field of children's affairs is emerging'* (1998, p28). He concluded that the economic status of families with children is satisfactory, while acknowledging that they have on average a lower per capita income than families without children. He suggested that the worries in Denmark were not so much about children in poor families as about children in families who for some reason are not able to take reasonable care of their children, such as *'children in families affected by drug or alcohol abuse'* (p31). The Consolidation Act on Social Services 2004 continues to reflect this focus on prevention. The aims of the act are expressed as being to *'offer general services designed to serve as preventative measures'* and the object of the Act is to *'improve the capacity of the individual recipient to be self-reliant, or to facilitate his/her daily life and enhance the quality of life'* (Consolidation Act on Social Services, 2004).

While the Danish welfare state is relatively generous by the standards of the rest of Europe, there are still significant problems for minority communities who may not have become integrated into Danish society. This is particularly noticeable with young people who have become alienated from the school, welfare and social protection systems.

Octopussy (Blæksprutten, Avedøre, Copenhagen)

Octopussy is a project based in a flat in Avedøre , part of Hvidovre municipality in Copenhagen. The area has one of the largest concentrations of ethnic minorities in Copenhagen, estimated to be between 30 per cent and 40 per cent of the local population. The area is one of social housing which provides accommodation for approximately 5,600 people. Octopussy is part of the SSP initiative (school, social services, police) which seeks to provide services for young people who are disadvantaged and/or socially excluded. It works with a large number of ethnic minority young people, the majority of whom are Turkish or Pakistani in origin, although there are children attending the project from Germany and from other Scandinavian countries. The aim of the project is to provide a safe environment for young people, to recognise the various reasons they may not be currently attending local schools, and to seek to gain their reintegration into school. The project is headed by a Kurdish social pedagogue, the first non-Danish social pedagogue to qualify in Denmark. It employs five or six staff including social pedagogues, a teacher and a social adviser.

The project organises its work with the young people by concentrating resources on the most at-risk children, who are divided into A and B grades. The A group is the group with the greatest social needs, and the most intensive work is done with them. They are provided with resources to improve their integration to Danish society. The B group have a more tangential relationship to the project, using it as a drop-in centre.

The work of Octopussy has been chosen for discussion because it had an anti-racist agenda, although it did not specifically work with Gypsies or Roma, who are relatively rare in Scandinavia. The research involved interviewing five members of staff: four pedagogues and one teacher. (All quotes in this section are from interviews conducted in Denmark during 1998–2000.) At the time of the research one of the pedagogues was untrained but was due to undertake training soon. The others had qualified some time previously. The teacher had only been with the project since the end of the previous year. In addition I interviewed four young people. It was clear during my interviews with the workers in the project that they were acutely aware of issues of racism. They described the experiences many of the young people had had in other parts of Copenhagen.

The most obvious and systematic elements of racism were less present in the immediate surroundings as it was very much a multi-cultural area where there appears to be a great degree of tolerance between the different groups living there. However, they were acutely aware that the young people they worked with would often have very acute experiences of racism, which brought them into contact with the criminal justice system as well as schools and social services. The project leader was particularly committed to the notion of combating racism in the local area. He was aware from his own experiences of the difficulties non-Danish people could experience. He was currently trying to influence the education of pedagogues and social advisers so that racism became a much more integral part of the training curriculum.

All the young people interviewed recounted instances of racism that they had experienced on a fairly regular basis. They also made the point that they did not experience racism within Octopussy itself, or even within the geographical area in which Octopussy was based. However, it was a major problem in other parts of Copenhagen and they spoke of their concern about the activities of the Green Jackets, a neo-Nazi group of young people who had adopted skinhead motifs and who promoted the idea of Denmark being for Danes.

Clearly the project adopts an explicit anti-racist perspective in the work in which it engages. Its methodology combined both casework and groupwork approaches and is clearly predicated on the need to enhance the self-esteem and self-confidence of the young people using the project. It also recognises the need to tackle the broader causes of social exclusion. The workers involved are seeking to influence the training of social professionals within Denmark, and they are also involved through their union in promoting a commitment to anti-racism in Denmark.

The project leader pointed out that this is not always easy. Describing the experience of the young people he worked with, he says:

> We want to create a more stable life, give them more security, let them know that they may have trouble in their situation, but they have control of themselves and can be masters of their situation. From my own experience, and my family's experience, I have not experienced racism but the stories in the media make me think. I think the ethnic minorities and social society need to enter dialogue. They both need to know about each other. This may not take all the discrimination away but it may minimise it.

One of his colleagues saw this as a major challenge for Danish pedagogy. He said that 'when we treat them [the young people] as individuals we want to make them strong, to be able to stand up and say, "Yes, I am Turkish, I have my identity. I am Turkish and I am able to fight as a Turk and I am strong in my person and am able to stand up for that when I go out"'.

One of the project leaders at Blæksprutten described the difficulties people often face when they try to explain the nature of their difficulties to people in agencies, including social care agencies:

A woman is living with a man in a family together, he is violent towards her. Whenever it happens she goes to some social assistants who really pity her. They say 'I feel really sorry for you'. She says that is not what she needs. She needs someone to cry out and say 'do something about it. Rise up and do something yourself.' The system does not really handle the problem, we do not really involve ourselves, we just listen.

Another project leader of a different community project pointed to the need for agencies to work with both excluded and mainstream people. He suggested that:

There are many voluntary institutions working with people to take care of them, but there are no resources to take them on. That is what's special about us. We try to work with the excluded and the majority. We feel that if you want to integrate people in society you have to work with all groups.

The Octopussy Project

Octopussy was part of the SSP project, which describes its work in the following way:

The SSP-network is meant to complement and to improve the children and youth initiatives and actions run separately by the police, the school sector and the sports clubs.

Thus SSP-network is building network and cooperation between the sectors – school, police, social services and sport clubs – to strengthen their individual and collective capacity to identify and share notions, perspectives and agree on joint actions, efforts and solutions.

Some preventive efforts are not directly addressing crime issues, although they may have a positive impact. In this context, 'indirect efforts' should also be considered part of the crime prevention.

(http://ccpa.eu/what-we-do/sport-school-police/introduction/, accessed 4/3/15)

ACTIVITY 7.3

Taking one of the above countries as an example, map the social work activity described against the Professional Capability Framework or National Occupational Standards community work (see Chapter 3). Outline three ways in which the PCF or NOS outlined at the beginning of this chapter could be met by the type of intervention described. Evaluate how that might contribute to a change of focus within your own training.

Comment

You may wish to look at the web addresses below to gain a further insight into the issues discussed.

The above examples illustrate a diversity of practice but a common thread. They are predicated on the belief that even those people facing the most extreme forms of marginalisation and exclusion have the capacity to engage with processes of social change. They provide an important model of the forms of practice outlined in Chapters 2 and 3 and a way of establishing the legitimacy of social work and community work practice. (For more European examples, see Hatton, 2013.)

C H A P T E R S U M M A R Y

This chapter has sought to take forward the discussion in Chapter 6 of international approaches to social work, particularly pedagogy. It attempts to show how social work across Europe, while sharing common concerns, is often a product of the particular national context within which it develops. It shows how the managerial discourses which have had such a significant impact on UK social work, while providing challenges to social work in other countries, are not so embedded in day-to-day practice.

The chapter then looked at the experience of an innovative range of projects in Ireland, the Czech Republic and Denmark. The Irish project, the Traveller Visibility Group, seeks to promote the empowerment of Irish Travellers and to challenge negative media projections of Travellers. The Czech discussion highlights the way in which the Roma in the Czech Republic are reacting against the discrimination they face and developing their own analysis of their situation. Both examples highlight the potential for radical social and community action highlighted in Chapters 2 and 3 and demonstrate the way in which people facing significant marginalisation and disadvantage can develop their own indigenous leadership, what MacLaughlin has called an 'ethnic intelligentsia' and Gramsci described as 'organic intellectuals'. They can also be seen to demonstrate the way European traditions of social work can have relevance to current UK practice both in terms of the radical agenda and in the way they develop interactions with the people with whom they work – the pedagogy agenda.

The chapter concluded with a discussion of a project for disaffected young people in Denmark, Blæksprutten, or Octopussy, which seeks to reintegrate them into society. It demonstrates how the pedagogic principles outlined in Chapter 6 are implemented in practice.

WEBSITES

Ireland

Combat Poverty Agency: www.cpa.ie

Irish Traveller Movement: http://www.itmtrav.ie/

National Consultative Committee on Racism and Interculturalism: www.nccri.ie

Czech Republic

Roma in the Czech Republic: www.romove.radio.cz/en

Sdružení Dženo: www.dzeno.cz

Romodrom: http://www.romodromcz.cz/new/index.php

Denmark

Ministry of Social Affairs – www.sm.dk/en

Consolidation Act on Social Services, Act no. 1093 5 September 2013 – sm.dk/en/files/consolidation-act-on-social-services-1.pdf **downloaded 30/07/15**

Centre for Alternative Social Analysis - www.casa-analyse.dk

Other

Centre for the Study of Poverty and Social Justice: www.brisrol.ac/sps/research/centres/poverty

Information for Practice: www.nyu.edu/socialwork/ip

European Roma Rights Centre: www.errc.org

Chapter 8

Conclusion: New parameters for social work

The preceding chapters have sought to outline some of the key challenges, opportunities and threats facing social work today. We have examined the way in which issues of inclusion, inter-professionalism and internationalism have remained significant within social work's agenda. Yet these debates have themselves been shown to be problematic. *Inclusion*, while a key emphasis in virtually all new policy and legal developments in social work/social care/health and education (perhaps surprisingly given the Coalition's broader agenda) is a contested concept. Many people using services have raised issues about the adequacy of the frameworks developed to implement this inclusion agenda. They point to the way that inclusion is often framed as an agenda item by those who control the social work agenda. They ask, how real is this involvement? What resources are available to support inclusion processes? What processes of evaluation and accountability have been built in to ensure that inclusion is properly participatory and, perhaps, more importantly, how can people using services and their carers gain control of the resources and services to fully ensure that their needs are met?

These questions are particularly pertinent given other key policy agendas, which include ensuring the joined-up nature of services, most commonly through notions of *partnership, collaboration and inter-professional working*. While successive enquiries identified gaps in existing provision and pointed to the need for greater cooperation and understanding between services, this must not be at the expense of the participation and partnership arrangements developed with service users and carers. As argued in the first edition of this book, a clear danger of this increased inter-professional activity could be the further erosion of the power of the user of services (Warren, 2007, pp52–6). As indicated earlier, inclusion and inter-professionalism, without an acknowledgement of power differentials, are a mere tokenistic response to the problems we identify.

The themes identified in the introduction are clearer. They cross-cut with each other to give us the beginnings of a framework for understanding how social work may develop in the future. Earlier chapters examined the way debates around inclusion, inter-professionalism and internationalism remain key to the future direction of social work. The drive behind these initiatives may well come from discourses within the current social policy agenda and the attempt to regulate social work in such a way that its aim to achieve meaningful social change is marginalised. This is particularly true within a philosophy which promotes the acquisition of knowledge and skills within a framework driven by the regulatory and validation bodies (HCPC and TCSW). However, the same frameworks, if interpreted within a discourse which seeks to empower users and carers within social work services, provides an opportunity to promote the social change perspective that has been critical to the development of social work since its inception (Kendall, KA, 2000; see also Chapters 2 and 3). As the introduction pointed out, there are, however, significant challenges posed by more recent policy developments, including:

- Questions around the way we **perform** social work, the control and regulatory functions of what we do and the challenge of working creatively so that we enhance the wellbeing and potential of the people we work with (see also discussion of social pedagogy, Hatton, 2013).

- The overall silence **on notions of power** as reflected in the minimal attention given to users'/carers' role in social work education or practice within these discourses.

- Whether the focus on the enhanced professional status of social work as a profession disempowers people who use services (Tew, 2006).

- The silence about **hierarchical power relationships** in organisations: Will this new professional identity enable social workers to exercise control over their work? Or is managerialism so entrenched that this will not happen? Earlier chapters have suggested that social workers have a greater capacity to transform their practice than they often appreciate (see discussions on street-level bureaucracy and radical social and community work).

In the first edition the author noted that 'the inter-cutting themes of the book can now be seen to converge'. As noted in Chapter 5, different policy developments have promoted the idea of participation and inclusion, yet have done so in a way that is not always measurable. They may in fact not only appear to be tokenistic, but if placed within an analytical framework that seeks to evaluate service user/care involvement may actually be shown to be so.

In turn, debates around professionalism cannot be separated from debates around inter-professionalism. If the development of our professional identity is predicated on the development of processes of inclusion and ways of protecting ourselves vis-à-vis other emergent and established professionals (precisely the process we have argued against in the development of our own professional identity), how much more powerful are these processes when we link with other professionals?

The final part of the equation occurs when we talk about partnership. Clearly this is not the same as inter-professionalism in that it suggests equality between partners and may occur at a range of levels – between agencies, agencies and service users/ carers, across networks and so on. However it occurs, how much can this notion of partnership be enhanced if we begin to engage with social workers in other countries, from whose traditions we can learn and with whom we can share elements of our best practice?

These potential points of connection can provide a possible framework for a new form of social work practice. The remainder of this chapter seeks to map out the way this may occur. Figure 8.1 illustrates how these processes occur and how they intersect with each other. The diagonal boxes show the interrelationships of the key factors; for example, the downward-facing triangle shows the relationship between the key themes in current social work of inter-professionalism and internationalism and that, if they are to be effective, they need to be underpinned by processes of inclusion. Instead of enhancing the power of social workers by making their decision making even more remote from the experience of people who use social work services, they are then grounded in the day-to-day reality of service users and carers. Such an inversion of the 'normal' relationships in social work helps to ensure its relevance to current societal developments. The discussion around discretion in the debate around street-level bureaucracy in Chapter 1 explores some of these tensions.

The upward-facing triangle reflects the underpinning issues that help achieve this goal. Partnership is integral to developing models of inclusion. Properly understood, it does not mean the enhancement of the effectiveness of the professional but has more to do with creating conditions of equality so that each partner's contribution is regarded as of equal value. Participation suggests that this process of partnership is active and is based on engagement and the empowerment of all people using social work services. This does not mean rejecting current moves to professionalise or re-professionalise social work, but it does mean developing new concepts of professionalism grounded in participation and partnership. It therefore suggests a model of professional practice that is reflexive, responsive and open and which does not use professionalism as a way to exclude either other professionals or service users and carers. This suggests that it is possible to develop a model of professional practice that, while conscious of the need to ensure standards of good practice, is also accountable, not just to other social workers but also to those who use social work services. Dominelli has called this the *'politics of practice'*, a process through which

> *social workers engage with others in activities that will change inegalitarian social relations ... [and will involve] ... recognition, representation and redistribution of resources.*

> (2010, pp172–3)

She argues that recognition *'focuses on the strengths of the people with whom practitioners work'*. Representation *'is about helping individuals and communities to represent their views and aspirations to power holders and decision-makers and lobbying them to eradicate exclusionary practices'*. Redistribution is about facilitating the fairer distribution of resources (Dominelli, 2010, p172–3).

These two sets of relationships – *internationalism, inter-professionalism and inclusion* and *professionalism, participation and partnership* – are based on a conception of power that is multi-faceted and which not only seeks to understand how power operates and influences social workers and those who use services, but also how power can be used to challenge inequality and disadvantage and promote more equitable social relationships. A central element in any newly configured social work is then about both recognising the power we have and wherever possible seeking to share it with the people with whom we work. A key task for social work is therefore the creation of an empowered and active group of service users and carers who hold us to account, share in our decision making and participate actively in the way we deliver our services. We need to re-conceptualise how we see professionalism. This book suggests that we need to move beyond formulaic and credentialist forms of professionalism and create a new democratic accountable professionalism (DAP).

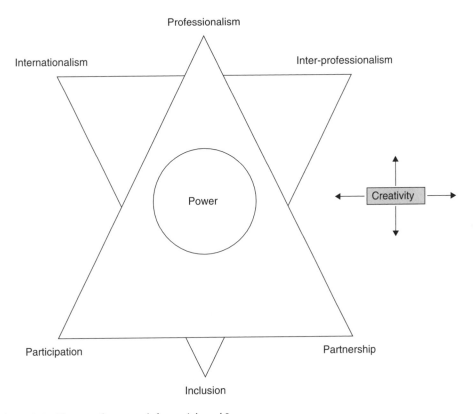

Figure 8.1   *The new framework for social work?*

The earlier chapters have provided some indications of how these processes can occur. Chapter 1 looked at models of policy analysis and asked how they reflected contemporary social work. Superficially the pluralist view seemed to suggest that power could be gained by well-organised groups while the structuralist argument appears to foreclose action to redress inequality because of the powerful interests currently wielding power and the unlikelihood of them relinquishing it. The book has sought to demonstrate that neither model provides a full account of the way we can achieve change as social workers. Indeed, the benefit of current developments around choice, control and independence may well be that we no longer see the acquisition of power as beyond our abilities or aspirations but as something attainable through the promotion of our own self-activity and that of the people we work with. The discussion of street-level bureaucracy suggested that, at a micro-level, we already exercise more power than we sometimes recognise through our use of discretion. It points to the way that this discretion can be either used positively to improve the lives of the people we work with or negatively to support organisational and policy imperatives imposed from above. Our understanding of, and ability to use power are key determinants in the outcomes of our interventions.

Chapters 2 and 3 took this analysis forward, arguing that social work has a rich tradition on which it should draw to revitalise its practice. Radical social and community work demonstrate how a focus on wider social structures can complement work at the individual level. Chapter 3 in particular shows how the core values of social work and community work share a common concern with tackling discrimination and promoting empowerment.

As a social work educator, the author is often told by qualifying and post-qualifying students that it is not possible to practise in any way other than through an instrumental and managerialist perspective within the statutory sector. Leaving aside the argument that this suggests a degree of control over social work by agencies of which even the Stasi would have been proud (and which is contradicted by earlier analysis in the book), it also denies the possibility that social workers can themselves be active change agents. It is almost as if empowerment is something that happens to others but not something to which we can aspire. Hopefully the lesson of this book is that it is possible to negotiate space to achieve such change. Indeed, Foucault has suggested that *'all of my investigations rest on a postulate of absolute optimism'* (Foucault, 1981, p174). He added that *'the problems I pose are always concerned with local and particular issues'* (p150). By analysing power, he suggests, *'those who are inserted in certain relations of power, who are implicated in them, might escape them through their actions of resistance and rebellion, might transform them in order not* to *be subjugated any longer'* (p174).

A useful counterpoint to the conservatism in some UK practice is provided by examples from the international arena. Rowe et al. (2000) interviewed 45 social workers from throughout the world, affiliated to the International Federation of Social Workers (IFSW). They found that for *'the majority of respondents and especially for those practising in developing countries, participation and empowerment were essential components of social and community development'* (p68). Their respondents mention women's rights, HIV/AIDS, child welfare, community development, disability and environmental degradation as issues with which it was possible to transcend national borders and develop new forms of practice.

Chapter 4 showed how these pressures towards a more conservative form of practice are not peculiar to statutory social work but are also present in the voluntary or third sector. It notes the changed terms of debate since the election of the Coalition government in 2010, particularly the focus on the 'Big Society', localism and social action. However, it demonstrates continuities with the previous governments' emphasis on communitarianism and the continual focus on neo-liberalism and the reduction of the role of the state. It seeks to show that agencies can resist these constraints and develop ways of working that are enabling and empowering.

It also suggests that we should be challenging the paradigms of those seeking to control the social work and wider welfare agenda by using Foucault's idea of reverse discourse to establish a radical agenda for social work, which suggests a transformative form of practice is possible.

Chapter 5 looked at how one response to these issues has continued to gain prominence. The involvement of service users and carers (or experts by experience) in social work is now at the core of all policy and legislative developments. This can present another set of problems – how can we be sure that any involvement that is developed is real and not merely tokenistic? The chapter suggests a model of participation and inclusion which places service users and carers in control of the interventions with which they are engaged. It introduces into the discussion the more widely developed concepts of personalisation and co-production. It develops Arnstein's model of participation through the integration of more complex analyses of power than that provided in Arnstein's analyses, and provides a clearer focus on the capacity and agency of people using social work services.

Chapters 6 and 7 then sought to suggest the importance of looking outside the UK for models with which we could take forward our own practices. These chapters argued that this is a reciprocal process but that we can learn a great deal from engaging with ideas from elsewhere. In particular, work by the Thomas Coram Research Unit, supported by the Department for Education and Skills and the Department of Health, looking at the relevance of social pedagogy to work with children and young people, provides an opportunity to consider ways in which our own practice can be revitalised. Chapter 6 develops the earlier book's discussion of social pedagogy, through a focus on the work of European writers on social pedagogy and with reference to the author's other published work, and focuses on the importance of creativity in social pedagogic discourses. Chapter 7 builds on these discussions by focusing on an updated analysis of social work in three European countries: Ireland, the Czech Republic and Denmark. This discussion provides useful examples of a more engaged form of practice in which service users not only develop their own organisations but form their own leadership and challenge traditional relationships between professionals and people using services. Their example indicates that the way we relate to people using services is in its infancy and that only when we begin to cede control of services to those using them will we be able to claim that we now have real, accountable and person-centred social and community services.

This final chapter seeks to bring the overall analysis together and asks how we can make our practice more relevant to the concerns of people who use services. The discussion of the 'common third' in Chapter 6 suggests a means of doing this. The common third is based on the idea of social workers/social pedagogues coming to situations as partners and creating, through music, drama and so on, a joint activity in which neither is the expert and in which each makes an equal contribution. The purpose is to develop the self-esteem and self-confidence of the person using the service so that they can take that new self-belief forward into other areas of their lives and become fully empowered citizens. Central to this approach is the notion of creativity, which we referred to throughout the book. The reintroduction of creativity into both the academic curricula and the practice environment is an important means of taking social work forward and reclaiming the traditions that placed person-centred, humanistic practice and social change at the top of the social work agenda. The model therefore places creativity as a core activity in the new social work framework. This creativity, however, is as important at the mezzo and macro levels as it can suggest new ways of transforming social professional (social work, community work, youth work) practice so that we can both 'imagine' and 'build' new ways of working that prefigure an alternative form of theory and practice.

It also begins to raise wider questions about how we can begin to tackle the broader structural oppression people who use and work in services face. This means rejecting the idea that the organisations we work in, or receive services from, are monolithic. We need to find the space in our organisations to pursue more radical policies. This means creating alliances beyond our immediate occupational spaces with other groupings – community organisations, single issue groups, those campaigning around difference and diversity, those in health, education, youth and community work, the trade unions – to create alliances which can generate an approach which struggles against and provides an alternative to the austerity agenda.

In addition to the range of factors outlined above we have to factor in poverty, privatisation and profit as countervailing forces which we need to produce alternatives to. This means thinking about how we receive and deliver our services (co-production and co-operatives), how we work together (socially and collectively) and how we oppose policies we disagree with (energetically and with critical awareness). Passivity does not work, as demonstrated by the demise of the College of Social Work. To paraphrase Gramsci (and as was echoed by Foucault), we need to have both *'pessimism of the intellect and optimism of the will'* to be either a person who uses or works in social or welfare services. If we want to shape a new, more egalitarian, future we will need both.

Generating optimism – Examples of creative social work at the University of Portsmouth

- **Create a group** – of service users/carers, students and staff from the Centre for Social work and the School of Creative and Performing Arts who work together to produce scenarios that illustrate the experience of people using social work services.

- **Creative workshops** – have been running since 2007. They are produced in partnership with the Social Work Inclusion Group, students (UK and international) and academic staff.

- **Curriculum** – at undergraduate level the exploration of issues of identity, difference and discrimination through creative activity. At postgraduate level the development of two units where the assessment is based on the production of creative artefacts such as performance, music, creative writing, poetry and so on.

- **Forum Theatre** – using theatre is a creative art form (Boal, 1998; Shah, 2006). The practitioner/social worker/social pedagogue works in a way that allows the audience to 'stop', 'rewind' and influence the direction of the performance. This methodology has the advantage of utilising creativity and providing a safe environment in which to make mistakes. The social work student is expected to demonstrate a cognitive flexibility that allows the gathering and analysis of multiple data types in a practice setting. This ability to reflect in action can be considered as one of principal tenets of the Critical Reflection and Analysis section of the TCSW's PCF. The challenge in social work education is to equip the student social worker not only with the theoretical models by which to do this but also with the practice experience of reflection in action. Forum Theatre presents the opportunity to Social Work Educators to engage students and service users in high-risk scenarios and to explore the possible pathways down which that may evolve. However, where it is potentially most powerful is as a teaching tool in providing a relatively risk-free environment in which to demonstrate and apply reflection in action. This method fits within the Portsmouth philosophy of engagement and inclusion and has been used with both undergraduate and post-graduate students.

- **The Black & White Project** – sees MSc students form partnerships with local service user groups to co-produce an audio visual presentation based around eight black and white photographs. The audio visual presentation is accompanied with a written reflective diary of the process. This form of direct co-production allows the student to apply recently learned theory relating to group working, empowerment and co-production itself and to explore the practicalities of the process. Critical to the process are the development of professional relationships with service users and the application of the principle of the common third.

Two short excerpts from the work of the Creative Writing Group at Portsmouth illustrate the core themes of the book:

See us as people, not just as a case

Others are just as important

Come, learn what we have to say

I am the expert on my case

Authority and power should come from us

Listen!

Work with us

Our experiences are very valuable

Respect goes both ways

Knowledge is not just academic

(Creative Writing Working Party, Summer 2006)

Method

Take one Social Services Department.

Add a good SWIG of service users and carers and a promising mix of students.

Mix well and brew slowly for three years.

Leave open for experience.

(Creative Writing Working Party, Summer 2006)

Appendix 1
Professional Capabilities Framework

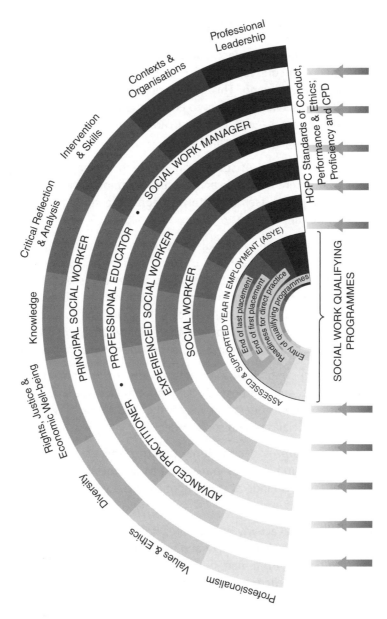

(Reproduced with kind permission of The College of Social Work)

Appendix 2

Subject Benchmark for Social Work

Defining principles (QAA, 2008)

4.1 As an applied academic subject, social work is characterised by a distinctive focus on practice in complex social situations to promote and protect individual and collective wellbeing. This underscores the importance of partnerships between HEIs and service providers to ensure the full involvement of practitioners, managers, tutors, service users and carers with students in both academic and practice learning and assessment.

4.3 Contemporary definitions of social work as a degree subject reflect its origins in a range of different academic and practice traditions. The precise nature and scope of the subject is itself a matter for legitimate study and critical debate. Three main issues are relevant to this:

- Social work is located within different social welfare contexts. Within the UK there are different traditions of social welfare (influenced by legislation, historical development and social attitudes) and these have shaped both social work education and practice in community-based settings including residential, day care and substitute care. In an international context, distinctive national approaches to social welfare policy, provision and practice have greatly influenced the focus and content of social work degree programmes.

- There are competing views in society at large on the nature of social work and on its place and purpose. Social work practice and education inevitably reflect these differing perspectives on the role of social work in relation to social justice, social care and social order.

- Social work, both as occupational practice and as an academic subject, evolves, adapts and changes in response to the social, political and economic challenges and demands of contemporary social welfare policy, practice and legislation.

4.6 Social work is a moral activity that requires practitioners to recognise the dignity of the individual, but also to make and implement difficult decisions (including restriction of liberty) in human situations that involve the potential for benefit or harm. Honours degree programmes in social work therefore involve the study, application of, and critical reflection upon, ethical principles and dilemmas. As reflected by the four care councils' codes of practice, this involves showing respect for persons, honouring the diverse and distinctive organisations and communities that make up contemporary society, promoting social justice and combating processes that lead to discrimination, marginalisation and social exclusion. This means that honours undergraduates must learn to:

- recognise and work with the powerful links between intrapersonal and inter-personal factors and the wider social, legal, economic, political and cultural context of people's lives;

- understand the impact of injustice, social inequalities and oppressive social relations;

- challenge constructively individual, institutional and structural discrimination;

- practise in ways that maximise safety and effectiveness in situations of uncertainty and incomplete information;

- help people to gain, regain or maintain control of their own affairs, in so far as this is compatible with their own or others' safety, wellbeing and rights;

- work in partnership with service users and carers and other professionals to foster dignity, choice and independence, and effect change.

4.7 The expectation that social workers will be able to act effectively in such complex circumstances requires that honours degree programmes in social work should be designed to help students learn to become accountable, reflective, critical and evaluative. This involves learning to:

- think critically about the complex social, legal, economic, political and cultural contexts in which social work practice is located;

- work in a transparent and responsible way, balancing autonomy with complex, multiple and sometimes contradictory accountabilities (for example, to different service users, employing agencies, professional bodies and the wider society);

- exercise authority within complex frameworks of accountability and ethical and legal boundaries;

- acquire and apply the habits of critical reflection, self-evaluation and consultation, and make appropriate use of research in decision making about practice and in the evaluation of outcomes.

References

Aabro, C. (2004) *The Common Third*. Written correspondence with author.

Abbott, P. and Wallace, C. (1990) *An Introduction to Sociology: Feminist Perspectives*. London: Routledge.

Abrahamson, P. (1997) 'Combating poverty and social exclusion in Europe', in W. Beck, L. van der Maesen and A. Walker (eds), *The Social Quality of Europe*. Bristol: The Policy Press.

Ackerson, B.J. and Harrison, D. (2000) 'Practitioners' perceptions of empowerment', *Families in Society: The Journal of Contemporary Human Services*, 81 (3): 238–45.

Adams, A. Erath, P. and Shardlow, S. (2000) *Fundamentals of Social Work in Selected European Countries*. Lyme Regis: Russell House Publishing.

Adams, A. Erath, P. and Shardlow, S (2001) *Key themes in European Social Work: Theory, practice and perspectives*. Lyme Regis, Russell House Publishing.

Adams, R. (2008) *Empowerment, Participation and Social Work*, 4th edn. Basingstoke: Palgrave Macmillan.

Adams, R., Dominelli, L. and Payne, M. (2005*) Social Work Futures: Crossing Boundaries, Transforming Practice*. Basingstoke: Palgrave Macmillan.

Ahmad, B. (1990*) Black Perspectives in Social Work*. Birmingham: Venture Press.

AIEJI (2010) *The Profession of Social Education in Europe: Comparative Survey*. Barcelona: Consejo General de Colegios de Educadoras y Educadores Sociales.

Alcock, P. (2012) *The Big Society: A New Policy Environment for the Third Sector*, Third Sector Research Centre, Working Paper 82. Birmingham: University of Birmingham.

Alden, S. (2014) 'Discretion on the frontline: The street-level bureaucrat in English statutory homelessness services', *Social Policy and Society*, 14 (1): 63–77.

Alinsky, S. (1971*) Rules for Radicals*. New York: Random House.

Allman, P. (2001) *Revolutionary Social Transformation: Democratic Hopes, Political Possibilities and Critical Education*. Westport, CT: Bergin and Garvey.

Aluffi-Pentini, A. and Lorenz, W. (1996) *Anti-Racist Work with Young People: European Experiences and Approaches*. Lyme Regis: Russell House.

Aniagolu, C. (1997) 'Being black in Ireland', in E. Crowley and J. MacLaughlin (eds) *Under the Belly of the Tiger: Class, Race, Identity and Culture in the Global Ireland*. Dublin: Irish Reporter Publications.

Arnstein, S. (1969) 'A ladder of citizen participation', *Journal of the American Institute of Planners*, 35 (4), 214–24.

Aspis, S. (1997) 'Self-advocacy for people with learning difficulties; does it have a future?', *Disability and Society*, 12 (4), 647–54.

Aspis, S. (2002) 'Self-advocacy: Vested interests and misunderstandings', *British Journal of Learning Disabilities*, 30: 3–7.

Association of Chief Executives of Voluntary Organisations (ACEVO) (2014) '*Remaking the State' Commission Report*. London: ACEVO. Available from www.acevo.org.uk/news/acevo-commission-chaired-will-hutton-and-rob-owen-tackle-'care-deficit'-public-services (accessed 30/07/15).

ATD Fourth World (2005) *Getting the Right Trainers: Enabling Service Users to Train Social Work Students and Practitioners about the Reality of Family Poverty in the UK.* London: ATD Fourth World.

Atkinson, D. (1999) *Advocacy: A Review.* York: Joseph Rowntree Foundation.

Avramov, D. (1997) 'Homelessness in the European Union: Changes and continuities', in D. Avramov (ed.), *Youth Homelessness in the European Union.* Brussels: FEANTSA.

Bailey, R. and Brake, M. (eds) (1975) *Radical Social Work.* London: Edward Arnold.

Bailey, R. and Brake, M. (1980) 'Contributions to a radical practice in social work', in M. Brake and R. Bailey (eds), *Radical Social Work and Practice.* London: Edward Arnold.

Baistow, K. (1994) 'Liberation and regulation? Some paradoxes of empowerment', *Critical Social Policy*, 14 (3): 34–46.

Bamfield, L. (2005) Making the public case for tackling poverty and inequality, Poverty, no 121, Child Poverty Action Group.

Barnard, H. and Turner, C. (2011) *Poverty and Ethnicity: A Review of the Evidence.* York: Joseph Rowntree Foundation.

Barry, M. (1998) 'Social exclusion and social work: An introduction', in M. Barry and C. Hallett (eds), *Social Exclusion and Social Work: Issues of Theory, Policy and Practice.* Lyme Regis: Russell House.

Barry, M. and Hallett, C. (eds) (1998) *Social Exclusion and Social Work: Issues of Theory, Policy and Practice.* Lyme Regis: Russell House.

Bateman, N. (2006) *Practising Welfare Rights.* London: Routledge/Community Care.

Bauman, Z. (2001) *Community-seeking Safety in an Insecure World.* Cambridge: Polity Press.

Bennett, F. and Roberts, M. (2004) *From Input to Influence: Participatory Approaches to Research and Inquiry into Poverty.* York: Joseph Rowntree Foundation.

Benwell Community Development Project (1974) *Final Report.* London: HMSO.

Beresford, P. (1996) 'Challenging the "them" and "us" of social policy research', in H. Dean (ed.), *Ethics and Social Policy Research.* Bedfordshire: University of Luton Press/Social Policy Association.

Beresford, P. (2013) 'Service user issues: Rights, needs and responsibilities', in B. Littlechild and R. Smith (eds), *A Handbook for InterProfessional Practice in the Human Services: Learning to Work Together.* Harlow: Pearson.

Beresford, P. and Campbell, J. (1994) 'Disabled people, service users, user involvement and representation', *Disability and Society*, 9 (3): 315–24.

Beresford, P. and Croft, S. (1993) *Citizen Involvement: A Practical Guide.* Basingstoke: Macmillan.

Beresford, P. and Croft, S. (1995) 'It's our problem too: Challenging the exclusion of poor people from poverty discourse', *Critical Social Policy*, 44/45.

Beresford, P. and Hoban, M. (2005) *Participation in Anti-poverty and Regeneration Work and Research: Overcoming Barriers and Creating Opportunities.* York: Joseph Rowntree Foundation.

Beresford, P. and Holden, C. (2000) 'We have choices: Globalisation and welfare user movements', *Disability and Society,* 15 (7): 973–89.

Beresford, P., Green, D., Lister, R. and Woodward, K. (1999) *Poverty First Hand: Poor People Speak for Themselves.* London: Child Poverty Action Group.

Berridge, D., Biehal, N., Lutman, L. and Palamores, M. (2011) *Raising the Bar? Evaluation of the Social Pedgogy Pilot Programme in Residential Children's Homes,* Research Report DFE-RR 148. London: Department of Education.

Berry, J.W., Pootinga, Y.H., Segall, M.H. and Dasen, P.R. (2002) *Cross Cultural Psychology: Research and Applications*, 2nd edn. Cambridge: Cambridge University Press.

Berry, L., Cannan, C. and Lyons, K. (1992) *Social Work in Europe*. Basingstoke: Macmillan.

Boal, A. (1998) *Legislative Theatre: Using Performance to Make Politics*. London: Routledge.

Boddy, J., Cameron, C., Hepinstall. E., McQuail, S. and Petrie, P. (2003) *Working with Children: Social Pedagogy and Residential Child Care in Europe (Draft Report)*. London: Department of Health.

Boddy, J., Cameron, C., Moss, P., Mooney, A., Petrie, P. and Statham, J. (2005) *Introducing Pedagogy into the Children's Workforce: Children's Workforce Strategy: A Response to the Consultation Document*. London: Thomas Coram Research Unit.

Bolger, S., Corrigan, P., Docking, J. and Frost, N. (1981) *Towards Socialist Welfare Work*. Basingstoke: Macmillan.

Borghill, L. (2004) 'The empowerment of young people at risk through sport and outdoor activities'. Unpublished undergraduate dissertation, Portsmouth University.

Bown, K. (2004) 'Involving young people in research – some reflections'. Paper presented to the PIMHS Research Group, University of Portsmouth.

Boylan, J. and Ing, P. (2005) '"Seen but not heard" – young people's experience of advocacy', *International Journal of Social Welfare*, 14: 2–12.

Brah, A. (1992) 'Difference, diversity and differentiation', in J. Donald and A. Rattansi (eds), *'Race', Culture and Difference*. London: SAGE/Open University.

Brake, M. and Bailey, R. (eds) (1980) *Radical Social Work and Practice*. London: Edward Arnold.

Brammer, A. (2010) *Social Work Law*. Oxford: Oxford University Press.

Braye, S. (2000) 'Participation and involvement in social care', in H. Kemshall and R. Littlechild (eds), *User Involvement and Participation in Social Care: Research Informing Practice*. London: Jessica Kingsley.

Brayne, H. and Carr, H. (2013) *Law for Social Workers*, 12th edn. Harlow: Pearson Education.

Breen, C. (2008) 'The policy of direct provision in Ireland: a violation of asylum seekers' right to an adequate standard of housing', *International Journal of Refugee Law*, 20 (4): 611–636.

Brueggemann, W.G. (2006) *The Practice of Macro Social Work*, 3rd edn. Belmont, CA: Thomson Brooks/Cole.

Buckley, H., Skehill, C. and O'Sullivan, E. (1997) *Child Protection Practices in Ireland: A Case Study*. Dublin: Oak Tree Press.

Burns, D., Hambleton, R. and Hoggett, P. (1994) *The Politics of Decentralisation: Revitalising Local Democracy*. Basingstoke: Macmillan.

Burr, V. (1995) *An Introduction to Social Constructionism*. London: Routledge.

Byers, C. and Creating Links (2013a) 'Member of the team? Carers' experience of interprofessional working: key issues in current policy and practice', in B. Littlechild and R. Smith (eds), *A Handbook for InterProfessional Practice in the Human Services: Learning to Work Together*. Harlow: Pearson.

Byers, C. and Creating Links (2013b) 'The barriers presented by power, control and agency agendas on carer participation in interprofessional working: promoting inclusionary practice', in B. Littlechild and R. Smith (eds), *A Handbook for InterProfessional Practice in the Human Services: Learning to Work Together*. Harlow: Pearson.

Byrne, D. (1999) *Social Exclusion*. Buckingham: Open University Press.

Cabinet Office and HM Treasury (2006) *The Future Role of the Third Sector in Social and Economic Regeneration: Interim Report*. London: HMSO.

Callan, T. and Nolan, B. (1994) 'Income poverty in Ireland', in B. Nolan and T. Callan (eds) *Poverty and Policy in Ireland*. Dublin: Gill and Macmillan.

Callan, T., Nolan, B., Whelan, B.J., Whelan, C.T. and Williams, J. (1996) *Poverty in the 1990s: Evidence from the Living in Ireland Survey*. Dublin: Oak Tree Press.

Cameron, C. (2004) 'Social pedagogy and care: Danish and German practice in young people's residential care', *Journal of Social Work*, 4 (2): 133–51.

Cameron, C., McQuail, S. and Petrie, P. (2007) *Implementing the Social Pedagogic Approach for Work Force Training and Education in England: A Preliminary Study*. London: Thomas Coram Research Unit.

Cameron, C., Petrie, P., Wigfall, V., Kleipoedszus, S. and Jasper, A. (2011) *Final report of the Social Pedagogy Pilot Project: Development and Implementation*. London: Thomas Coram research Unit/Institute of Education, University of London.

Campbell, J. and McColgan, M. (2002) 'Social work in Northern Ireland', in M. Payne and S. Shardlow (eds), *Social Work in the British Isles*. London: Jessica Kingsley.

Campbell, J. and Oliver, M. (1996) *Disability Politics: Understanding Our Past, Changing Our Future*. Basingstoke: Macmillan.

Carr, S. (2004) *Has Service User Participation Made a Difference to Social Care Services?* Position Paper No 3. London: Social Care Institute of Excellence.

Carrington, D. (2002) *The Compact – the Challenge of Implementation*. London: Active Community Unit, Home Office.

Casey, L. A. (2012) *Listening to Troubled Families: A Report to the Department for Communities and Local Government*. London: Department for Communities and Local Government.

Cassell, P. (1993) *The Giddens Reader*. Basingstoke: Macmillan.

Castells, M. (2000*) End of the Millenium*. Chichester: Wiley.

Centre for Enterprise and Economic Development Research (CEEDR) (2001) *Final Report to the Small Business Service*. London: Middlesex University Business School.

Chambers, H. (2004) *Creative Arts and Play for the Well-being of Looked After Children*, Highlight no. 212. London: National Children's Bureau.

Charity Commission (2007) *Stand and Deliver: The Future for Charities Providing Public Services*. Liverpool: Charity Commission.

Children's Rights Alliance and National Youth Council of Ireland (2002) *Hearing Young Voices*. Dublin: The Open Your Eyes to Child Poverty Initiative. Available from www.youth.ie/sites/youth.ie/files/Hearing YoungVoices-Full.pdf (accessed 16/2/15).

Chouan, K., Esmail, U., Joseph, J., Mathal, K. and Modayil, J. (1996) *Anti-racism and Black Experiences and Approaches*. Lyme Regis: Russell House.

Christie, A. (2003) 'Unsettling the "social" in social work: Responses to asylum-seeking children in Ireland', *Child and Family Social Work*, 8: 223–31.

Chytil, O. (1998) 'Social work in the Czech Republic', *Social Work in Europe*, 5 (3): 48–55.

Chytil, O. and Popelkova, R. (2000) 'Social policy and social work in the Czech Republic', in A. Adams, P. Erath and S. Shardlow (eds), *Key Themes in European Social Work: Theory, Practice, Perspectives*. Lyme Regis: Russell House.

Clarke, J., Langan, M. and Williams, F. (2001) 'Remaking welfare: The British welfare regime in the 1980s and 1990s', in A. Cochrane, J. Clarke and S. Gewirtz (eds), *Comparing Welfare States,* 2nd edn. London: SAGE/Open University.

Cohen, S. (1975) 'It's all right to talk: Political and sociological manifestos for Social Work Action', in M. Brake and R. Bailey (eds), *Radical Social Work and Practice*. London: Edward Arnold.

Commission for Social Care Inspection (2005) *Making Every Child Matter.* Newcastle: Office of the Children's Rights Inspector.

Commission for Social Care Inspection (2006a) *Real Voices, Real Choices.* Newcastle: Office of the Children's Rights Inspector.

Commission for Social Care Inspection (2006b) *Young People's Views on Leaving Care.* Newcastle: Office of the Children's Rights Inspector.

Commission for Social Care Inspection (2007) *Care Matters: Children's Views on the Government Green Paper.* Newcastle: Office of the Children's Rights Inspector.

Community Development Projects (1974) *Inter-project Report.* London: HMSO.

Community Development Projects (1977) *Gilding the Ghetto.* London: HMSO.

Consolidation Act on Social Services Act no. 1093 5 September 2013 (CASS) Ministry of Social Affairs, Copenhagen, Denmark. available at sm.dk/en/files/consolidation-act-on social-services-1.pdf

Coote, A. (2011) *The 'Big Society' and the New Austerity.* London: New Economics Foundation.

Corkey, D. and Craig, C. (1978) 'CDP: Community work and class politics', in P. Corno (ed.), *Political Issues in Community Work.* London: Routledge & Kegan Paul.

Cornwell, N. (1994) 'Social work education and practice sans frontiers', *Issues in Social Work Education*, 14: 1.

Corrigan, P. and Leonard, P. (1978) *Social Work Under Capitalism.* Basingstoke: Macmillan.

Coulshed, V. and Orme, J. (2012) *Social Work Practice*, 5th edn. Basingstoke: Palgrave Macmillan.

Council of Europe (2003) *Report by Mr Alvaro Gil-Robles, Commissioner for Human Rights on his visit to the Czech Republic, 24 – 26 February*, CommDH (2003)10.

Council of Europe (2004) *Final Report of the Activity Carried out in 2003–2004.* European Committee for Social Cohesion (CDCS), Group of specialists on User Involvement in Social Services and Integrated Social Services Delivery (CS-US). Strasbourg: Council of Europe.

Courtiox, M. and Davies Jones, H. (1984) *Socialpedagog I Europa.* Denmark: Fédération Internationale des Communautés d'Enfants.

Cowden, S. and Singh, G. (2009) 'The social worker as intellectual', *European Journal of Social Work*, 12 (4): 479–93.

Craig, G. and Mayo, M. (1995) *Community Empowerment: A Reader in Participation and Development.* London: Zed Books.

Craig, G., Gorman, M. and Vercseg, I. (2004) 'The Budapest Declaration: Building civil society through community development', *Community Development Journal*, 39 (40): 423–9.

Craig, G., Taylor, M. and Parker, T. (2004) 'Protest or partnership? The voluntary and community sectors in the policy process', *Social Policy and Administration*, 38 (3): 221–31.

Creative Writing Working Party (2006) *Poems from the Creative Writing Working Party.* Portsmouth: University of Portsmouth.

Croft, S. and Beresford, P. (1998) 'Postmodernity and the future of welfare: Whose critiques, whose social policy?', in J. Carter (ed.), *Post-modernity and the Fragmentation of Welfare.* London: Routledge.

Croisedale-Appleby, D. (2014) *Re-visioning Social Work: An Independent Review.* London: Department of Health.

Crouch, C. (1999) *Social Change in Western Europe.* Oxford: Oxford University Press.

Cullen, P. (2000) *Refugees and Asylum Seekers in Ireland.* Cork: Cork University Press.

Curno, A. (1982) *Women in Collective Action*. London: Routledge & Kegan Paul.

Dalrymple, J. (2004) 'Developing the concept of professional advocacy: An examination of the role of child youth advocates in England and Wales', *Journal* of *Social Work*, 4 (2): 179–97.

Dalrymple, J. and Boylan, J. (2013) *Effective Advocacy in Social Work*. London: SAGE.

Dalrymple, J. and Burke, B. (2006) *Anti-oppressive Practice*, 2nd edn. Maidenhead: Open University Press.

Davies Jones, H. (1984) Socialpedagogens arbejde I dagens samfund, in M. Courtiox (ed.) *Socialpedagog I Europa*. Denmark: Fédération Internationale des Communautés d'Enfants.

Davis, A. and Wainwright, S. (2005) 'Combating poverty and social exclusion: Implications for social work education', *Social Work Education,* 24 (3): 259–73.

Dawson, P. and Palmer, W. (1993) *Taking Self-advocacy Seriously*. Nottingham: EMFEC.

Day, G. (2006) *Community and Everyday Life*. London: Routledge.

Delanty, G. and Strydom, P. (eds) (2003) *Philosophies of Social Science: The Classic and Contemporary Readings*. Buckingham: Open University Press.

Department for Communities and Local Government (2012/2014) *Helping Troubled Families Turn Their Lives Around*. Available from www.gov.uk/government/policies/helping-troubled-families-turn-their-lives-around (accessed 16/2/15).

Department for Education (2012) *Newly Qualified Social Worker Programme Final Evaluation Report (2008 to 2011)*. London: Department for Education.

Department for Education (2014) *Knowledge and Skills for Child and Family Social Work*. London: Department for Education.

Department for Education and Skills (2005) *Youth Matters Green Paper*. London: HMSO.

Department for Education and Skills (2006) *Care Matters: Transforming the Lives of Children and Young People in Care*. London: HMSO.

Department for Education and Skills and Department of Health (2006) *Options for Excellence: Building the Social Care Workforce of the Future*. London: Department of Health.

Department for Work and Pensions (2005) *Opportunity for All: A Summary of the Seventh Annual Report*. London: HMSO.

Department of Health (1995) *Messages from Research*. London: HMSO.

Department of Health (1998) *Modernising Social Services: Promoting Independence, Improving Protection, Raising Standards*. London: HMSO.

Department of Health (2000*) Framework for the Assessment for Children in Need and their Families*. London: HMSO.

Department of Health (2001) *Valuing People: A New Strategy for Learning Disability for the 21st Century*. London: HMSO.

Department of Health (2005a) *Independence, Well-being and Choice*. London: HMSO.

Department of Health (2005b) 'Responses to the consultation on adult social care in England; analysis of feedback from the Green Paper, Independence, well being and choice'. London: Department of Health.

Department of Health (2006) *Our Health, Our Care, Our Say*. London: HMSO.

Department of Health (2007) *Putting People First*. London: HMSO.

Department of Health (2010a) *A Vision for Adult Social Care: Capable Communities and Active Citizens*. London: Department of Health.

Department of Health (2010b) *Personalisation through Person-Centred Planning*. London: Department of Health.

Department of Health (2013) *Working Together for Change*. London: HMSO.

Department of Health (2014) *Draft Knowledge and Skills Statement for Social Workers in Adult Services: A Consultation*, prepared by the Chief Social Worker for Adults. London: Department of Health. Available from www.gov.uk/government/uploads/system/uploads/attachment_data/file/362491/knowledge_and_skills_for_adult_social_work_consultation.pdf (accessed 16/2/15).

Department of the Environment, Transport and the Regions (DETR) (1998) *Guidance on Enhancing Public Participation in Local Government*. London: DETR.

Dickinson, H., Allen, K., Alcock, P., Macmillan, R. and Glasby, J. (2012) *The Role of the Third Sector in Delivering Social Care*. Birmingham: NIHR School for Social Care Research, University of Birmingham.

Doel, M. and Williams, C. (2002) 'Social work in Wales', in M. Payne and S. Shardlow (eds), *Social Work in the British Isles*. London: Jessica Kingsley.

Dominelli, L. (1990) *Women and Community Action*. Birmingham: Venture Press.

Dominelli, L. (1997a) *Anti-racist Social Work*, 2nd edn. Basingstoke: Macmillan.

Dominelli, L. (1997b) *Sociology for Social Work*. Basingstoke: Palgrave.

Dominelli, L. (1998) 'Anti-oppressive practice in context', in R. Adams, L. Dominelli and M. Payne (eds), *Social Work: Themes, Issues and Critical Debates*. Basingstoke: Macmillan.

Dominelli, L. (1999) 'Neo-liberalism, social exclusion and welfare clients in a global economy', *International Journal of Social Welfare*, 8: 14–22.

Dominelli, L. (2004) *Social Work: Theory and Practice for a Changing Profession*. Cambridge: Polity Press.

Dominelli, L. (2010) *Social Work in a Globalizing World*. Cambridge: Polity Press.

Dominelli, L. and Hoogvelt, A. (1996) 'Globalisation and the technocratisation of social work', *Critical Social Policy*, 16 (2), 45–62.

Drake, R.F. (1999) *Understanding Disability Policies*. Basingstoke: Macmillan.

Driver, S. and Martell, L. (1998) *New Labour: Politics after Thatcherism*. Cambridge: Polity Press.

Dunst, C.J., Trivette, C.M. and Deal, A. (1994) 'Meaning and characteristics of empowerment', in C.J. Dunst, C.M. Trivette and A.G. Deal (eds), *Supporting and Strengthening Families: Methods, Strategies and Practices*. Cambridge, MA: Brookline Books.

Eichstellar, G. and Raper, D. (2006) 'Treasure hunt: Searching for pedagogic ideas within youth work in Portsmouth'. Paper presented at the *What is a pedagogue?* conference, Thomas Coram Research Unit, London.

Ellis, K. (2007) 'Direct payments and social work practice: The significance of "street-level bureaucracy" in determining eligibility', *British Journal of Social Work*, 37 (3): 405–422.

Ellis, K. (2011) '"Street-level bureaucracy" revisited: The changing face of frontline discretion in adult social care in England', *Social Policy and Administration*, 45 (3): 221–44.

Erath, P., Hamalainen, J. and Sing, H. (2000) 'Comparing social work from a European perspective: Towards a comparative science of social work', in A. Adams, P. Erath and S. Shardlow (eds), *Key Themes In European Social Work: Theory, Practice, Perspectives*. Lyme Regis: Russell House.

Etzioni, A. (1993) *The Spirit of Community*. London: Fontana Press.

European Commission (1995) 'Final report on the implementation of the Community programme concerning the economic and social integration of the economically and socially less privileged groups in society', *Poverty 3* (1989–94). Brussels: Commission of the European Communities.

European Commission (1999) *White Paper on Modernisation of the Rules Implementing Articles 85 And 86 of The EC Treaty*. Brussels: Commission of the European Communities.

European Roma Rights Centre (1999) *A Special Remedy: Roma and Schools for the Mentally Handicapped in the Czech Republic*. Budapest, Hungary: ERRC.

European Roma Rights Centre Vzajemme Souziti, Peacework Development Fund and the Centre, on Housing Rights and Evictions in Europe (2006) *Submission to the United Nations Human Rights Commission concerning Implementation of the United Nations Human Rights Covenant on Civil and Political Rights ((ICCPR) in the Czech Republic*. Brussells: ERRC.

Evans, T. and Harris, J. (2004) 'Street-level bureaucracy and the (exaggerated) death of discretion', *British Journal of Social Work*, 34: 871–95.

Evers, A. (2004) 'Current strands in debating user involvement in social services', in B. Munday (ed.), *User Involvement in Personal Social Services*. University of Kent with the assistance of the Group of Specialists on User Involvement in Social Services (CS-US). Strasbourg: Council of Europe.

Fanon, F. (1971) *The Wretched of the Earth*. London: Penguin.

Fanon, F. (1978) *Black Skin, White Masks*. London: Penguin.

FEANTSA (2009) *Homeless in Europe Magazine*, Spring. Available from www.feantsa.org/spip.php?article1027& lang=en (accessed 16/2/15).

Featherstone, B. (2011) 'The current economic crisis in Ireland: Why social work needs to be part of the challenge to a discredited system', *Communiania, International Journal of Social Work and the Social Sciences*, 1: 17–29.

Federation for Community Development Learning (2015) Community Development National Occupational Standards. Available from www.fcdl.org.uk (accessed 30/7/15).

Feldon, P. (1975) 'Radical soft cops destroy capitalist society by withdrawing their labour permanently', *Case Con, 19*.

Ferge, Z. (2000) 'Poverty in Hungary and in central and eastern Europe'. In D. Gordon and Townsend, P. (eds) *Breadline Europe: The Measurement of Poverty*. Bristol: Policy Press.

Ferguson, H. (1996) 'Protecting Irish children in time: Child abuse as a social problem and the development of the child protection system in the Republic of Ireland', *Administration*, 44 (2): 5–36.

Ferguson, H. and Powell, F. (2002) 'Social work in late modern Ireland', in M. Payne and S. Shardlow (eds), *Social Work in the British Isles*. London: Jessica Kingsley.

Ferguson, I. and Woodward, R. (2009) *Radical Social Work in Practice: Making a Difference*. Bristol: Policy Press.

Festis, G., Ostlin, P., Mckee, M. and Adany, R. (2012) 'Policies to improve the health and well-being of Roma people: The European experience', *Health Policy*, 105: 25–32.

Fletcher, K. (2006) *Partnerships in Social Care: A Handbook for Developing Effective Services*. London: Jessica Kingsley.

Fook, J. (1999) 'Critical reflectivity in education and practice', in B. Pease and J. Fook (eds), *Transforming Social Work Practice: Postmodern Critical Perspectives*. London: Routledge.

Fook, J. (2002) *Social Work: Critical Theory and Practice*. London: SAGE.

Foucault, M. (1980) *Power/knowledge: Selected Interviews and Other Writings*. Brighton: Harvester Wheatsheaf.

Foucault, M. (1981) *Remarks on Marx*. New York: Semiotext(e).

Fox Harding, L. (1997) *Perspectives in Child Care Policy*, 2nd edn. Harlow: Longman.

Frazer, H. (2001) 'Racism, poverty and community development', in F. Farrell and P. Watt (eds), *Responding to Racism in Ireland*. Dublin: Veritas Publications.

Freeman, F., Morrison, A., Lockhart, F. and Swanson, M. (1996) 'Consulting service users: The views of young people', in M. Hill and J. Aldgate (eds), *Child Welfare Services: Developments in Law, Policy, Practice and Research*. London: Jessica Kingsley.

Freeman, R., Chamberlayne, P., Cooper, A. and Rustin, M. (1999) 'Conclusion: A new culture of welfare', in P. Chamberlayne, A. Cooper, R. Freeman and M. Rustin (eds), *Welfare and Culture in Europe: Towards a New Paradigm in Social Policy*. London: Jessica Kingsley.

Freire, P. (1972) *Pedagogy of the Oppressed*. London: Penguin.

Fremeaux, I. (2005) 'New Labour's appropriation of the concept of community: A critique', *Community Development Journal*, 40 (3): 265–74.

Fridberg, T. (1998) *Denmark* in *European Observatory on National Family Policies: Developments in Family Policies in 1996*. Keighley: European Commission.

Gallagher, A. (1977) 'Women and community work', in M. Mayo (ed.), *Women in the Community*. London: Routledge & Kegan Paul.

Gardiner, F. (2014) *Being Critically Reflective*. London: Palgrave Macmillan.

Giarchi, G.G. and Lankshear, G. (1998) 'The eclipse of social work in Europe', *Social Work in Europe*, 5 (3): 25–36.

Giddens, A. (1971) *Capitalism and Modern Social Theory: An Analysis of the Writings of Marx, Durkheim and Max Weber*. Cambridge: Cambridge University Press.

Gil, D.G. (1998) *Confronting Injustice and Oppression: Concepts and Strategies for Social Workers*. New York: Columbia University Press.

Gilchrist, A. (1994) *Community Work Skills Manual*. Newcastle: Association of Community Workers. pp. 20–21.

Gilchrist, A. (2009) *The Well-connected Community: A Networking Approach to Community Development*. Bristol: Policy Press.

Gilligan, R. (1991) *Irish Child Care Services*. Dublin: Institute of Public Administration.

Ginsburg, N. (1992) *Divisions of Welfare: A Critical Introduction to Comparative Social Policy*. London: SAGE.

Glennerster, H. (1999) 'Which welfare states are most likely to survive?', *International Journal of Social Welfare*, 8: 2–13.

Gojova, A. (2011) 'Community work and the ideas of empowerment and participation in a changing social context', in F.W. Seibel, G.J. Freisenhahn, W. Lorenz and O. Chytil (eds), *European Developments and the Social Professions*. Brno: European Centre for Community Education.

Golightley, M. (2008) *Social Work and Mental Health,* 3rd edn. Exeter: Learning Matters.

Goodley, D. (1997) 'Locating self-advocacy in models of disability: understanding disability in the support of self-advocates with learning difficulties', *Disability and Society*, 12 (3): 367–79.

Goodley, D. (2011) *Disability Studies: An Interdisciplinary Introduction*. London: SAGE.

Gordon, D. and Townsend, P. (2000) *Breadline Europe: The Measurement of Poverty*. Bristol: Policy Press.

Gordon, G. (1980) *Michel Foucault Power/Knowledge: Selected Interviews and Other Writings 1972–1977*. Brighton: Harvester Wheatsheaf.

Gould, A. (1993) *Capitalist Welfare Systems: a Comparison of Japan, Britain and Sweden*. Harlow: Longman.

Gramsci, A. (1971) *Selections from the Prison Notebooks*. London: Lawrence and Wishart.

Gray, M., Healy, K. and Crofts, P. (2003) 'Social enterprise: Is it the business of social work?', *Australian Social Work*, 56 (2): 141–53.

Groch, S.A. (1994) 'Oppositional consciousness: its manifestation and development. The case of people with disabilities', *Sociological Inquiry*, 64: 4.

Guerin, P. (2002) 'Racism and the media in Ireland: setting the anti-immigrant agenda', in R. Lentin and R. McVeigh (eds), *Racism and Anti-Racism in Ireland*. Belfast: Beyond the Pale Publications.

Gutierrez, L. (1990) 'Working with women of color: An empowerment perspective', *Social Work*, 35 (2): 149–53.

Gutierrez, L.M. and Lewis, E.A. (1999) *Empowering Women of Color*. New York: Columbia University Press.

Gutierrez, L., Glenmaye, L. and Delois, K. (1995) 'The organizational context of empowerment practice: Implications for social work administration', *Social Work*, 40: 2.

Hallerod, B. and Heikkila, M. (1999) 'Poverty and social exclusion in the Nordic countries', in M. Kautto, M. Heikkila, B. Hvinden, S. Marklund and N. Ploug (eds) *Nordic Social Policy: Changing Welfare States*. London: Routledge.

Hallerod, B. and Heikkila, M. (1999) 'Poverty and social exclusion in the Nordic countries', in M. Kautto, M. Heikkila, B. Hvinden, S. Marklund, M. Heikkila and I. Julkunen (eds) (2004), *Obstacles to an Increased User Involvement in Social Services*. Brussels: Group of Specialists in Social Services, Council of Europe.

Hamalainen, J. (2003) 'The concept of social pedagogy in the field of social work', *Journal of Social Work*, 3 (1): 70–80.

Hanmer, J. and Statham, D. (1999) *Women and Social Work: Towards Women-Centred Practice*. Basingstoke: Macmillan.

Hardcastle, D.A. (2004) 'Globalisation, welfare states and social work', in T. Ngoh-Tiong and A. Rowlands (eds), *Social Work Around the World III*. Berne: International Federation of Social Workers.

Harder, M. (1997) 'Child protection in Denmark', in M. Harder and K. Pringle (eds), *Protecting Children in Europe: Towards a New Millenium*. Aalborg: Aalborg University Press.

Haringey Local Safeguarding Children Board (2010) *Serious Case Review 'Child A'*. London: Department for Education.

Harris, A. (1994) *Community Work Skills Manual*. Newcastle: Association of Community Workers.

Hatton, K. (1999) 'Developing post-graduate social work training: European cooperation around curricular design and delivery'. Paper presented at the EAIE Conference, Maastricht.

Hatton, K. (2001) 'Translating values: Making sense of different value bases – reflections from Denmark and the UK', *International Journal of Social Research Methodology*, 4 (4): 265–78.

Hatton, K. (2006) 'Europe and the undergraduate programme', in K. Lyons and S. Lawrence (eds), *Social Work in Europe: Educating for Change*. Birmingham: BASW/Venture Press.

Hatton, K. (2008) *New Directions in Social Work Practice*. Exeter: Learning Matters.

Hatton, K. (2009) 'Creating new identities'. Paper presented at the JSWEC Conference, University of Hertfordshire.

Hatton, K. (2011) 'Changing professional identities: Towards a structural social pedagogy', in F.W. Seibel, G.L. Freisenhahn, W. Lorenz and O. Chytil (eds), *European Developments and the Social Professions*. Brno: European Centre for Community Education.

Hatton, K. (2012a) 'Le travail communautaire au Royaume-Uni durant les années 1970–1980 souvenirs d'un temps revolu?', *Vie Sociale*, 2: 99 –110.

Hatton, K. (2012b) 'Youth inclusion and social pedagogy: A UK perspective'. Paper presented at the *Biennale internationale de l'education de la formation et des pratiques professionnelles,* Paris.

Hatton, K. (2013) *Social Pedagogy in the UK: Theory and Practice.* Lyme Regis: Russell House.

Hatton, K. (2015) 'Community work', in N.J. Smelser and P.B. Baltes (eds), *International Encyclopedia of the Social and Behavioural Sciences,* 2nd edn. Oxford: Elsevier.

Hatton, K. and Nugent, C. (1993) 'Empowerment: Professionalism's Achilles heel'. Paper presented at the *Facing the European Challenge – the Role of the Professions in a Wider Europe* conference, Leeds University.

Haughey, M. (1991) 'Confronting the pedagogical issues', *Open Learning,* 6 (3): 14–23.

Hautekeur, G. (2005) 'Community development in Europe', *Community Development Journal,* 40 (4): 385–98.

Hawtin, M., Hughes, G. and Percy-Smith, J. (1994) *Community Profiling: Auditing Social Needs.* Buckingham: Open University Press.

Hayden, C., Goddard, J. Gorin, S. and Van Der Spek , N. (1999) *State Child Care: Looking After Children?* London: Jessica Kingsley.

Health and Care Professions Council (2013) *Service User and Carer Involvement in Education and Training Programmes – Consultation Response and Our Conclusions.* London: HCPC.

Healy, K. (2000) *Social Work Methods and Skills: The Essential Foundations of Practice.* Basingstoke: Macmillan.

Healy, K. (2005) *Social Work Theories in Context.* Basingstoke: Palgrave Macmillan.

Healy, K. (2012) *Social Work Methods and Skills: The Essential Foundations of Practice.* Basingstoke: Palgrave.

Healy, S. and Reynolds, B. (1998) *Social Policy in Ireland: Principles, Practice and Problems.* Dublin: Oak Tree Press.

Heikkila, M. and Junkunen, I. (2003) 'Obstacles to an increased user involvement in social services', in B. Munday (ed.), *User Involvement in Personal Social Services.* University of Kent with the assistance of the Group of Specialists on User Involvement in Social Services (CS-US). Strasbourg: Council of Europe.

Helleiner, J. (1997) '"Women of the itinerant class": gender and anti-traveller racism in Ireland', *Women's Studies International Forum,* 20 (2): 275–87.

Henderson, P. and Glen, A. (2006) 'From recognition to support: Community development workers in the UK', *Community Development Journal,* 41 (3): 277–92.

Henderson, P. and Thomas, D.N. (1980) *Skills in Neighbourhood Work.* London: National Institute for Social Work, Allen and Unwin.

Henderson, P. and Vercseg, I. (2010) *Community Development and Civil Society: Making Connections in the European Context.* Bristol: Policy Press.

Hepple, B. (2013) 'Back to the future: Employment law under the Coalition Government', *Industrial Law Journal,* 42 (3): 203–223.

Hersov, J. (1992) 'Advocacy - issues for the 1990s', in T. Thompson and P. Mathia (eds), *Standards in Mental Handicap.* London: Bailliere and Tindall.

Higham, P. (2001) 'Changing practice and an emerging social pedagogue paradigm in England: The role of the personal adviser', *Social Work in Europe,* 8 (1): 21–8.

Hill, M. (2005) *The Public Policy Process,* 4th edn. Harlow: Pearson/Longman.

Hindess, B. (1996) *Discourses of Power: From Hobbes to Foucault.* Oxford: Blackwell.

Hirschman, A.O. (1970) *Exit, Voice and Loyalty.* Cambridge, MA: Harvard University Press.

HM Government (2003) *Every Child Matters.* London: The Stationery Office.

HM Government (2009) *Valuing People Now: A New Three-Year Strategy for People with Learning Disabilities: 'Making it happen for everyone'.* London: HMSO.

HM Government (2013) *Working Together to Safeguard Children.* London: HMSO.

Hodgkinson, S. and Robbins, G. (2013) 'The return of class war conservatism? Housing under the UK Coalition Government', *Critical Social Policy*, 33 (57): 57–77.

Hoggett, P. (ed.) (1997) *Contested Communities: Experiences, Struggles, Policies.* Bristol: Policy Press.

Hokenstad, M.C. and Midgely, J. (eds) (1997) *Issues in International Social Work: Global Challenges for a New Century.* Washington, DC: NASW Press.

Homelessness Action Research Team (2006) *Nowhere to Go.* Portsmouth: University of Portsmouth.

Homeless Link *Get Creative: Arts for All.* Available at http://www.homeless.org.uk/our-work/national-projects/get-creative-arts-for-all (accessed 30/7/15).

Honey, P. and Mumford, A. (1992) *The Manual of Learning Styles*, 3rd edn. Maidenhead: Peter Honey Publications.

Horncastle, J. and Brobeck, H. (1995) 'An international perspective on practice teaching for foreign students', *Social Work in Europe*, 2 (3): 48–52.

Horner, N. (2006) *What is Social Work? Context and Perspectives*, 2nd edn. Exeter: Learning Matters.

Horner, N. (2013) *What is Social Work? Context and Perspectives*, 4th edn. London: Sage/Learning Matters.

Hudson, A. (1989) 'Feminist social work', in M. Langan and P. Lee (eds), *Radical Social Work Today.* London: Unwin Hyman.

Hudson, B., Dearey, M. and Glendinning, C. (2004) *A New Vision for Adult Social Care: Scoping Service Users' Views.* York: Department of Health/University of York.

Hughes, G. (1998) 'A suitable case for treatment? Constructions of disability', in S. Saraga (ed.), *Embodying the Social: Constructions of Difference.* London: Routledge.

Hugman, R. (1991) *Power and the Caring Professions.* Basingstoke: Macmillan.

Hugman, R. (1998) *Social Welfare and Social Value.* Basingstoke: Macmillan.

Hugman, R. (2005) *New Approaches in Ethics for the Caring Professions.* Basingstoke: Palgrave Macmillan.

Hugman, R. (2010) *Understanding International Social Work: A Critical Analysis.* Basingstoke. Palgrave Macmillan.

Humphries, B. (1996) *Critical Perspectives on Empowerment.* Birmingham: Venture Press.

Humphries, B. (2000) 'Resources for hope: Social work and social exclusion', in J. Batsleer and B. Humphries (eds), *Welfare Exclusion and Political Agency.* London: Routledge.

Hupe, P. and Hill, M. (2007) 'Street-level bureaucracy and public accountability', *Public Administration*, 85 (2): 279–99.

Husband, C (1980) 'Culture, context and practice: racism in social work', in M. Brake and R. Bailey (eds), *Radical Social Work and Practice.* London: Edward Arnold.

Husen, M. (1996) Det fælles tredje – om fællesskab og værdier i det pædagogiske arbejde, in B. Pécseli (red.): *Kultur & pædagogik*, København: Socialpædagogisk Bibliotek. Munksgaard/Rosinante.

Ife, J. (1997) *Rethinking Social Work: Towards Critical Practice.* Sydney: Longman Pearson.

Ife, J. (1999) *Community Development: Creating Community Alternatives – Vision, Analysis and Practice.* Sydney: Longman Pearson.

Institute for Economic Affairs Health and Welfare Unit (1996) *Charles Murray and the Underclass: The Developing Debate.* London: IEA/Sunday Times.

International Federation of Social Workers (IFSW) (2014) *Global Definition of Social Work.* Berne: IFSW. Available from ifsw.org/get-involved/global-definition-of-social-work, (accessed 30/7/15).

Irish Government (1963) *Commission on Literacy.* Dublin: Stationery Office.

Irish Government (1995) *Report of the Task Force on the Travelling Community.* Dublin: Stationery Office.

Irish Government (1999) *Equal Status Bill.* Dublin: Stationery Office.

Jakes, S. and Cassidy, L. (n.d.) *Evaluating the National Outcomes: Programme Outcomes For Communities, Citizen Development.* Available from http://ag.arizona.edu/sfcs/cyfernet/nowg/cd_indicators.html (accessed 16/2/15).

Jamous, H. and Peloille, B. (1970) 'Professions or self-perpetuating systems? Changes in the French University Hospital system', in J.A. Jackson (ed.), *Professions and Professionalisation.* Cambridge: Cambridge University Press.

Johannesen, T. (1997) 'Social work as an international profession: Opportunities and challenges', in M.C. Hokenstad and J. Midgely (eds), *Issues in International Social Work: Global Challenges for a New Century.* Washington, DC: NASW Press.

Johns, R. (2014) *Using the Law in Social Work,* 6th edn. London: Sage/Learning Matters.

Johnson, N. (1999) *Mixed Economies of Welfare: A Comparative Perspective.* London: Prentice Hall, Europe.

Johnson, N., Jenkinson, S., Kendall, I., Bradshaw, Y. and Blackmore, M. (1998) 'Regulating for quality in the voluntary sector', *Journal of Social Policy,* 27 (3): 307–328.

Jones, C. (1983) *State Social Work and the Working Class.* London: Routledge & Kegan Paul.

Jones, C. and Novak, T. (2014) *Poverty and Inequality: Critical and Radical Debates in Social Work.* Bristol: Policy Press.

Jones, D. (1975) *Community Work Two.* London: Routledge & Kegan Paul.

Jones, D. and Mayo, M. (1974) *Community Work One.* London: Routledge & Kegan Paul.

Jordan, B. (1996) *A Theory of Poverty and Social Exclusion.* Cambridge: Polity Press.

Jordan, B. (2006) *Social Policy for the Twenty-first Century.* Cambridge: Polity Press.

Jordan, B. (2007) *Social Work and Well-being.* Lyme Regis: Russell House.

Jordan, B. (2011) 'Making sense of the "Big Society": Social work and the moral order', *Journal of Social Work,* (May): 1–17.

Jordan, B. and Drakeford, M. (2012) *Social Work and Social Policy under Austerity.* Basingstoke: Palgrave Macmillan.

Jordan, B. and Jordan, C. (2000) *Social Work and the Third Way: Tough Love and Social Policy.* London: SAGE.

Joseph Rowntree Foundation (2006) *Findings (0406): The Value Added by Community Involvement in Governance.* York: Joseph Rowntree Foundation.

Jowitt, M. and O'Loughlin, S. (2012) *Social Work with Children and Families,* 3rd edn. London: Sage/Learning Matters.

Kemshall, H. (2002) *Risk, Social Policy and Welfare.* Buckingham: Open University Press.

Kendall, J. (2000) 'The mainstreaming of the third sector into public policy in England in the late 1990s: Whys and wherefores', *Policy and Politics,* 28 (4): 541–62.

Kendall, K.A. (2000) *Social Work Education: Its Origins in Europe.* Alexandria: Council of Social Work Education.

Koehn, E. (2001) 'Assessment of communications and collaborative learning in civil engineering education', *Journal of Professional Issues in Engineering Education and Practice*, 127: 160–5.

Krakesova, M. (1973) *Vychovna socialni terapie* I Praha:Ministerstvo prace a socialnich veci.

Laming, Lord (2003) *The Victoria Climbié Inquiry.* London: The Stationery Office.

Laming, Lord (2009) *The Protection of Children in England: A Progress Report.* London: The Stationery Office.

Langan, M. (2002) 'Radical social work', in R. Adams, L. Dominelli and M. Payne (eds), *Social Work: Themes, Issues and Critical Debates* 2nd edn. Basingstoke: Macmillan.

Langan, M. and Lee, P. (eds) (1989) *Radical Social Work Today.* London: Unwin Hyman.

Langager, S. (2009) 'Social pedagogy and "at risk" youth: societal changes and new challenges in social work with youth', in J. Kornbeck and N. Rosendal Jensen (eds) *The Diversity of Social Pedagogy in Europe, Studies in Comparative Social Pedagogies and International Social Work*, Vol VII. Bremen: Europp ischer Hochschulverlag.

Lavalette, M. and Ferguson, I. (2007) *International Social Work and the Radical Tradition.* Totten: BASW.

Law Centres Federation (2001) *Law Centres: Putting Justice on the Social Exclusion Agenda.* London: Community Fund.

Lawrence, S., Lyons, K., Simpson, G. and Huegler, N. (eds) (2009) *Introducing International Social Work.* Exeter: Learning Matters.

Ledwith, M. (1997) *Participating in Transformation: Towards a Working Model of Community Empowerment.* Birmingham: Venture Press.

Le Grand, J. (1991) 'Quasi-markets and social policy', *Social Security*, 37: 32–45.

Leonard, P. (ed.) (1975) *The Sociology of Community Action. Sociological Review* Monograph 21.

Levin, E. (2004) *Involving Service Users and Carers in Social Work Education*, Resource Guide 2. London: Social Care Institute of Excellence.

Levitas, R. (2005) *The Inclusive Society? Social Exclusion and New Labour*, 2nd edn. Basingstoke: Macmillan.

Lewington, W. and Clipson, C. (2004) *Advocacy for Equality.* London: Independent Advocacy Campaign.

Lipsky, M. (1980) *Street Level Bureaucracy: Dilemmas of the Individual in Public Services.* New York: The Russell Sage Foundation.

Lister, R. (1998) 'In from the margins: Citizenship, inclusion and exclusion', in M. Barry and C. Hallett (eds), *Social Exclusion and Social Work: Issues of Theory, Policy and Practice.* Lyme Regis: Russell House.

Local Authority Circular/Department of Health (2008) London: Department of Health.

Lorenz, W. (1994) *Social Work in a Changing Europe.* London: Routledge.

Lorenz, W. (1995) 'Nationalism and racism in Europe: A challenge for pedagogy', *Social Work in Europe*, 2 (3): 34–9.

Lorenz, W. (1998) 'The ECSPRESS approach: The social professions between national and global perspectives', *Social Work in Europe*, 5 (3): 1–8.

Lorenz, W., Aluffi-Pentini, A. and Kniephoff, A. (1998) 'Erasmus evaluation: The experience of the social professions – European report', in F.W. Seibel and W. Lorenz (eds), *Social Professions for a Social Europe*, Erasmus Evaluation Conference, Koblenz, Frankfurt, IKO-Verlag fur Interkulturelle KommunikationThematische Netzwerkprojekte (TNP) und Ergänzende Maßnahmen (CME) in SOKRATES/ERASMUS Materialien des DAAD-Seminars am 4. März 1998 in Hannover, Bonn, o.J. (1998).

Lowndes, V. and Pratchett, L. (2012) 'Local governance under the Coalition Government: Austerity, localism and the "Big Society"', *Local Government Studies*, 38 (1): 21–40.

Lukes, S. (1975) *Power: A Radical View.* Basingstoke: Macmillan.

Lukes, S. (2004) *Power: A Radical View,* 2nd edn. Basingstoke: Palgrave Macmillan.

Lymbery, M. (2003) 'Negotiating the contradictions between competence and creativity in social work education', *Journal of Social Work,* 3 (1): 99–117.

Lymbery, M. (2004) 'Responding to crisis: The changing nature of welfare organisations', in M. Lymbery and S. Butler (eds), *Social Work Ideals and Practice Realities.* Basingstoke: Palgrave.

Lymbery, M. (2010) 'A new vision for adult social care? Continuities and change in the care of older people', *Critical Social Policy,* 30 (1): 5–26.

Lymbery, M., Charles, M., Christopherson, J. and Eadie, T. (2000) 'The control of British social work education: European comparisons', *European Journal of Social Work,* 3 (3): 269–82.

Lyons, K. (1999) *International Social Work: Themes and Perspectives.* Aldershot: Ashgate.

Lyons, K. and Lawrence, S. (2006a) 'Setting the scene: Europe and social work', in K. Lyons and S. Lawrence (eds), *Social Work in Europe: Educating for Change.* Birmingham: Venture Press/BASW.

Lyons, K. and Lawrence, S. (2006b) *Social Work in Europe: Educating for Change.* Birmingham: Venture Press/BASW.

Lyons, M. (2006) 'The best of both worlds', *Guardian,* 4 October 2006. Available from www.theguardian.com/society/2006/oct/04/public.services.guardiansocietysupplement .

Mac An Ghaill, M. (1999) *Contemporary Racisms and Ethnicities: Social and Cultural Transformations.* Buckingham: Open University Press.

MacInnes, T., Aldridge, H., Bushe, S., Kenway, P. and Tinson, A. (2013) *Monitoring Poverty and Social Exclusion 2013.* York: Joseph Rowntree Foundation/ New Policy Institute.

MacLaughlin, J. (1995) *Travellers and Ireland: Undercurrents.* Cork: Cork University Press.

Malin, N., Wilmot, S. and Manthorpe, J. (2002) *Key Concepts in Health and Social Policy.* Buckingham: Open University Press.

Manthorpe, J., Harris, J., Hussein, S., Cornes, M. and Moriarty, J. (2014) *Evaluation of the Social Work Practices with Adults Pilots: Summary Report.* London: Social Care Workforce Research Unit, King's College London.

Marynowicz-Hetka, E., Piekarski, J. and Wagner, A. (1999) 'Issues in social work: An invitation to a discussion', in E. Marynowicz-Hetka, A. Wagner and J. Piekarski (eds), *European Dimensions in Training and Practice of the Social Professions.* Katowice: Slask.

Mayo, M. (1980) 'Beyond CDP: reaction and community action', in M. Brake and R. Bailey (eds), *Radical Social Work and Practice.* London: Edward Arnold.

Mayo, M. (1980) 'Community work', in R. Adams, L. Dominelli and M. Payne (eds), *Social Work: Themes, Issues and Critical Debates.* Basingstoke: Palgrave Macmillan.

Mayo, P. (1999) *Gramsci, Freire and Adult Education.* London: Zed Press.

McCabe, A. (2010) 'Below the radar in a Big Society? Reflections on community engagement, empowerment and social action in a changing policy context', Working Paper 51, December, Joint ESRC, OCS Barrow Cadbury Third Sector Research Centre. Birmingham: University of Birmingham.

McCann, M., Ó Siochain, S. and Ruane, J. (1994) *Irish Travellers: Culture and Ethnicity.* Belfast: The Institute of Irish Studies, The Queen's University Belfast

McNay, M. (1994) 'European social work - a degree', *Social Work in Europe*, 1 (2): 15–17.

Melhbye, J. (1993) 'Denmark', in M.J. Colton and W. Hellinckx (eds), *Child Care in the EC: A Country Specific Guide to Foster and Residential Care*. Aldershot: Arena.

Memmi, A. (1990) *The Colonizer and the Colonized*. London: Earthscan.

Midgely, J. (1995) *Social Development: The Developmental Perspective in Social Welfare*. Thousand Oaks, CA: SAGE.

Midgley, J. (1997) 'Social work and international social development: Promoting a developmental perspective in the profession', in M.C. Hokenstad and J. Midgely (eds), *Issues in International Social Work: Global Challenges for a New Century*. Washington, DC: NASW Press.

Miles, S. (2007) 'Different journeys at different speeds: Young people, risk and the challenge of creative learning', *Journal of Youth Studies*, 10 (3): 271–84.

MIND (2005) *Factsheet: User Empowerment 1 – The User/Survivor Movement*. London: MIND.

Ministry of Health (1994) Middellevetidsudvalget [Working group on life expectancy]. Life expectancy in Denmark. Copenhagen: Ministry of Health.

Ministry of Social Affairs (1995a) *Report on the Seminar on Transfer of Know-how and Good Practice from Poverty*. Copenhagen: Ministry of Social Affairs.

Ministry of Social Affairs (1995b) *The Good Society*. Copenhagen: Ministry of Social Affairs.

Ministry of Social Welfare/Ministry of Health and Prevention (2008) *National Report on Strategies for Social Protection and Social Inclusion 2008–10*. Copenhagen: Government of Denmark.

Monshengwo, K. (2001) 'The potential of public awareness programmes', in F. Farrell and P. Watt (eds), *Responding to Racism in Ireland*. Dublin: Veritas.

Morison, J. (2000) 'The government–voluntary sector compacts: governance, governmentality and civil society', *Journal of Law and Society*, 27 (1): 98–132.

Mullaly, M. (1993) *Structural Social Work*. Toronto: McClelland & Stewart.

Mullaly, R. (2006) *The New Structural Social Work*. Ontario: Oxford University Press.

Mullard, M. and Spicker, P. (1998) *Social Policy in a Changing Society*. London: Routledge.

Munday, B. (1996) 'Introduction: Definitions and comparisons in European social care', in B. Munday and P. Ely (eds), *Social Care in Europe*. London: Prentice Hall/Harvester Wheatsheaf.

Munro, E. (2011) *The Munro Review of Child Protection: Final Report*. London: HMSO.

Murray, C. with Phillips, M. (2001) *The Underclass +10: Charles Murray and the Underclass Debate*. London: Civitas/Sunday Times.

Narey, M. (2014) 'Making the education of social workers consistently effective'. Report of Sir Martin Narey's independent review of the education of children's social workers. London: Department of Education.

National Anti-Poverty Strategy (1997) *Sharing in Progress*. Dublin: Stationery Office.

National Occupational Standards (2009) *National Occupational Standards for Community Development*. London: Lifelong Learning. Available from http://www.communitydevelopmentworkforcewales.org.uk/wp-content/uploads/2011/01/NOS_CD_EngINT.pdf (accessed 16/2/15).

National Strategic Partnership Forum (2006) *Making Partnerships Work: Examples of Good Practice*. London: Department of Health.

Nett, J.C. and Spratt, T. (2012) Child Protection Systems: An international comparison of 'good practice examples' of five countries (Australia, Germany, Finland, Sweden, United Kingdom) with recommendations for Switzerland. Zurich: Fonds suisse pour des projets de protection de l'enfance. Available from http://kinderschutzfonds.ch/wp-content/uploads/Bericht_Nett_EN.pdf (accessed 15/2/15).

Nonneman, G., Niblock, T. and Szajkowski, B. (1997) *Muslim Communities in the New Europe.* Reading: Ithaca Press.

North Shields Community Development Project (1974) *Final Report,* Volumes 3 and 4. London: The Home Office.

OECD (2014) *Society at a Glance 2014: OECD Social Indicators.* Paris: OECD Publishing. Available from http://dx.doi.org/10.1787/soc_glance-2014-en (accessed 16/2/15).

Office of the Deputy Prime Minister (2005) *Improving Services, Improving Lives.* London: Cabinet Office.

Office of the Third Sector (OTS) (2006) *Social Enterprise Action Plan: Scaling New Heights.* London: Cabinet Office.

O'Halloran, C., Hean, S., Humphris, D. and Macleod-Clark, J. (2006) 'Developing common learning: The New Generation Project undergraduate curriculum model', *Journal of Interprofessional Care,* 20 (1): 12–28.

O'Loughlin, M. and O'Loughlin, S. (2008) *Social Work with Children and Families,* 2nd edn. Exeter: Learning Matters.

O'Malley, J. (1977) *The Politics of Community Action.* London: Spokesman Books.

Oppenheim, C. (1998*) Poverty the Facts.* London: Child Poverty Action Group.

Osborne, S.P. and McLaughlin, K. (2002) 'Trends and issues in the implementation of local "Voluntary Sector Compacts" in England', *Public Money and Management: Integrating Research with Policy and Practice,* (January–March): 55–63.

Palmer, G., Carr, J. and Kenway, P. (2004) *Monitoring Poverty and Social Exclusion 2004.* York: Joseph Rowntree Foundation.

Parker, S., Fook, J. and Pease, B. (1999) 'Empowerment: The modernist social work concept par excellence' in B. Pease and J. Fook (eds), *Transforming Social Work Practice: Postmodern Critical Perspectives.* London: Routledge.

Parsloe, P. (ed.) (1996) *Pathways to Empowerment.* Birmingham: BASW/Venture Press.

Parton, N. and O'Byrne, P. (2000) *Constructive Social Work; Towards New Theory and Practice.* New York: Palgrave Macmillan.

Payne, M. (2014) *Modern Social Work Theory,* 4th edn. Basingstoke: Palgrave Macmillan.

Peacock, M. and Bissell, P. (2011) *Briefing Paper 3: The Social Determinants of Health Inequalities: Implications for Research and Practice.* Sheffield: National Institute for Health Research, CLAHRC for South Yorkshire.

Pease, B. and Fook, J. (eds) (1999) *Transforming Social Work Practice.* London: Routledge.

Penna, S., Paylor, I. and Washington, J. (2000) 'Globalisation, social exclusion and the possibilities for global social work and welfare', *European Journal of Social Work,* 3 (2): 123–38.

Petrie, P. (2001) 'The potential of pedagogy/education for work in the children's sector in the UK', *Social Work in Europe,* 8 (3): 23–5.

Petrie, P. (2003) 'Coming to terms with "pedagogy": Reconceptualising work with children', in B. Littlechild and K. Lyons (eds), *Locating the Occupational Space for Social Work: International Perspectives.* Birmingham: BASW/Venture Press.

Petrie, P. (2004) 'Briefing paper: Pedagogy – a holistic, personal approach to work with children and young people, across services. European models for practice, training, education and qualification'. London: Thomas Coram Research Unit.

Petrie, P., Boddy, J., Cameron, C., Heptinstall, K., McQuail, S., Simon, S. and Wigfall, V. (2009) *Pedagogy – a holistic personal response to work with children and young people, across services: European models for practice, training education and qualification, Briefing Paper, Update*, Thomas Coram Research Unit, Institute of Education, University of London.

Phillips, A. (1999) *Which Equalities Matter.* Cambridge: Polity Press.

Pierson, J. (2000) *Tackling Social Exclusion.* London: Routledge/Community Care.

Pinker, R. (1999) 'Do poverty definitions matter?', in D. Gordon and P. Spicker (eds), *The International Glossary on Poverty.* London: Zed Books/CROP.

Pinkney, S. (1998) 'Reshaping of social work and social care', in G. Hughes and G. Lewis (eds), *Unsettling Welfare: The Reconstruction of Social Policy.* London: Routledge/Open University.

Policy Action Teams (1999) *National Strategy for Neighbourhood Renewal, Enterprise and Social Exclusion.* London: HM Treasury.

Pollock, A.M. and Price, D. (2011) 'The final frontier: The UK's new coalition government turns the English National Health Service over to the global health care market', *Health Sociology Review*, 20: 294–305.

Popple, K. (1995) *Analysing Community Work.* Buckingham: Open University Press.

Popple, K. and Redmond, M. (2000) 'Community development in the voluntary sector in the new millennium: The implications of the third way in the UK', *Community Development Journal*, 35 (4): 391–400.

Portsmouth City Council (2007) *Review of Youth Services*, May 2007. Portsmouth: Portsmouth City Council.

Powell, F. (1998) 'The professional challenge of reflexive modernisation: social work in Ireland', *British Journal of Social Work*, 28: 311–28.

Powell, F. (2001) *The Politics of Social Work.* London: SAGE.

Power, A. (2014) 'Personalisation and austerity in the crosshairs: Government perspectives on the remaking of adult social care', *Journal of Social Policy*, 43 (4): 829–46.

Pridhova, A. (1999) 'Social and legal protection of children and youth in the Czech Republic', *Social Work in Europe*, 6 (3): 38–44.

Priestley, M. (1999) *Disability Politics and Community Care.* London: Jessica Kingsley.

Pringle, K. (1997)' Child protection in England and Wales', in M. Harder and K. Pringle (eds), *Protecting Children in Europe: Towards a New Millenium.* Aalborg: Aalborg University Press.

Pringle, K. (1998) *Children and Social Welfare in Europe.* Buckingham: Open University Press.

Prins, K. (2004) *Problem-based Project Work.* Written communication with author.

Prins, K. (2013) 'Social pedagogy'. Paper presented at the School of Health Sciences and Social Work Research Seminar, University of Portsmouth.

QAA (2008) *Social Work 2008.* Mansfield: The Quality Assurance Agency for Higher Education. Available from www3. shu.ac.uk/HWB/placements/SocialWork/documents/QAABenchmarkstatementsw.pdf (accessed 16/2/15).

Quinney, A. (2006) *Collaborative Social Work Practice.* Exeter: Learning Matters.

Rambouskova, J., Dlouhy, P., Krizova, E., Prochazka, B., Hrncirova, D. and Andel, M. (2009) 'Health behaviours, nutritional status and anthropometric parameters of Roma and non-Roma mothers and their infants in the Czech Republic', *Journal of Nutrition Education and Behaviour*, 41 (1): 58–64.

Ramscharan, P., Roberts, G., Grant, G. and Borland, J. (1997) 'Citizenship, empowerment and everyday life: Ideal and illusion in the new millenium', in P. Ramscharan, G. Roberts, G. Grant and J. Borland (eds), *Empowerment in Everyday Life: Learning Disability.* London: Jessica Kingsley.

Ramsden, S. (2010) *Practical Approaches to Co-production: building effective partnerships with people using services, families and citizens*, prepared for the DoH. London: HMSO.

Rapaport, J., Manthorpe, J., Moriarty, J., Hussein, S. and Collins, J. (2005) 'Advocacy and people with learning disabilities in the UK: How can local funders find value for money?', *Journal of Intellectual Disabilities*, 9 (94): 299–319.

Regional Youth Work Unit – North East (2010) *A Study on the Understanding of Social Pedagogy and its Potential Implications for Youth Work Practice and Training*. Sunderland: University of Sunderland.

Revans, L. (2001) 'People with learning difficulties in from the cold', *Community Care*, (March): 10–11.

Reverda, N. (2001) 'The role of the personal adviser: Some observations on social pedagogy from the Netherlands', *Social Work in Europe*, 8 (1): 29–30.

Ritchie, T. (2004) *Relationer i Teori og Praksis*. Copenhagen: Billeso and Baltzer.

Robinson, L. (1998) *'Race', Communication and the Caring Professions*. Buckingham: Open University Press.

Rotelli, F., Mezzina, R., De Leonardis, O., Georgen, R. and Evaristo, P. (n.d.) *Is Rehabilitation a Social Enterprise?* Geneva: Division of Mental Health, World Health Organisation. Available from www.triestesalutementale.it/english/doc/rotelli-et-al_xxxx_rehabilitation.pdf (accessed 16/2/15).

Rowbotham, S., Segal, L. and Wainwright, H. (1980) *Beyond the Fragments: Feminism and the Making of Socialism*. London: Merlin.

Rowe, W., Hanley, J., Moreno, E.R. and Mould, J. (2000) 'Voices of social work practice: reflections on the effects of globalisation', in Social Work and Globalisation, special issue of *Canadian Social Work*, 2 (1): 65–87.

Ruch, G., Turney, D. and Ward, A. (2010) *Relationship Based Social Work: Getting to the Heart of Practice*. London: Jessica Kingsley.

Sapey, B.J. and Oliver, M. (2006) *Social Work with Disabled People*, 3rd edn. Basingstoke, Palgrave Macmillan.

Savage, S.P. and Atkinson, R. (eds) (2001) *Public Policy under Blair*. Basingstoke: Palgrave.

Schulze, H.J. and Wirth, W. (1996) *Who Cares? Social Service Organizations and Their Users*. London: Cassell.

Service User Inclusion Group (SUIG) (2005) *Evaluation of Service User Training*. Portsmouth: University of Portsmouth.

Shah, S. (2006) 'Sharing the world: The researcher and the researched', *Qualitative Research*, 6 (2): 207–220.

Shar, A. (1989) 'Anti-racist social work', in M. Langan and P. Lee (eds) *Radical Social Work Today*. London: Unwin Hyman.

Shardlow, S. and Payne, M. (eds) (1998) 'Finding social work in Europe', in S. Shardlow and M. Payne (eds), *Contemporary Issues in Social Work: Western Europe*. Aldershot: Arena.

Shepperd, M. (2006) *Social Work and Social Exclusion: The Idea of Practice*. Aldershot: Ashgate.

Silver, H. (1994) 'Social exclusion and social solidarity: Three paradigms', *International Labour Review*, 1333 (5–6): 531–78.

Simmons, R. and Birchall, J. (2005) 'A joined-up approach to user participation in public services: Strengthening the "participation chain"', *Social Policy and Administration*, 39 (3): 260–83.

Skehill, C. (1999) *The Nature of Social Work in Ireland*. Ceredigion: Edward Mellen Press.

Skills for Care (2006) *Learning Resource Network, Review of Progress April 2003 – March 2006*. Leeds: Skills for Care.

Skills for Care and Skills for Health (2009) *Common Core Principles to Support Self-Care: A Guide to Support Implementation*. Leeds/Bristol: Skills for Care/Skills for Health.

Smale, G., Tuson, G. and Statham, D. (2000) *Social Work and Social Problems: Working Towards Social Inclusion and Social Change*. Basingstoke: Macmillan.

Smethurst, E. (2010) 'Becoming a social care worker in the voluntary sector', *Guardian*, 3 June.

Social Care Institute for Excellence (2004a) *Position Paper No 3: Has service user participation made a difference to social care services*, Bristol, Policy Press

Social Care Institute of Excellence (2004b) *Resource Guide No 2: Involving service users and carers in social work education*, London, SCIE

Social Care Institute for Excellence (SCIE) (2013) *Co-production in Social Care: What It Is and How to Do It*, SCIE Guide 15. London: Social Care Institute for Excellence.

Social Work Action Network (2010) *Social Work and Social Justice: A Manifesto for a New Engaged Practice*. Paisley: SWAN. Available from www.socialworkfuture.org/about-swan/national-organisation/manifesto (accessed 16/2/15).

Social Work Action Network (n.d.) *Privatization of Children's Services: Independent 'Social WorkPractices'*. Paisley: SWAN. Available from www.socialworkfuture.org/attachments/article/151/SocialworkPractice-SWAN-briefing2010.pdf (accessed 16/2/15).

Social Work Inclusion Group (2006) *Creative Writing Working Party*. Portsmouth: University of Portsmouth.

Social Work Reform Board (2011) *Building a Safe and Confident Future*. London: HMSO.

Social Work Task Force (2009) *Facing Up to the Task: Interim Report of the Social Work Task Force*. London: DoH/DCSF.

Spear, R. (2006) *National Profiles of Work Integration Social Enterprises: United Kingdom*. Brussels: European Research Network.

Spicker, P. (1999) 'Definitions of poverty: Eleven clusters of meaning', in D. Gordon and P. Spicker (eds), *The International Glossary on Poverty*. London: Zed Books/CROP.

Stepney, P. and Popple, K. (2008) *Social Work and the Community : A Critical Context for Practice*. Basingstoke: Palgrave.

Stoesz, D. and Midgley, J. (1991) 'The radical right and the welfare state', in H. Glennester and J. Midgley (eds), *The Radical Right and the Welfare State: An International Assessment*. Brighton: Harvester Wheatsheaf.

Storo, J. (2013) *Practical Social Pedagogy: Theories, Values and Tools for Working With Children and Young People*. Bristol: Policy Press.

Tan, H. (1998) *Communitarianism: A New Agenda for Politics and Citizenship*. Basingstoke: Macmillan.

Taylor, M. (2003) *Public Policy in the Community*. Basingstoke: Palgrave.

Taylor, Z. (1999) 'Values, theories and methods in social work education: A culturally transferable core?', *International Social Work*, 42 (3): 309–18.

Taylor-Gooby, P. and Stoker, G. (2011) 'The coalition programme: A new vision for Britain or politics as usual', *The Political Quarterly*, 82 (1): 4–15.

Teasdale, S. (2011) 'What's in a name? Making sense of social enterprise discourses', *Public Policy and Administration*, (May). Available from http://ppa.sagepub.com/content/early/2011/05/25/0952076711401466 (accessed 16/2/15).

Tew, J. (2006) 'Understanding power and powerlessness: Towards a framework for emancipatory practice in social work', *Journal of Social Work*, 6 (1): 33–51.

The College of Social Work (2012) *Professional Capabilities Framework*. London: The College of Social Work. Available from www.tcsw.org.uk/pcf.aspx (accessed 16/2/15).

Thompson, J., Alvy, G. and Lees, A. (2000) 'Social entrepreneurship – a new look at the people and the potential', *Management Decision*, 38 (5): 328–38.

References

Thompson, N. (2001) *Anti-discriminatory Practice.* Basingstoke: Macmillan.

Thompson, N. (2005) *Understanding Social Work: Preparing for Practice,* 2nd edn. Basingstoke: Palgrave.

Thompson, N. and Campling, J. (1998) *Promoting Equality: Challenging Discrimination and Oppression in the Human Services.* Basingstoke: Macmillan.

Tonnies, F. (1955) *Community and Association.* London: Routledge and Kegan Paul.

Took, L. (2006) 'DH social care workforce policy'. Paper presented at the Hants/IOW Learning Resource Network Conference, November.

Toren, N. (1969) 'Semi-professionalism and social work: A theoretical perspective', in A. Etzioni (ed.), *The Semi-Professions and their Organisation: Teachers, Nurses, Social Workers.* London: Collier-Macmillan.

Travellers Visibility Group (2007) *Annual Report.* Cork: Ireland.

Treseder, P. (1995) 'Involving and empowering children and young people: Overcoming the barriers', in C. Cloke and M. Davies (eds), *Participation and Empowerment in Child Protection.* London: Pitman.

Turner, M. and Beresford, P. (2005) *Contributing on Equal Terms: Service User Involvement and the Benefits System,* Adult Services Report 08. Bristol: Social Care Institute of Excellence/Policy Press.

Ungerson, C. (ed.) (1997) *Women and Social Policy:* A *Reader.* Basingstoke: Macmillan.

UNICEF Innocenti Research Centre (2010) Report Card 9 – *The Children Left Behind: A League Table of Inequality in Child Well-being in the World's Richest Countries.* Florence: UNICEF.

University of London/Cabinet Office/Department for Education and Skills.

University of Portsmouth (2003) *Making Service User Involvement Effective.* Portsmouth: University of Portsmouth.

University of Portsmouth (2009) *Pilot Project for Newly Qualified Social Workers.* Leeds: Skills for Care.

Vaisanen, R. (2010) 'Social pedagogical approach in youth social work', *Journal Europeen D'Education Sociale,* 18/19: 23–34.

Vass, A. (1980) 'The myth of a radical trend in British community work', *Community Development Journal,* 14: 1.

Verick, S. (2009) *Who Is Hit Hardest during a Financial Crisis? The Vulnerability of Young Men and Women to Unemployment in an Economic Downturn,* IZA Discussion Paper No. 4359. Bonn: Institute for the Study of Labor. Available from http://nbn-resolving.de/urn:nbn:de:101:1–20091105792 (accessed 16/2/15).

Vygotsky, L. (2004) 'Imagination and creativity in childhood', *Journal of Russian and East European Psychology,* 42 (1): 7–97.

Waddington, P. (1979) 'Looking ahead – community work in the 1980s', *Community Development Journal,* 14 (3): 224–34.

Wales Social Security Campaign (1989) *Repay or Don't Claim – Poverty and Social Security in Wales.* Cardiff: WSSC.

Walmsley, J. (1993) 'Women first: lessons in participation', *Critical Social Policy,* 38, Autumn: 86–99.

Ward, C. (1995) Women in situations of disadvantage', in Cork Federation of Women's Organisations (ed.), *Women and Leadership: Redefining Power.* Cork: Bradshaw Books.

Warren, J. (2007) *Service User and Carer Participation in Social Work.* Exeter: Learning Matters.

Whittington, C. (2003) *Learning for Collaborative Practice With Other Professions and Agencies: A Study to Inform the Development of the Degree in Social Work.* London: Department of Health.

Wilkinson, R.G. and Pickett, K.E. (2006) 'Income inequality and population health: A review of the evidence', *Social Science and Medicine,* 62 (7): 1768–84.

Wilkinson, R.G. and Pickett, K.E. (2007) 'The problems of relative deprivation: Why some societies do better than others', *Social Science and Medicine*, 65: 1965–78.

Wilkinson, R.G. and Pickett, K.E. (2009) *The Spirit Level: Why Equality is Better for Everyone*. London: Penguin.

Williams, C., Soydan, H. and Johnson, M.R.D. (1998) *Social Work and Minorities: European Perspectives*. London: Routledge.

Williams, F. (1999) 'Balancing polarities: Developing a new framework for welfare research', in F. Williams, J. Popay and A. Oakley (eds), *Welfare Research: A Critical Review*. London: UCL Press.

Williams, F., Popay, J. and Oakley, A. (1999) 'Changing paradigms of welfare', in F. Williams, J. Popay and A. Oakley (eds), *Welfare Research: A Critical Review*. London: UCL Press.

Williams, G.A. (1979) *When was Wales?* BBC Wales Annual Radio Lecture, 12 November, Cardiff.

Williams, J. and Simpson, G. (2009) 'Understanding international social work', in S. Lawrence, K. Lyons, G. Simpson and N. Huegler (eds), *Introducing International Social Work*. Exeter: Learning Matters.

Williams, P. (2006) *Social Work With People With Learning Difficulties*. Exeter: Learning Matters.

Williams, R. (1976) *Keywords*. Glasgow: Fontana.

Wilson, A. and Beresford, P. (2000) '"Anti-oppressive practice": Emancipation or appropriation?', *British Journal of Social Work*, 30: 553–73.

Wilson, D. (2006) 'Seduced by the politics of penal populism', *Independent*, 16 August. Available from www.rethinking.org.nz/assets/Penal%20Populism/M2 (accessed 16/2/15).

Wilson, E (1980) 'Feminism and social work' in M. Brake and R. Bailey (eds), *Radical Social Work and Practice*. London: Edward Arnold.

Winter, S.C., Dinesen, P.T. and May, P.J. (2008) *Implementation Regimes and Street-Level Bureaucrats: Employment Service Delivery in Denmark*, Working Paper 12:2008. Copenhagen: Danish National Centre for Social Research.

Wirth, W. and Schulze, H.J. (1996) 'Individual clients in international networks: Perspectives of social service integration and user involvement in Europe', in H.J. Schulze, and W. Wirth (eds), *Who Cares? Social Service Organizations and their Users*. London: Cassell.

Wistow, G. (2005) *Developing Social Care: the past, present and the future*. London: SCIE.

Witz, A. (1992) *Professions and Patriarchy*. London: Routledge.

Wyatt, M. (2002) 'Partnerships in health and social care: The implications of government guidance in the 1990s in England, with particular reference to voluntary organisations', *Policy and Politics*, 30 (2): 167–82.

Yeates, N. (ed.) (2014) *Understanding Global Social Policy*, 2nd edn. Bristol: Policy Press.

Young, R.E. (1996) *Intercultural Communication: Pragmatics, Geneology, Deconstruction*. Avon: Multi-Lingual Matters Ltd.

Index

Added to a page number 'f' denotes a figure and 't' denotes a table.